Requiem for a Family Business

Jonathan Guinness, third Lord Moyne, was born in March 1930, the son of Bryan Guinness, later second Lord Moyne, and Diana Mitford who was later married to Sir Oswald Mosley. Jonathan Guinness went to Eton and read modern languages at Oxford. From 1953 to 1956 he worked at Reuters News Agency in London and Bonn. He then switched to merchant banking where he worked at Erlangers until it was taken over by Philip Hill, later to be a component of Hill Samuel. With some colleagues, he bought control of Leopold Joseph in 1962. He worked there as an Executive Director until 1968, then left to join the building ceramics firm, Red Bank and live in Leicestershire.

He joined the Monday Club, a pressure group within the Conservative Party, in 1968. In 1970 he became the Club's chairman, a post he held for two years. From 1960 to 1974 he was a member of Leicestershire County Council. He was Parliamentary Candidate for Lincoln in 1973 and for Coventry North West in 1974 and 1975. From 1961 Jonathan Guinness was a non-executive family member of the Board of Guinness PLC.

Jonathan Guinness has been married twice and has eight children. His father died in 1992 and he inherited the title and seat in the House of Lords. This is his third book.

Jonathan Guinness

Requiem for a
Family Business

PAN BOOKS

First published 1997 by Macmillan

This edition published 1998 by Pan Books
an imprint of Macmillan Publishers Ltd
25 Eccleston Place, London SW1W 9NF
and Basingstoke

Associated companies throughout the world

ISBN 0 330 32364 4

1 3 5 7 9 8 6 4 2

A CIP catalogue record for this book is available from
the British Library.

Phototypeset by Intype London Limited
Printed and bound in Great Britain by
Mackays of Chatham plc, Chatham, Kent

Contents

Acknowledgements

This book could not have been written without the generous help of many people.

From Guinness PLC, Chris Davidson, who has been in charge of public relations ever since the time of which I am writing, and who was frank as well as unstinting in his help, and Sue Garland, the efficient and helpful head of archives in the Park Royal Brewery.

Among former staff and directors of Guinness PLC I had immense help from: Alan Scrine, Company Secretary before, during and after the Distillers takeover and an old friend and colleague, his information was of priceless value; Shaun Dowling, who was in immediate charge of solving the problems after the takeover; Anthony Purssell, Ernest Saunders' immediate predecessor; Brian Baldock, Executive Director in charge of brewing at the time of the Distillers takeover; the late Lord Moyne, my father, who gave me much help before his death, and my sister Rosaleen Mulji, who is in charge of his archive; the late Benjamin, 3rd Earl of Iveagh, and his widow, Miranda, Countess of Iveagh; Simon 2nd Viscount Boyd and my brother, Dr Finn Guinness, who both helped me with their memory of events; Edward Guinness was most informative about the crucial part he played in the crisis; Peter Guinness, in an interview and subsequent letter, clarified the events surrounding Ernest Saunders' appointment; the late Owen Williams, chief brewer in the 1950s, not only gave me much information when I stayed with him in Guernsey, but also let me have his 'Nonsense Book', a series of notes giving an invaluable insight into Guinness as it was in the early years of the 20th century; Dr Arthur Hughes, who ran the Dublin Brewery for many years, was most informative about the post-war period; Michael Ogle gave me a helpful interview about his part of the business; Michael Hadfield gave me a useful interview about the years when Ernest Saunders was in charge.

Of those unconnected with the Company, Roger Seelig, formerly of Morgan Grenfell, gave me a frank interview which helped me to gain insight into some of the events. Lord Spens, formerly of Ansbachers, not only patiently explained much that had been obscure, but gave me access to his comprehensive and immaculately kept archive. To him and his wife Barbara I am indebted for hospitality as well as help. Horst Tiefenthaler, formerly of Bank of Vienna, was frank and helpful. John Chiene, of Wood Mackenzie, gave me a good insight into Guinness's relationship with that firm and with the Stock Exchange in general. My mother, Lady Mosley, was informative about family discussions about the Brewery in the late 1920s. This book was also originally her idea.

Jonathan Guinness
London, August 1997

ONE

The Brewery

Arthur Guinness signed his name clearly, with a firmly knotted capital A and at the end an eighteenth-century double s. In his day self-assertion was expressed not, as nowadays, by reducing one's signature to a squiggle; rather by enhancing it with a flourish. Arthur's flourish was a fine one, sweeping and curling, not without grace, from the cross of the t. This energetic signature still appears on every bottle and can of his firm's stout. Stout? That good old word is dying out, lingering among geriatric members of the Guinness family who still distinguish their own name from that of the product. To the rest of the world the stuff is Guinness. For an individual to be called Guinness is like being called Biro or (in England) Hoover. Even to me my name evokes blackness and beige foam, the tang of hops, the sting of carbon dioxide. It recalls the days when the Brewery was one of the sights of Dublin; every visitor to Ireland could view the stages in the brewing process, and most of them did. Guinness! The connection with the product has made the name seem designed to fit it, from the gargle at the beginning to the final hiss.

The Dublin Brewery is no longer quite such an attraction to visitors as it was. The Company still does its best, and many tourists still come; but the brewing process is now less visible, more enclosed. The main features today are an exhibition and an explanatory film: no substitute for traipsing up and down the staircases and catwalks among the pipes ('mains') and the

1

gigantic brewing vessels, accompanied by a knowledgeable and fluent guide as versed in legend as in fact. So let me take you round it as it was in the late 1940s when I first got to know it.

We'll start at the maltings, a great low-ceilinged room with iron pillars, its floor covered about 6 inches deep with gently steaming barley, moistened and warmed to make it sprout and produce the diastase that will convert its starch into soluble malt sugar. Then we climb six floors to the top storey of another building, dark and dusty, where our guide removes one of many manholes and lowers a light on a long rubber-covered flex, down, down; an empty vessel, white with dust, ready to receive the malt when it has been dried.

Brewing starts in one of the great kieves; in lesser breweries these are known as mash tuns. A kieve is a circular vessel, about 15 feet across, with a copper lid which can be lifted by a pulley, a perforated floor, and rotating metal arms which spray boiling water on to the mash, which is a mixture of malt, flaked barley and roasted barley. As the guide lifts the lid we see dimly, through the steam, the arms going sedately round discharging trickles of water from multiple holes. This process of 'sparging' continues until all the soluble matter has gone from the mash; the water thus charged, now known as 'wort', goes through a main to a copper, where the hops will be added. We will make a detour through the hop store with its huge, tightly packed sacks or 'pockets' of hops giving off an overpowering smell. It takes a bit of getting used to, that hop smell. If one had insomnia, the hop store would be the place to set up a camp-bed. Sleep would be instantaneous.

The copper is indeed made of gleaming copper, on the outside at any rate. It is a rounded cone like a gigantic version of an eleventh-century helmet, as worn on the Bayeux tapestry. It stretches two storeys down; we are on the top storey, and take it in turns to mount a few steps and look through a thick glass porthole at the wort, already dark from the roasted barley in the mash, which is boiling with its quota of hops, cascading like a shimmering brown crinoline from a central fountain. We then follow the hopped wort to the great square fermentation tun. A red bar is placed diagonally over the opening, reading 'TUN DANGEROUS'. Inside the great vessel, as big as a swimming bath and illuminated by a weak bulb, viscous foam mounts and subsides in slow motion; the yeast is at its mysterious work making sugar, $C_6 H_{12} O_6$, into $2 \times C_2 H_5$ OH (ethyl alcohol) and $2 \times CO_2$ (carbon dioxide). To fall in would mean instant death; the carbon dioxide has completely replaced all the air and, being comparatively heavy, is invisibly streaming out at the bottom of the opening, where one can take a good sniff of it and get a stinging in the nose.

From there we climb to the skimmers, wide flat vessels where the dun-coloured, viscous bubbles of yeast rise to the top, to be skimmed off periodically with a special sort of plank with handles, and gaze down through a trough at the edges. About an eighth of the yeast will be used again; the rest is turned into cattle food or yeast extract; Marmite is the best-known brand. After the skimmers, the vats like huge barrels with staves and hoops, where the beer matures for a bit together with a small amount of unskimmed beer so that there is enough yeast to make it fizz. Then comes the racking shed where the barrels are filled. They are still wooden barrels of different sizes; $4\frac{1}{2}$-gallon pins, 9-gallon firkins, 18-gallon kilderkins, 36-gallon barrels, 54-gallon hogsheads or great butts containing 108 gallons. (Those are for the English trade; an Irish barrel is 32 gallons and some of the Scottish sizes are different again.) Each cask is attached by a rubber tube to the big cylindrical racking vessel, for all the world like piglets sucking from their mother.

Then we see the cooperage, a Kingdom of Noise or Wagnerian Nibelheim full of clanging and banging, where the casks are made; the coopers, our guide explains, cut the staves entirely by eye, as we can see for ourselves. One cooper has placed his staves in their bottom hoop, splayed like the petals of a great flower. He lowers a steam-driven device to pull them together and they turn miraculously into a watertight barrel. He bangs on the final hoops and then fires the cask inside with a sort of flame-thrower.

We leave the cooperage deafened by the noise and awed by the skill we have seen displayed, our attitude to the humble beer barrel changed for ever. We go up on to a roof, from where we see right down the Liffey across Dublin, its townscape largely unchanged since the days of the first Arthur Guinness, to the green domes of the Four Courts and the Customs House. Finally we repair to a bar where we are each given a drink. Guinness, it is explained to us, is made in four varieties whose main difference is in strength. There is Extra Stout, which accounts for the overwhelming majority of the production and is what the British and Irish public think of as Guinness; there is Porter, drunk only in Dublin and Belfast, which is rather weaker; then on the other hand there is Export, which is stronger and consumed mostly in Continental Europe; finally there is Foreign, the real Guinness drinker's drink, as strong as Export but with an extra dose of hops, the Guinness that goes overseas to sustain the British Empire.

Generations of visitors made this trip, regaled between stops with the lore of the Brewery. They heard tales of ghosts, of men drowned in tuns, of the 'troubles' at independence, of the Battle of the River Poddle when old Arthur and his workers expelled the men sent by Dublin Corporation who wanted to cut off his water which then came from that Liffey tributary. Yes, the Brewery had its glamour. Just what effect this had on sales one can only guess, but it certainly had some. Many of the visitors were British and Irish publicans, and their glimpse of the Brewery will have added subliminally to their respect for the product. And a publican will often influence his customers.

Not that they needed much influencing. Years before there

was any systematic advertising campaign, the Guinness image was already in place. Some aspects of this image were and are a bit mysterious, notably the rumour that it is brewed from the water of the polluted Liffey which flows past the Brewery and carries the product on stately barges down to the port of Dublin. Reference to this libel was one of the few ways in which one could get a rise out of my great-uncle Rupert Earl of Iveagh, normally an equable man; he was Chairman between 1927 and 1963. He was wrong to get worked up, for the story added in a strange way to the product's attraction. When I was nine or so, an older boy at my preparatory school told me that Mars bars were made of what he called Chinese eggs, tiny and sinister objects composed of dog meat and worse; the centre of a gobstopper, according to him, was also a Chinese egg. Being hopelessly gullible I believed him, but this did not, as perhaps he had hoped, make me hand him my supplies. On the contrary, it made gobstoppers and Mars bars all the more glamorous. I believe the Liffey water story had some such effect on the Guinness-drinking public.

In this and other ways, the image of Guinness always had a sort of glamour. Is this word too pretentious? 'Mystique' or 'magic' is no better, 'charm' seems a bit tame, because the image also contained a certain mystery. Glamour it shall be. Possibly the term is endangered if discussed, but I doubt it. The image has been endlessly dissected already by friend and foe, and it has remained quite unaffected. 'Obdurate', Alan Wood called it, his respect tinged with exasperation. As Public Relations Director in the early 1970s he was in charge of the image, and found it was something that could not be tinkered with. This insight, by an exceptionally effective and sensitive executive, certainly contributed to the feeling of depression that crept up on the Board when it seemed that the Guinness image would not satisfy the new tastes of a new generation. If it could not be changed, what was there left but the prospect of slow and seedy decline? But this is to anticipate.

The Chinese egg factor could not, to be sure, be made explicit. On the contrary: the part of Guinness's reputation which was to pay best was the general view that it was *wholesome*. People have always enjoyed drinking Guinness, but the enjoyment has never been seen as particularly uproarious, considering that Guinness is an alcoholic drink. It was powerfully reinforced by a feeling that it was good for the health. This was already around long before 1929, providing that powerful moral reinforcement that works such magic with consumers in the British Isles. I call it the Filboid Studge effect, after Saki's short story in which a breakfast cereal sweeps the country when given this grim name. A poster shows a man being roasted by devils; the caption is 'He Can't Get his Filboid Studge Now'. What we came up with was, of course, 'Guinness is Good for You'.

Is Guinness in fact good for you? On the whole it is. The yeast residue and the malt both provide some B vitamins as well as nourishing carbohydrate and protein, the humulone content from the hops, higher than in most beers, acts as a mild sedative. (Hop pillows used to be prescribed for insomniacs.) Guinness is therefore both nourishing and relaxing. Doctors used to prescribe it to nursing mothers and people who were 'run down'; perhaps they still do. I'm sure it helps the patients, cheering them up as well as calming and feeding them. Cynics will say that all this ignores what most Guinness drinkers have always really gone for, which is the alcohol content; but I for one am prepared to meet them head on and say that of course the alcohol assists the cheering effect, and why not? To be sure, one can get as abjectly drunk on too much Guinness as on any other booze. But an alcoholic who concentrated on Guinness would be less malnourished than if he confined himself to, say, vodka.

In fact few Guinness drinkers are alcoholics. They are not even 'bingers'. In the 1960s it was calculated that 70 per cent of Guinness was drunk by people who drank it every day. Guinness becomes a habit; its devotees take a daily pint or two, and that is all. It rarely appeals to the new drinker; the high hop rate and the roasted barley combine to make it rather bitter. Young people are also less interested in their health, so are less susceptible to the Filboid Studge effect. Guinness drinkers, therefore, have usually tended to be getting on in years: a fact that has often worried the marketing men who fear that the poor old things may just die out one day without the rising generation acquiring the taste. Every now and then a campaign used to be suggested with a 'Y. G. Twist' – young generation, that is. At most times, this worry has proved unfounded. Alan Wood had no doubts, writing in 1975: 'Guinness, fortunately, has always been very conservative about modifying itself. For example, its image tends to be too bitter. This comes up in every piece of research. It remains too bitter. In consequence, our advertising strategy is to say, not "new, less bitter", but "a touch of bitterness".' Although by the mid-1970s the threat to the brand from lager was beginning to look serious, this defensive tactic did keep together the hard core of Guinness drinkers pending the arrival of Ernest Saunders who, coming new to the Company and to the industry, refused to accept that people would avoid the product until their hair went grey.

Some of the glamour is associated with the vague, misty, occasionally sinister magic associated in the British mind with Ireland. There, Guinness's Brewery had come to dominate the beer trade by the late nineteenth century. So had its product, stout; most other breweries in Ireland also came to concentrate on it. Nobody will ever quite know why this was. In the eighteenth century the Brewery produced ale as well as stout, as indeed it does again. But starting towards the end of that century, demand for ale in Ireland diminished until stout and its lighter version, porter, became almost the only beer that was drunk there; Guinness eventually became keenly concerned not to monopolize its production, perceiving that this would be politically dangerous. Stout has been such a part of everyday life in Ireland, such a staple, that it became known as 'plain', as readers of J. P.

Donleavy's *The Ginger Man* will remember. The expression is also celebrated in a verse by Brian O'Nolan:

> *When things go wrong and will not come right,*
> *Though you do the best you can,*
> *When life looks black as the hour of night,*
> *A PINT OF PLAIN IS YOUR ONLY MAN.*
>
> *When money's tight and is hard to get*
> *And your horse has also ran,*
> *When all you have is a heap of debt,*
> *A PINT OF PLAIN IS YOUR ONLY MAN.*

The Brewery, by the time it became a public company in 1886, was far and away the most important undertaking in Ireland outside Ulster. Dublin was dominated by it; in at least one way this remains true, for to this day the whole city smells of brewing when the prevailing west wind spreads the odours over it. Everybody wanted a job there. In handpicking among applicants for employment, the Brewery did not favour its own customers. On the contrary, it liked to employ people who belonged to the Temperance movement, reliability being rated higher than love of the product.

Another poem, unpublished as far as I know, of which someone once gave me a typescript (since lost), averred that

> *The Garden of Eden described in the Bible*
> *Was Guinness's Brewery, mentioned by Joyce.*

Before the Fall of Man, we were told:

> *Nothing existed but Guinness's Brewery,*
> *Guinness's Brewery occupied all.*

Any Dubliner, certainly of the older generation, will see what the unknown poet was getting at. As to being 'mentioned by Joyce', so the Brewery most certainly is, repeatedly, although as usual with this author it always suffers a 'sea-change into something rich and strange'. In *Finnegans Wake* we find Guinnghis Khan and Allfor Guineas; *Ulysses* features 'the foaming ebon ale which the noble twin brothers Bungiveagh and Bungardilaun brew ever in their devine alevat, cunning as the sons of deathless Leda'.

Dublin intellectuals were not always so genial about the Brewery. Brian O'Nolan, author of the poem about the pint of plain, wrote to Chief Brewer Owen Williams (9 August 1963):

> Guinness grows every week in the public's detestation . . . I believe it can be said of the brewery that it is the only large industrial concern in Europe in which Catholics . . . are totally barred except for the most menial positions . . . I am myself becoming more and more horrified by this Liffey-side huddle of shabby, wealthy Protestant nitwits, many bearing ludicrous 'titles' and indefatigably concerned to prove they are not Paddies . . .

Williams comments:

> I never quite understood why I was the fortunate recipient of this magnificent polemic. I was on reasonably friendly terms with [O'Nolan] . . . He was at this time [shortly before his death] generally plunged into melancholy and it required a number of large Irish whiskeys to get him out of it. He was then brilliant and fascinating for about an hour and a half until the drink finally took possession of him . . . The last time I saw him . . . he wanted us to provide some money for some project he had in mind, I cannot remember what. I blew rather cold on it and this may have been why he wrote me this letter.

This outburst shows how the Dublin intelligentsia could sometimes feel a sort of Third World rancour. *In vino veritas:* O'Nolan was not the only 'lovely character' among the Irish literati to reveal such feelings in his cups. Yet most Dubliners of all classes and religions have seemed friendly to the Brewery and proud of it.

In Ireland, in Dublin especially, the glamour has attached more to the huge and fragrant Brewery than to the everyday plain that gushes out of it. In England it has naturally been the other way round; it is the 'obdurate image' that has kept people drinking Guinness. In the days when most pubs were owned or controlled by rival brewers, those brewers found increasingly that it paid better to sell Guinness than to promote their own stouts. Whitbread's Mackeson, the largest apparent exception, is much sweeter, and a blindfold drinker would be more likely to confuse it with a brown ale than with Guinness. The last important dry stout to rival Guinness in England until the last few years was Reid's, which belonged to Watneys; the owners found it worth their while to sell the brand to Guinness and stop brewing it. Now things are changing; an ancient dread of the Guinness Board has been realized, with the increased penetration into England of Murphy and Beamish financed by the powerful companies that own the brands. But now that Guinness the Company no longer depends on Guinness the brand, this matters less.

What is the Guinness secret? Is there one? There have been all sorts of rumours, including some which were clearly put about by the enemies of the business; the Liffey water story is only one of these and not the most offensive. I remember being solemnly told that a man had been drowned in a vat and that the Guinness that year had been particularly delicious. The facts are more ordinary. Guinness is made from malt with a proportion of roasted barley, hops, yeast, and of course water, which if the product is not to be spoilt has to be pure. As to brewing techniques, the knack which the first Arthur acquired and which subsequent generations improved could in theory have been duplicated by anybody at any time. Yet it was not; the Brewery outpaced all rivals and grew to be the biggest in the world, long before systematic advertising began in February 1929. Day to day, this was achieved by careful quality control and continuous improvement of production methods. Good customer relations were also important, as was marketing; and although in the days of the original Arthur Guinness and his immediate descendants the word marketing was not yet used in this sense, they certainly practised it intelligently.

Intelligently: this is the key. If Guinness had a secret it was, quite simply, brainpower. The early Guinnesses were exceptionally bright, and also quite evidently possessed the ability to attract other bright people to work in their business.

Arthur, the founder of the Brewery, was the son of Richard Guinness, a Protestant born about 1690. As a young man Richard became steward and land agent to the Revd Arthur Price, Church of Ireland Rector of Celbridge, near Dublin. Richard Guinness prospered as his master advanced in the Church, in due course becoming Archbishop of Cashel; to be steward to an Archbishop was to be somebody. Very probably Richard called his son Arthur after his employer. When he grew up Arthur also worked for the Archbishop, evidently as brewer to the household, for when in 1756 Price died and left him £100 he invested it in a small brewery at Leixlip, a few miles from Celbridge. Arthur did well enough there to move to Dublin, where he brought a 9,000-year lease on a larger brewery at St James's Gate. It stood on about 4 acres of land which included a dwelling house, garden and fishpond. The start of the Guinness business is always taken as being 1759, the date of this move.

Living at first on the premises, Arthur brewed all the types of beer which existed at that date, including the dark beer known as porters' ale or porter. The colour was obtained by including in the mash, with the ordinary pale malt, a proportion of malt that was roasted until virtually black. Nowadays the roast material consists not of malt, but of unmalted barley. Infusions from it, cooked in coffee machines by the Brewers to test the colour of each sample, taste and indeed are identical to the ersatz coffee prevalent on the Continent just after the war. About 10 per cent of the Guinness mash consists of this roast barley.

In Arthur's day brewing was still an art, not a science; Louis Pasteur was as yet unborn, and there were no laboratories to analyse samples of barley and hops; the brewer's eye was the only measuring tool. As to yeast, it is a living organism, and a quick-breeding one; and even now with strict scientific control it can develop a genetic mutation so inconvenient as to require the destruction of an entire batch. Arthur must have mastered all these problems better than most.

In particular, he was among the first Irishmen to become really good at producing the black porter. There was money in this. Porter had first been produced in London in the mid-seventeenth century. It became popular enough to be exported to Ireland; the transport cost made it into a premium drink, more expensive than ordinary beer of comparable strength, therefore more profitable to brew for anyone who had the knack. (The position of lager in modern England has been similar; higher profit margins could be obtained because it was supposed to be foreign.) Once Arthur Guinness and the other Irish brewers – he had competitors – had cracked the technical problem and produced a porter as good as that which came from London, it was worth their while to concentrate on it. Soon the Irish product not only equalled the London porter, but surpassed it; after conquering the Dublin market, Irish porter became in demand in Britain. It was brewed in different strengths, and the exports were of strong or extra stout porter, later known simply as stout. (In modern times, however, all beer has become steadily weaker, and today's stout has much less strength than the porter of 1914.) This success in the English market was achieved in the teeth of an extra tax which penalized beer imported from Ireland. When this was removed in 1795 it cleared the way for the Brewery to give up ale-brewing altogether in 1799 and concentrate on porter and stout, much of it for the export trade.

When he had made enough money, Arthur moved to the country, buying a house of grey stone at Beaumont, near Dublin, built with the sober grace of the Irish eighteenth century, to accommodate his enormous family. He had married Olivia Whitmore in 1761 and she bore him twenty-one children of whom ten lived to grow up. He started the family tradition of good works by founding the Dublin Sunday School, the first in Ireland. He took an interest in politics, being a friend and patron of the Irish statesman Henry Grattan, whom he assisted in his campaign for the emancipation of the Roman Catholic majority in Ireland from the penal laws that deprived them of many elementary rights.

Arthur died in 1803 at the age of seventy-eight. His eldest son Hosea had become a clergyman, but three of his other sons were already running the Brewery and it was to them that he left the business. Chief of them, and Arthur's effective successor, was his second son, also called Arthur, born in 1768. Of the others, Benjamin died in 1826 and William Lunell in 1842, so the second Arthur did not attain sole ownership until he was seventy-four, but he was always effectively in control. As a leader of Irish business he became in 1820 Governor of the Bank of Ireland, in which capacity he united the Irish pound with sterling. He was a devout supporter of the Evangelical movement of Low Church enthusiasm; his letters to his family could have been written by one of those earnest Dissenters who were building British industry in the North of England and in Ulster. Many of the Guinness family were conspicuously religious; besides his elder brother in holy orders, the second Arthur had three daughters married to clergymen, and his nephew, Henry Grattan Guinness, was to become one of the most celebrated preachers of his age and beget a formidable family of missionaries. However, despite his Low Church inclinations, the second Arthur followed his father in supporting Roman Catholic emancipation. In 1829, when the Duke of Wellington as Prime Minister finally enacted it, he said in a speech: 'Hitherto, although always a sincere advocate for Catholic freedom, I could never look my Catholic neighbour confidently in the face . . . We shall henceforth meet as equals.'[1]

It was during the time of the second Arthur that Guinness stout became familiar in England. Already in 1814 Irish beer exports exceeded imports, although Guinness was not yet preponderant in this trade, which was at first dominated by the Cork brewers. One of these, Beamish and Crawford, was the largest brewery in Ireland at the time; this firm comes into our story again in the 1960s. Its production at about 100,000 barrels a year was roughly half as much again as that of Guinness.[2] All the same, Guinness was already the leader of the Dublin brewers, with a growing reputation. As early as the Battle of Waterloo we find a British officer drinking a glass of Guinness. Later, in 1837, Disraeli records dining on Guinness and oysters at the Carlton Club; by that time Guinness had far outpaced all its Irish rivals. Later still, the illustrator of Dickens's *Pickwick Papers* shows Sam Weller composing his valentine in a pub with a point-of-sale Guinness advertisement on the mantelpiece, proof that Guinness advertising existed well before 1929 when it is supposed to have started.

After the end of the Napoleonic Wars came a severe recession all over the British Isles, which apart from radicalizing opinion and eventually bringing about the Reform Bill also caused Guinness the sharpest and most sudden setback in its history. By 1820, sales were only 41 per cent of their 1815 peak, and not until 1833 did they recover to that level.[3] This was what made the second Arthur push the export trade, with tremendous success; by 1840 the strong double or extra stout, mostly sold in the English market, accounted for 82 per cent of output.[4]

Some time in the 1840s the second Arthur retired; his third son, Benjamin Lee, took over the running of the business. Shortly afterwards Ireland was hit by the disastrous Potato Famine. Arthur wrote to Benjamin from retirement in Torquay in 1849, when the famine was into its third year:

> May the Lord in his infinite mercy direct our Government and all individuals also possessing means to do so to the use of measures to relieve if possible the sufferings of our wretched poor people. I wish to know any mode in which we might be able to aid in the work. You know my dear Ben that my purse is open to the call.

Benjamin's elder brother Arthur Lee had already responded to the emergency. His workpeople gave him a miniature replica in green marble of an obelisk in Stillorgan Park with the inscription:

> *1847. To Arthur Lee Guinness Esq. To mark the veneration of his faithful labourers who in a period of dire distress were protected by his generous liberality from the prevailing destitution, this humble testimonial is respectfully dedicated consisting of home materials. Its colour serves to remind that the memory of benefits will ever remain green in Irish hearts.*

Arthur Lee had started in the Brewery but had not enjoyed it; he was a country gentleman and lifelong bachelor, a dilettante and a collector. When he was young his puritanical father used to lecture him for extravagance; it is to old Arthur's credit that he allowed his son to leave the business on generous terms, paid his debts and never interfered. Arthur Lee's nephew Edward Cecil, future Earl of Iveagh, must have known him as a boy; it may have been this kindly philanthropist who started the interest in paintings which ultimately led to the collection in Kenwood House.

The second Arthur died in 1855 at the age of eighty-seven, leaving the Brewery to his son Benjamin Lee who was already running it. The same year marked the start of a considerable advance in the Irish market, largely powered by the building of the Irish railways. Dublin porter sales multiplied sixteen-fold between 1855 and 1880.[5] Exports continued to progress as well. Benjamin Lee also took part in public affairs, becoming Mayor of Dublin in 1851. He married his first cousin, Elizabeth Guinness, daughter of the second Arthur's brother Edward, a failed iron-master. (Cousin marriages have been common in the Guinness family; Benjamin's son Edward Cecil was also to marry a Guinness cousin, though a less close one.)

Benjamin had a large house on St Stephen's Green in Dublin is well as a country estate, but he also spent time in London, especially after 1865 when he became Member of Parliament for Dublin City. He sent his first two sons to Eton. Spending less time in Dublin, he had to delegate much of the day-to-day running of the Brewery to the manager, John Tertius Purser.

It was not only for the Guinnesses that the Brewery was a family business. At all levels it was usual for fathers to encourage their sons to follow them into the Brewery. John Tertius Purser represented the third generation in his family to work there. His grandfather John, a member of the Nonconformist Church known as the Moravian Brothers, had worked for the first Arthur but had left, or perhaps been sacked, following a quarrel with the old man. After Arthur's death, however, the second Arthur took John Purser back as head bookkeeper, and no fewer than seven of his descendants were to follow him in the business. His son, John Purser Junior, was promoted by the second Arthur to be a partner. Two sons and four grandsons of John Purser Junior followed him (see the family tree of Pursers and Geoghegans in Appendix B.)

John Tertius was born in 1809 and taken on in 1824 at the age of fifteen. He progressed steadily in the business, becoming manager under Benjamin Lee. He certainly made an important contribution to the continued growth in profits which enabled Benjamin Lee to pay for a complete restoration of St Patrick's Cathedral, a benefaction which is said to have been the main reason for his being awarded a baronetcy in 1867.

TWO

From Partnership to Company

Sir Benjamin died suddenly in May 1868, following a chill. He was seventy, but his death was unexpected. The Brewery now belonged in equal shares to his first and third sons, Arthur and Edward Cecil; the middle son, Lee, was a soldier. Arthur, now Sir Arthur, was twenty-eight and Edward Cecil only twenty-one, but it was the younger brother who was closer to the business, where he had been working since the age of sixteen. He was not sent to Eton like his elder brothers, although he did study at Trinity College, Dublin, which is not far from St James's Gate. He knew the Brewery well and everyone who worked there. So did Sir Benjamin's sudden death and the comparative remoteness of his elder brother mean that Edward ran the whole business? This view has got around, and can seem plausible in the light of Edward's later outstanding business success. All the same, it is not quite the case. At twenty-one, though already familiar with the working of the business, Edward Cecil was in many ways still learning, and he was by no means always at the Brewery. Much later in life, he was to comment following a visit to the United States: 'It is no place for a gentleman to live, because everyone works.' He could and did work hard when he had to, but work for its own sake held no appeal to him. He chose the right people and delegated to them; a talent he shared with his forebears and some of his descendants.

The most important man in the Brewery at this stage did not

have to be chosen; John Tertius Purser was already in place. When Sir Benjamin died, Purser was fifty-nine. He was utterly loyal to the family and innocent of any thought of supplanting it. Edward Cecil could rely on Purser to look after the business in his absence, which enabled him to keep up an active social and sporting life in London as well as Dublin. Edward bought the lease of a flat in Berkeley Square in 1870, a convenient spot then as now for London's picture galleries; he was already interested in paintings.

Edward Cecil married Adelaide Guinness in 1873; he was twenty-six, she was three years older. Her father was Richard Samuel Guinness, Member of Parliament for Kinsale, grandson of Samuel Guinness, goldsmith, who was the first Arthur's brother. Adelaide's father, like Sir Benjamin's father-in-law, had done badly in business. In Richard's case it was a small private bank which had failed. He had owned it in partnership with his older brother, Robert Rundell Guinness, who in due course left the partnership, taking with him John Ross Mahon with whom he founded another bank, Guinness and Mahon. This became an internationally known business and has survived, under various incarnations, to this day.

Richard recovered after a fashion, presumably with the help of Robert Rundell. In due course he returned to the House of Commons, this time representing Barnstaple. All the same he was never prosperous, and when he died in 1857 his widow Katherine and eight children were left in what Adelaide herself later described as 'grinding poverty'. Actually the family's circumstances seem rather to have answered to Nancy Mitford's phrase 'poor – but not like poor people', for Adelaide's mother always managed to keep servants. She ought to have been delighted at her daughter's engagement to one of the richest men in Ireland, but when one came of an old Gloucestershire family and one's father was Sir Thomas Jenkinson, Baronet, one's daughter ought not to marry a brewer. When she was finally brought to yield, she grumbled at losing her daughter: 'Who will walk the dogs?' she wondered.

In fact the match was to prove good for two of her sons as well as for her daughter. In 1881 Edward took on Adelaide's younger brother Claude at the Brewery at the age of twenty-nine, with the idea that he should succeed John Tertius Purser when the old man retired. Quite apart from being a member of the family, Claude was generally regarded as brilliantly clever. He would have been a catch for any business, with his first-class degree from Oxford; he was an athlete as well, foreshadowing the twentieth-century managers and directors who also often combined scholarship with being good at games. Also, when the Brewery became a public company in 1886 an older brother of Adelaide and Claude, Reginald Robert, was made a director and became Chairman when Edward Cecil temporarily retired from the Board.

Sir Arthur Guinness had already married Lady Olivia White, daughter of the Earl of Bantry, in 1872. Like his father, he sat in Parliament for Dublin City as a Unionist. His primary interest was politics. Disraeli was to elevate him to the peerage as Baron Ardilaun in 1880 after he lost his Commons seat. As owner of a half-share of the Brewery he did less work and drew more money than his brother; the two of them shared the profits unequally and in proportions that seem wholly haphazard. To Edward Cecil he was an expensive passenger. Sir Benjamin had provided in his will that if either brother wished to leave the partnership, the other had the right to buy him out for £30,000. Considering that annual profits in 1868 were already £102,000 and rising strongly, this was already hopelessly inadequate even at the time of Sir Benjamin's death, and clearly Sir Arthur would not settle for such a meagre sum. Production had doubled in eight years, from 350,000 barrels in 1868 to 700,000 in 1876, and profits had risen more than commensurately. There was certainly some hard bargaining between the brothers.

The deal was achieved in December 1876. Sir Arthur accepted a price of £680,000, payable in instalments, representing a capital payment of £600,000 plus a profit share of £80,000. In those days this was a tidy sum – for the modern equivalent it should be multiplied by at least fifty – and certainly Ardilaun was a rich man to the end of his life, indeed one of the richest men in Ireland. All the same, it was not long before the deal showed itself to have been a bad one for him, for in that very year, 1876, the profits of the business turned out at £302,000, and ten years afterwards it went public for £6 million.

Ardilaun's enduring claim to fame is that he bought the land enclosed by St Stephen's Green, Dublin, paid to have it landscaped and presented it to the public. He thus created perhaps the finest city square in Europe, big enough to be thought of as a park; his statue still stands there, self-confident and severe. In life he was a strange mixture. Generous to every sort of charity, and especially to the Church of Ireland, as a politician he was crotchety and unconstructive. The idea of any sort of Irish Home Rule horrified him. At the turn of the century he opposed the agricultural cooperative movement promoted by the progressive Unionist Sir Horace Plunkett; Edward Cecil, on the other hand, supported this, as did most sensible people, because its aim was to help Irish farmers to make better profits. Extremes met in their opposition to Plunkett; the Irish republicans also detested his cooperatives and their 'creameries', which the IRA used to burn down.

Ardilaun and his wife had no children; they gave elaborate parties both in Dublin and in London, where they lived at 11 Carlton House Terrace. Dublin society accorded them deep respect, with a tinge of mockery. Any slight impropriety made people ask; 'What will Lady Ardilaun say?'

In 1885 Edward Cecil was made a baronet as the result of his help with the State visit to Dublin that year of the Prince of Wales, later Edward VII. It was a distinctly tricky time for such a visit. Three years before, terrorists had shot two high-ranking Government officials in Phoenix Park. In the year of the visit itself, there had been a General Election in which Charles Parnell's Irish Party had won eighty-five seats, overwhelmingly a majority in Ireland. From that time on there could be no doubt either that the Catholic majority in Ireland wanted separation from the United Kingdom, or that in some form they would get it. Even if such a separation was only partial, as Gladstone's Government intended, it would transform the Irish political establishment. New people would gain influence in Dublin, and others would lose it. Parnell held the balance of power in Parliament, so the change looked not only inevitable, but imminent.

Inevitable it was, but not imminent. Scandal in the Irish Party and a split among the Liberals combined to postpone it for nearly forty years. But in 1885 the smart money was on some form of Home Rule within a short time, and so there were those in Dublin who wondered whether it was wise to be seen to welcome the Prince too warmly. For this very reason, the authorities needed the visit to be a success. Edward Cecil was High Sheriff of Dublin at the time, and cajoled or shamed the magistrates into making an effort. This succeeded; Edward Cecil earned his baronetcy.

In the meantime, the Brewery had become by the mid-1880s the largest brewery in the world, 'with a unique product, an unrivalled output, technical leadership and soaring profits'.[1] With profits for 1885 of £647,662, Edward Cecil reckoned it was time to cash in some of his gains by making the business a public company quoted on the London stock market. Today this thinking would be routine; in those days, when most businesses were still private partnerships, it was more of an event. Edward Cecil made the move in 1886, just ten years after buying out his brother, using Baring Brothers as his merchant bank. Barings were apparently his second choice; he is said to have first informally approached Rothschilds, who did not want to be associated with a brewing issue and accordingly turned him down.

The price was £6 million. Edward Cecil received not the full amount but £5,486,000, of which £825,000 was in ordinary shares at their par value and the balance of £4,661,000 in cash. The deductions consisted of issue expenses at £125,000 and a deficiency of £82,000 by which the final valuation of the Brewery stocks fell short of what had been promised in the prospectus. There was no fuss about this; Edward simply subtracted the sum from the amount due to him from the new Company. He also had to repay £307,000 which had been deposited with the business, mainly by employees who used it as their bank. From the balance, he gave four weeks' wages to the workmen, cheques of an unspecified amount to the clerks, and to the Brewers ordinary shares to the value of three months' salary. He gave presents of money to members of his family, the largest being £150,000 to his brother Lee, now a captain in the Royal Horse Guards, who had never shared in the prosperity of the Brewery. He gave £500 in ordinary shares to Father Healy of Bray, a stout priest whom Edward Cecil liked because he amused him, and who had been disappointed in his share application; a situation in which, as we shall see, he was by no means alone.

John Tertius Purser was also offered a gift, but refused it. He was by then seventy-seven, but a lifetime of dour Nonconformist abstemiousness had left him with scarcely diminished vigour, still running the Brewery day to day. He turned down £2,500 in ordinary shares and £2,500 in preference shares before retiring in dudgeon. Conceivably he thought the offer rather mean, though it was higher than was allotted to any other employee. Purser's position was unique. He had worked in the Brewery for sixty-two years; for much of that time he had more or less run it. He had even helped to finance it; of the depositors whom Edward Cecil repaid by far the largest was Purser, with £217,000, an astonishing fortune to leave on deposit. Purser's deposit account must have been distinctly helpful to Edward Cecil in getting together the cash to buy out his brother, a deal which made him, literally, millions. But the amount offered by Edward Cecil was probably irrelevant to Purser. He wanted no part of any public company.

All the same, the Purser family remained friends with the Guinnesses down the generations. I myself was taken as a child to tea with Miss Sarah Purser, John Tertius's daughter, for her nine-tieth birthday. She had a huge cake with ninety candles on it.

After the issue the ordinary shares climbed steadily, not only because they had been undervalued at the time of the issue, but also because Edward Cecil dealt on a large scale. Sometimes he sold, but mostly he was a buyer; by February 1888 he had added more than £500,000 to his holding, giving him over 50 per cent and control. Today any company chairman operating in this way would be compelled by law to reveal his dealings. At that time Edward Cecil's operations did not excite any particular attention; certainly nobody thought the worse of him. The shares are thought to have cost him an average price of nearly £20 each, or twice their par value. All the same, Edward did well out of the operation because of the gearing factor. The sale of £3.5 million worth of fixed interest securities had concentrated the future appreciation of the business on the ordinary shares and released a huge amount of capital for him to invest at will.

This was the composition of the Board at the time of the issue:

Sir Edward Cecil Guinness, Chairman
Claude Guinness, Managing Director
Reginald Robert Guinness
Viscount Castlerosse
Henry R. Glyn
Herman Hoskier
James R. Stewart

Reginald Robert Guinness, it will be remembered, was an elder brother of Adelaide and of Claude; he was to be knighted in 1897 and would be Chairman of the Company for a short time.

Viscount Castlerosse was son of the Earl of Kenmare and a crony of Edward Cecil's. Henry Glyn and Herman Hoskier were bankers, directors respectively of Glyn Mills and Brown Shipley. James Stewart was a solicitor.

All this was quite straightforward. The handling of the issue was another matter. The behaviour of Barings can only be described as 'hot', traditional City slang meaning more or less disreputable. Edward Cecil suffered, and so did the subscribing public. The valuation of the Company at £6 million did Edward Cecil out of a very large sum, probably more than £1 million. Given the chance, a merchant bank likes to keep the price of an issue moderate so as to be certain that the issue will appeal to investors; in this case, though, the way in which the public 'stagged' (oversubscribed) the securities offered proves not only that the price was far too low but that this was obvious to all. Barings had even tried to get Edward Cecil to accept £5 million, but he stuck out for £6 million. He cannot have been best pleased when Claude Guinness told him that an expert had valued the Brewery property at £8,640,000.

The new Company which acquired the business from Edward Cecil for £6 million issued the following securities:

Ordinary shares of £10	£2,500,000
6 per cent preference shares of £10	2,000,000
Share capital	4,500,000
5 per cent debenture stock	1,500,000
Total	6,000,000

The largest profit could be expected in the ordinary shares, which would participate in the future growth of the Company; but in those non-inflationary times there was also a sure profit in the 6 per cent preference shares, because the interest rate, for a security with virtually no risk, was comparatively high. Sure enough, the ordinary were to jump by 65 per cent on the first day of dealing, and the preference by 35 per cent. The two classes of shares totalled £4.5 million, for which applications were received for £114 million, mostly from the general public. Edward Cecil received £825,000 in ordinary shares as part of his consideration, leaving £3,575,000 to be issued.

Thousands rushed to submit applications. Anticipating this, Barings had secured a special police presence outside their Bishopsgate premises to control the crowd of applicants. The mob broke through the cordon and milled about; one of Barings' outer doors was broken. It was said that one or two desperate applicants on the edge, despairing of getting in, wrapped their application forms round stones and threw them through the windows. When forms ran out, people were prepared to buy them for 21 shillings.

Nowadays, when an issuing house is faced by a large over-subscription, it normally scales down the large applications and puts the smaller ones into a ballot, thus achieving a sort of rough justice. Often the smaller applicant from the general public is actually favoured, as happened in many of the privatization issues. Barings had no truck with such pandering to the common man. This was how most of the securities were apportioned:

Baring Bros, as a firm	(over) £800,000
Thomas Charles Baring	70,000
Thomas Baring	20,000
Lord and Lady Ashburton (family name Baring)	35,000
Lt General Baring	10,000
Colonel Baring	2,000
Subtotal, Baring Tribe	(over) £937,000
Glyn Mills	250,000
Hambros	105,000
Morgans	100,000
Rothschilds	350,000
Subtotal, City firms	805,000
Lord Rosebery (married to a Rothschild)	40,000
TOTAL favoured applications	(over) £1,882,000

26

This left the wretched public with less than £1,693,000, and gave Barings and their connections a profit of at least £500,000, quite apart from their fees.[2]

The favouring of other City firms shown in this list cannot quite be classed with the allocations to the Baring family and firm. It was part of a practice of mutual help which then, as now, stabilized the whole system by making it less likely for a firm to collapse. Only four years later Barings were to get into deep trouble with Argentine loans in the episode known as the Baring Crisis; in the end they were bailed out by the Bank of England, but other City firms also rallied round, Rothschilds prominent among them.

Barings had broken no law. Standard practice had not been established, and in fact this episode was one of those which helped to do this. But Philip Ziegler is too lenient when he says: 'By the standards of the day their behaviour can hardly even be described as immoral.'[3] Views of morality current at different times do vary, it is true, so the test of whether an action has offended the moral standards of its time is the way in which contemporaries saw it. Barings fail this test; people perceived, quite as clearly as they would today, that they had hogged too much for themselves. The Press was outraged; many people wrote angry letters to Barings. One writer told them that they had perpetrated 'one of the most disgraceful frauds on the public that in my experience has ever been concocted'; another returned a prospectus for another issue saying he was resolved 'if I can possibly help it to have no further dealings with your firm of any kind'.[4] So although Barings got away with their loot, it was at considerable cost in public relations. They lost an issue for another brewery, Walkers of Liverpool, as the result of their behaviour, and also because Lord Revelstoke, their senior partner, was too arrogant to accept criticism. 'During the discussion some strong words were used in Lord Revelstoke's presence. He pointed to the door, and the firm lost the quarter million or so which might have accrued from the business.'[5] Another brewery, Combe & Company, did give Barings their issue, but insisted that two of their directors should be present when Barings decided the allotments.[6]

City insiders were comparatively charitable, and this was only partly because they were in on similar operations themselves. It was mainly because they saw, more clearly than the general public, that new issues were dangerous. Failures, often ruinously costly, had to be balanced by a reasonable profit when there was a success. Edward Cecil Guinness probably realized this, for there is no record of his having objected to being short-changed by Barings. Yet there are surely limits in these matters.

So the story of Guinness as a family-dominated public company started with a historic City scandal, just as it was to end with another a century later. That of the 1880s was the simpler, in that it was purely a matter of greed; the public soon forgot it, and the City took its lessons on board in due course. That of the 1980s was far more complex. Greed there was, but it was joined by others of the Seven Deadly Sins. Pride, in the form of ambition, was at least as important as greed in powering events; fear and envy played their part. So, as a family member I have to admit, did sloth. Politicians and civil servants had dammed the river of human avarice for all the world like busy beavers, producing backwaters, locks and swamps. Later in this story we shall find indications that there is much amiss with the system they have produced. But nostalgia for the old City which was, we are told, ruled by gentlemen should be tempered by the memory of how some of those gentlemen actually behaved.

The organization of the business had already been remoulded before the issue. Until 1877, the Brewers who were taken on to manage the business were Protestant Irishmen educated in Ireland, often recruited through family connections; most of them were members of the Guinness family through the male or female line (see Appendix B) or of other brewery families such as the Pursers and Geoghegans (Appendix C). From 1877 on, Edward Cecil ceased to recruit senior employees in this way, finding them instead among public school-educated science graduates throughout the British Isles, never accepting anyone with less than a second-class degree. This was an up-to-date way of ensuring that Guinness would continue to be run by intelligent people. By the inter-war period degrees had to be in science, usually chemistry or physics, or engineering. This pattern, which lasted in essentials until the time of Ernest Saunders, by no means prevented sons from following in their fathers' footsteps (see Appendix C). It produced managers who were cultured as well as competent and who were often also talented sportsmen. Their science degrees ensured that they had technical knowledge, their public school background had taught them the humanities. The atmosphere within the Guinness Board used to be compared with that in a college common room. Outside the Brewery, too, the Brewers cut a dash in Dublin society. Invitations by the Viceroy to Dublin Castle were automatic; Owen Williams tells us that 'a brewer on early duty would not infrequently appear in knee breeches and buckled shoes, complete with sword'.[7]

The Brewers constituted the firm's aristocracy. 'Who is the Brewer in charge of advertising?' someone was to ask Thomas Marks, when he took charge of Guinness publicity in the 1960s. 'There is no brewer in charge of advertising,' Marks replied tartly. In his mind, as a newcomer, the word brewer had no capital letter; it meant somebody who brewed beer. To his questioner, the word denoted a figure of authority. A Guinness Brewer, once hired, had a well-paid job, hours (though subject to occasional shift-work) from nine till four, six weeks' 'leave' (*sic*: as in the public services this term was used rather than 'holidays'), plenty of scope for promotion, civilized colleagues and a good pension at the end.

The old guard was for some time suspicious of the graduates. William Purser Geoghegan was Head Brewer from 1880 to 1897 and Claude Guinness was in effect put in over his head. Under the old system Geoghegan would certainly have succeeded his uncle as Managing Director. He showed no direct resentment of this, but did not allow the new university-educated young gentlemen to do a proper job. Owen Williams tells us: 'The Brewers bought horses, looked after the Luncheon Room, harried the Medical Officers, but did little else [other] than the work later carried out by the Junior Brewery Office' – which was entirely routine. Geoghegan kept all the reins in his own hands, and it was not until after his day that the new Brewers were given proper responsibility.

Thomas Case was the first scientist to be taken on by the Brewery, in 1893. A sign of the times, this; brewing was becoming more science than art. It soon became apparent that one young Brewer, with a degree in natural science but no qualifications as a chemist, was not enough, even though Case was an able man who later became Managing Director of the Company. There were cases of passing off: a publican would sell as Guinness a product which was brewed elsewhere, and the Company would then sue, usually with success. But a certain D'Arcy, of Ballsbridge, cannier and better off than most publicans, hired a defending barrister. The barrister asked E. L. Phillips, the senior Brewer detailed to give evidence in these cases, if he was a chemist; he had to admit he was not, and the case was thrown out.

So the management looked for a real chemist, and in 1896 they engaged, on a three-year contract, a formidable twenty-four-year-old Scotsman called Alexander Forbes Watson. He needed to be formidable: the Brewers had no wish for any scientist to disturb their routine. Watson was told to act under the Brewery Office, to avoid friction, to 'start no new hares' and make himself useful in teaching Brewers. But he soon broke out of this modest role. He discovered how to make use of the beer at the bottom of the vats, which had hitherto been useless because the yeast sludge made it cloudy. Watson found that if this beer was heated to

180°F the yeast would sink to the bottom, clarifying it to the point where it was usable. He patented the process and sold it to the Company, greatly improving the profit margin.

This did not placate the Brewers; about halfway through his three-year contract it was decided not to re-employ Watson when the period had expired. But he was not so easily got rid of. Somebody was still needed to analyse samples for prosecution in passing-off cases. Watson proposed that he should continue to work for the Brewery as an outside contractor, and this arrangement was agreed. When it came to the ears of Edward Cecil he was angry, for he knew all about Watson and was acutely aware of his value and potential. He gave orders that the Company should take Watson on again and give him a laboratory of his own. This was kept entirely separate from the Brewers' Laboratory under Case, and relations remained cool. But from now on, the technique of brewing Guinness was based firmly on scientific principles.

THREE

Good for You

The flotation of the Company made Edward Cecil a national figure. Having acquired a very large sum in cash, he set to work to spend a lot of it. His charitable work was important, he did a good deal for science outside the Brewery as well as within it, he assembled one of the period's most important collections of paintings. He also became prominent for his lavish contribution to the period's rather ponderous amusements. In the summer he went for cruises on his large steam yachts, while the autumn and winter were the time for shooting. For this purpose he bought Elveden Hall in Suffolk with about 30,000 acres of poor land suitable for the rearing of pheasants. He held elaborate house-parties, mostly organized round the shoots in which sometimes 5,000 pheasants would be slaughtered in a day. The Prince of Wales was a regular guest; the future Edward VII had no objection to money made through trade, whatever Edward Cecil's mother-in-law might have thought. Over the years he became quite a friend, as did his son, later George V, who was once seen by Elizabeth Countess of Fingall shooting 'two birds coming up, and then, taking his second gun from the loader, two going back'.[1] The Elveden house-parties were by no means always pompous affairs. Edward Cecil's grandson Bryan wrote: 'I well remember my grandparents' old Irish friends staying there in happy informality.' He and his cousins, as children, had 'loved all those corridors and staircases for the escape routes they provided when we played hide-and-seek'.[2]

Bryan certainly wrote this with the conscious purpose of countering the image of his grandfather's displays of wealth; apart from belonging to a less self-confident generation, he had a very personal disapproval of ostentation and squirmed all his life at his family's reputation for affluence. But Edward Cecil was of his period. Adelaide Iveagh herself complained of another couple: 'My dear, I do think it is too much when *two* people bring five servants!' Lord and Lady Howe had come to stay bringing a valet, a maid, a secretary, a footman and a pony-boy.[3]

Edward Cecil's charitable work was as prominent as his conspicuous consumption. In 1890 he founded the Guinness Trust to clear slums and provide decent housing in London and Dublin. The idea came from his friend Lord Rowton, another Irishman. Originally named Montagu Lowry-Corry, Rowton had been private secretary to Disraeli, who made him a peer in 1880, at the same time as Lord Ardilaun. Philanthropy was in Rowton's family; his mother was the sister of the great Lord Shaftesbury. He created the Rowton Houses, extinct now but still remembered; they were 'common lodging houses' where people who were very poor but not quite destitute could obtain lodging in dormitories for a few pence a night.

The Guinness Trust dealt in cheap flats for working families, not beds for dossers. Rowton was the first Chairman, to be succeeded on his death in 1903 by Edward Cecil himself. The Guinness Trust was a fairly close imitation of the larger Peabody Trust, which dated from 1862. Peabody had shown what could be done in the way of slum clearance, but much more was needed. Edward Cecil himself had demolished and rebuilt a slum around Bull Alley in Dublin at a cost of about £220,000. The Guinness Trust, Dublin Fund, now added £50,000 for the same purpose, and was amalgamated with the Bull Alley scheme to form the Iveagh Trust. The London Fund amounted to £200,000 to which a further £100,000 was added later. It retained the name Guinness Trust. Its Trust Deed stipulates that the rents charged shall give a surplus after expenses amounting to 'a fair, low rate of interest', to ensure a steady expansion. The Trust is now one of the largest housing associations in Britain. Its expansion was steady rather than spectacular until the 1970s when, with the aid of Government finance, it greatly accelerated, and its properties are now valued (in modern pounds, to be sure) at £100 million.

We have seen how Edward Cecil steered the Brewery towards scientific competence in the matter of Alexander Forbes Watson. An accident induced him to fund scientific research outside the business. An Elveden farm worker called Jim Jackson, who looked after the carthorses, was bitten by his dog, which had rabies. The injections that Louis Pasteur had recently invented were only available at the Pasteur Institute in Paris, so Edward Cecil sent the patient there. The course of injections was painful – it is still the same today, forty jabs in the stomach – but it worked. Edward Cecil decided that the treatment ought to be available in London, and gave £255,000 to the recently founded Lister Institute, setting it on its feet.

Edward Cecil was made a baron in 1891, no doubt through Rowton's influence. He chose the title of Iveagh, to the irritation of the *Saturday Review* which saw it as a claim of descent from the old aristocratic Magennises of Iveagh, a claim of which the newspaper was rightly sceptical. It blamed the genealogist Sir Bernard Burke, again rightly. Edward Cecil's father had consulted Burke when he became a baronet, and if one hires a genealogist one accepts his opinion. (See Appendix A for consideration of the family's descent.) Edward Cecil was promoted to viscount in 1905 and to earl in 1919. The last promotion was probably due to his purchase, and gift to the public, of Kenwood House in London which he filled with the best of his collection of Old Master paintings.

He kept a shrewd eye on the business, even though mostly

34

from a distance. Nobody ever disputed that he was the boss, whatever his official status or shareholding, but his own attitude fluctuated; sometimes he felt like withdrawing, at other times he renewed his involvement. In 1886, at the time of the issue, he retained only a third of the ordinary share capital; then, as we have seen, he bought back enough to put him over 50 per cent. In July 1890 he resigned from the Chairmanship and even from the Board, appointing Reginald Guinness as his successor. However, he went back on the Board in 1898 and became Chairman again in 1902.

Early in 1895 there was a catastrophe; the brilliant Claude Guinness suddenly went off his head and had to be taken away in a straitjacket. No details survive of the incident; in those days people did not talk openly of such things and tried to forget them. Whatever happened was so painful and embarrassing that someone even went to the lengths of tearing out the page in the Brewery log for that day. There was private talk, of course, and later my father gleaned a little from word of mouth (he was not born at the time of the incident). He told me that the trouble was general paralysis of the insane, otherwise known as quaternary syphilis. If Claude was indeed suffering from syphilis he must have contracted it after the birth of his children, for he left healthy descendants. He died on 18 April 1895, aged forty-three. His brother Reginald succeeded him for a time, combining the posts of Managing Director and Chairman, but the real power was exercised by C. D. La Touche who was appointed Managing Director in 1902 when Reginald resigned, Edward Cecil resuming the Chairmanship at this time.

In July 1903 Edward Cecil again played a leading part in a royal visit to Dublin. By then his friend the Prince of Wales had succeeded to the throne as Edward VII. On this occasion there was no hesitation among the Irish notables of the kind they had shown in 1885. The people, too, cheered the King to the echo, as recounted in the *Morning Leader* of 25 July 1903:

There was practically nothing done in the way of decoration, only a solitary flag here and there hung out of a window. But the people assembled in their many hundreds to offer a greeting to the monarch. Hundreds of children, without shoes or stockings, women with shawls thrown over their heads, men in clothing which in England the ragman would despise – these formed the throng which gave welcome to the King . . . In the meagre streets, the King walked about unaffectedly, and bowed frequently to the cheering people. Youngsters in their bare legs scrambled between the police and were nearly trodden on by the monarch.

Had there been no First World War, Ireland might have contentedly progressed towards an agreed Home Rule, in which case the royal visit of 1903 might have come to be seen in the same light as that of George IV to Edinburgh in 1822, with Edward Cecil playing the part of an Irish Sir Walter Scott.

Among those who welcomed the King to the Iveagh Trust buildings was the eldest of Edward Cecil's three sons, Rupert, who was to succeed him as Chairman of the Brewery. Rupert was born in 1874, and educated at Eton, where he was wrongly thought to be stupid because he suffered from what is now known as dyslexia. (Family legend has it that he once spelled 'wife' 'yph', but this was probably a self-parody.) He also had a slight speech handicap. His last report from Eton glosses over his academic weakness and says: 'I think that his character is one of the most perfect I have ever met with in a boy here . . . I wish that his ability approached his character in excellence.' He was a brilliant oarsman, and won the Diamond Sculls at Henley. To all appearances, he was quite reconciled to his own deficiencies, such as they were. Many people throughout his long life looked on him as something approaching a saint.

Rupert joined the Board of the Brewery in 1899, and soon after that went out to the Boer War in charge of the Irish Hospital

First Aid Unit. This was paid for by Edward Cecil and staffed by seventy-two people from the Brewery and the Royal Irish Constabulary. On the ship out to South Africa Rupert won a prize for fancy dress; he dressed as a baby, complete with monstrous rattle. Often, throughout his life, people would say their babies looked like Rupert; he was pink and white and chubby. He was mentioned in despatches for the work of his Irish Hospital in South Africa.

Rupert went into politics; he was a Conservative of a type then common, an imperialist with a social conscience who admired Joseph Chamberlain. Chamberlain, a Birmingham ironmaster, had in his youth been on the radical wing of the Liberal Party. His opposition to Gladstone's policy of Home Rule for Ireland had led him to ally himself with the Conservatives, whom he later joined. He swung the Party over to a policy of Imperial Preference, infuriating those who wanted to retain free trade. He retained many of the social ideas of his youth; he was, for instance, a consistent advocate of old age pensions. The Empire, for Chamberlain, was both a cause to unite the country and a source of prosperity which should be spread among all classes. There is a parallel here with Bismarck, who had also combined pensions with imperialism.

Rupert promoted one side of Chamberlain's beliefs by investing a large amount of money in the Empire, and encouraging both his brothers to do so. Later, he and his erudite and serious young wife, born Lady Gwendolin (*sic*) Onslow, founded Overseas Training Schools to train people to go out to the colonies and man the Empire. The schools were at his country house, Pyrford, near Woking; his was for men and hers for women. He showed his social commitment in an even more remarkable way when in 1903 he moved with Gwendolin to Shoreditch in the East End of London where the couple devoted themselves to good works while Rupert nursed the constituency of Haggerston. There was no hope of his winning this at the General Election of 1906, which was a Liberal landslide, but he got in at a by-election in 1908, taking advantage of a split in the left-wing vote between a Liberal and a Social Democrat. Nonconformists who disapproved of 'the trade', as brewing used to be called, mounted a noisy campaign against Rupert, but to no avail. He held the seat for two years.

A keen yachtsman, Rupert was a member of the Royal Naval Reserve, in which capacity he was portrayed by the cartoonist Spy. More oddly, he was President of the National Society of Chauffeurs and Motor Cab Drivers Association; he had campaigned to get the speed limit raised. Later he was to become a pioneer of scientific farming. At Elveden, in particular, he made good farmland out of large areas of scrub that his father had bought for shooting.

Rupert was to succeed Edward Cecil as Chairman of the Company, but only as *primus inter pares*. Edward Cecil split his controlling interest in the Brewery more or less equally between Rupert, Ernest and Walter, being no doubt aware that they were unusually close to each other as brothers, and unlikely to fall out. They in their turn were to follow a similar policy among their children, which explains much about the relationship of Edward Cecil's descendants both with each other and with the Company in later years. Right down to the great-grandchildren of the three brothers it encouraged family solidarity, salted with a universal curiosity as to how much everyone else had. The arrangement continued to work for sixty years after Edward Cecil's death; until 1986, when Ernest Saunders brought about two resignations, there were descendants of all three brothers on the Guinness Board.

Gwendolin was by far the most intelligent and effective of Edward Cecil's daughters-in-law. She was to be a Member of Parliament for eight years, succeeding her husband as Member for Southend when he inherited his peerage; she was also to succeed him as Chairman of the Guinness Trust. Rupert's descendants were later to play a preponderant role in managing the family's interest in the Brewery: this was only partly because Rupert was the eldest of the three brothers. Another important factor was Gwendolin's influence.

The middle son, Ernest, born in 1876, was later made Vice-Chairman of the Company. He too was an outstanding oarsman; when Rupert won the Diamond Sculls it was after tossing with Ernest as to who should compete, for the two brothers would not row against each other. Ernest contributed a lot to the running of the business, without ever being formally part of the management. He liked facts – he always knew what the temperature was – and if the *Guinness Book of Records* had existed in his day he would have known it by heart. When he bought a house in England in 1928 he chose Holmbury near Guildford, Surrey, entirely because it was near an airfield. His family considered the house hideous. He was a quiet and private man, a lover of routine and an early bed. 'Every day he went for a walk in the morning, rain or shine,' his daughter Maureen remembers, 'and lights out was at ten.' His wife, Clotilde Russell, always known as Cloe, was attractive and spirited; in social life she certainly outshone her husband. But in the Brewery he was a different man. A natural engineer with considerable inventive powers, he introduced improvements into productive techniques which were genuinely important.[4] He developed the power-driven rakes fitted with angled scrapers in the kieves, or mash tuns; which, when scald (boiling water) had been run into them over the spent grains, enabled the kieves to be pumped out without any use of manual labour. He also improved the arrangements for returning hops to the copper after they were boiled up with the wort and transferred to a hopback; to replace an elevator in the centre of the hopback he worked out a mechanism where, as in the kieves, the hops were made liquid with wort and pumped back to the copper, again without resorting to manual labour. He had the coppers fitted with inside steam heaters instead of external coal-fire stokers, thus saving fuel, making the heat easier to control, and once again eliminating manual labour. He was the first person on the Brewery Board to suggest moving from coal-firing to oil with automatic temperature control; a suggestion that was not at first adopted because coal was cheap, but which came into its own when the price rose, paying off particularly during the fuel crisis of 1946/7 when coal was in short supply.

An Eton education, based almost entirely on the classics, was quite wrong for Ernest. His obituary notice in *Guinness Time* hints obliquely at this: 'His [engineering] knowledge was so much above that of the ordinary layman that had he been able to devote himself purely to this subject he would undoubtedly have achieved considerable distinction in the engineering field.' Yet Ernest was much luckier than many others whose talents were distorted or suppressed in the same way; his family's Brewery provided an outlet where he could shine, even without formal training.

Marriage to the flamboyant Cloe indicates a streak of romanticism in this outwardly staid man. Their three daughters, Aileen, Maureen and Oonagh, all took after her rather than him. All were blonde and beautiful; they were funny, too, and had a reputation for being rather wild. Ernest did not seem to mind such of their indiscretions as came to his ears, although they may have affected him more than he admitted. His granddaughter Caroline Blackwood, as a teenager, stayed with him for a dance and told him she was being taken there and back by a young man in his car. Ernest had already ordered a taxi; instead of cancelling it, he instructed the driver to shadow her and the young man both ways. One wonders what the taxi man was meant to have done, had the couple got up to anything naughty.

Walter, Edward Cecil's youngest son, was born in 1880; in the conventional sense he was the brightest of the three brothers and is supposed to have been his father's favourite. He married Lady Evelyn Erskine, daughter of the 14th Earl of Buchan. He had

Rupert's intelligence but none of his handicaps; he wrote and spoke well, and to the family conscientiousness he added a quick-wittedness that was all his own. He was brave, persuasive, energetic and charming, and also had scientific curiosity, gifts which ensured that he distinguished himself in a good many fields. Primarily he was a politician; a Conservative, but too cool and open-minded to be a really keen Party man. His systematic intellect and his objectivity made Prime Ministers value him as a 'good pair of hands'. Elected Member of Parliament for Bury St Edmunds in 1907, he served as Under-Secretary for War and as Minister of Agriculture. As a soldier he had a good record in the Boer War, when he was mentioned in despatches, and a brilliant one in the First World War, when he won the rare distinction of a DSO and bar. Anthony Eden, who knew him in the trenches, regarded him as utterly fearless. The journal he left of his experiences as a staff officer in France could almost have been written by Prince Andrew in *War and Peace*. There is the same effortlessness, the same balance, the same cool competence.

Between the wars Walter took to anthropology, using his ocean-going yacht to collect data on Pygmies and others in the Pacific and Eskimos in the North Atlantic. He was made Lord Moyne in 1932, choosing as supporters for his coat of arms a pair of macaque monkeys. 'He *would* have those wretched monkeys,' his secretary Dorothy Osmond remarked to me one day. 'Nobody else liked them, certainly Lady Evelyn didn't.' Despite his elegance and authority, despite his regular features, there was something of the monkey about Walter, especially as he grew older and the humorous wrinkles round his pale blue eyes deepened. The quality is caught in his portrait – not otherwise very good – that hangs at the Park Royal Brewery. He usually kept a monkey as a pet too. 'It is a healthy reminder of what human nature is really like,' he told Julian Amery, son of his old friend Leo Amery.[5]

During the Second World War Walter became Minister Resident in the Middle East, based in Cairo. In November 1944 he was assassinated there by Jewish terrorists on the orders of Yitzhak Shamir. Leo Amery, Secretary of State for India and a sympathizer with Zionism, commented in his diary: 'It is tragic that a man of such devotion to duty and kindliness to all men should be murdered by insane fanatics ... If they had only known how helpful Walter has been in all the Palestine discussions in finding fair and workable lines of solutions.' Quite so, but insane fanatics are not interested in fair solutions. The murderers were caught by Egyptian police and hanged. Although Chaim Weizmann and other top Zionists expressed regret at the time, the attitude of Israel's establishment changed when the Likud Party came to power, for its leaders included those who had ordered the assassination. Under the Camp David Agreement, Menachem Begin's Government recovered the bodies of the murderers from the Egyptians, reburied them with military honours and issued postage stamps in their memory.

Edward Cecil died in 1927 at the age of eighty; less than two years later, in 1929, the Company started full-scale advertising. Edward Cecil is said to have forbidden advertising during his lifetime, and the timing of the first campaign so soon after his death has been taken to imply that his sons and the other directors were longing to start the campaign and only waited for the old man's death to get it going. This is untrue, however, for the first experimental campaign in Scotland was decided on in August 1927, a few weeks before Edward Cecil's death. Brian Sibley may well be right in thinking that Edward Cecil was referring to advertising in his 1926 statement when he said; 'I believe very firmly that a business either goes forward or goes back – it seldom remains stationary – and when it arrives at that point, something ought to be done to get it moving again.'[6] Sales had levelled off, and the Board was concerned about this. The suggestion that Edward Cecil thought advertising vulgar has never seemed convincing. His brother, Lord Ardilaun, might have felt like this, but Edward Cecil was more hardheaded. It is more likely that until nearly the end of his life he saw advertising as unnecessary; why spend more money when the product was doing perfectly well? In any case the Board continued arguing about whether to advertise even during 1928, when there were clear signs that the pilot scheme in Scotland was proving a success; Ernest was against it, Walter was in favour. My mother, Diana Mosley, who became engaged to my father Bryan Guinness at that time, well remembers Walter talking about the controversy.

As advertising agency the Board chose S. H. Benson, whose accounts included Colman's Mustard and Bovril. It also thought up 'Did you Maclean your teeth today?', a slogan which, although it may have done wonders for the toothpaste, annoys the Scots, for they know the name should be pronounced *Maclane.* There are various versions of the way that Bensons clinched the Guinness account. Owen Williams claims that Philip Benson asked for four months to prepare the campaign. On his return to the Board, Rupert asked him: 'And what have you got for us, Mr Benson?'

'Just this,' he replied, and drew from his waistcoat pocket a small slip of paper. On it was written: GUINNESS IS GOOD FOR YOU.

Brian Sibley[7] has it that Oswald Greene, a director of the agency, and his junior Bobby Bevan, went round the pubs to find out what people were saying about Guinness, and they discovered that it was considered to be good for the health. They then reported this to the Board. Either one of them or, as some say, Ernest Guinness, then uttered the magic words.

The first advertisement in the nationwide campaign appeared on the front pages of the daily newspapers on Thursday, 7 February 1929. It was lengthy, pedestrian and pompous, but in its way it was also brilliantly clever.

THIS IS THE FIRST ADVERTISEMENT EVER ISSUED in a national newspaper to advertise GUINNESS. For over 150 years the House of Guinness have been engaged in brewing Stout. By concentrating on doing one thing well, they have produced a beverage which stands alone. Fortunes have been spent in study and development, going right back to the production of the kind of Barley seed that will enable the farmers to grow the Barley that makes the most suitable malt to make the best Stout. As the result of quality, and quality alone, the Guinness Brewery has grown to be by far the largest in the world.

ITS GREAT PURITY

Guinness is made solely from Barley, Malt, Hops and Yeast, and is naturally matured. No artificial colour is added; the colour of Guinness is due to the roasting of the Barley.

ITS HEALTH-GIVING VALUE

Guinness builds strong muscles. It feeds exhausted nerves. It enriches the blood. Doctors affirm that Guinness is a valuable restorative after Influenza and other weakening illnesses. Guinness is a valuable natural aid in cases of insomnia.

ITS NOURISHING PROPERTIES

Guinness is one of the most nourishing beverages, richer in carbohydrates than a glass of milk. That is one reason why it is so good when people are tired or exhausted.

GUINNESS
IS GOOD FOR YOU

This advertisement would be impossible now. One can imagine the grilling Rupert Iveagh would have faced from today's literal-minded busybodies.

'You say it builds strong muscles. Have you any clinical evidence of a correlation between consumption of Guinness and muscular development? You say that it feeds exhausted nerves. What does it feed them with? You go on to maintain that your product enriches the blood. Has there been any research on the blood corpuscle count of Guinness drinkers? On the composition of their plasma? You say certain doctors find that your product helps their patients to recover after influenza. What doctors, and what evidence do they adduce? Our analyst confirms that Guinness contains more carbohydrate than milk. We are informed, however, that Coca-Cola, brown ale, and tea with a sufficient quantity of sugar, also exceed not only milk, but also Guinness, in the matter of carbohydrates . . .'

As regards the doctors, at any rate, Rupert would have had a good case. They really did recommend it; Dr Charles Cameron, of the Irish Royal College of Surgeons, wrote in 1906 that he found Guinness to be a 'perfectly pure article' which 'has evidently been brewed from the best materials', adding that it 'contains nearly seven per cent of solid matter in solution and is, therefore, a food as well as a stimulant and tonic'. (Aficionados of pre-war advertising will remember that Bromo lavatory paper, too, was 'a perfectly pure article'.) When in 1936 the United States Federal Alcohol Administration of America objected to the claim that Guinness was good for you, the Company was able to inundate it with testimonials from the medical profession. It must also be remembered that much other advertising of the time made claims which would be considered outrageous by modern standards. For example, the ointment Zam-Buk, in 1937, was said to be an infallible (*sic!*) cure for eczema and impetigo, as well as for aches incurred during sport; this claim appeared in an advertisement, even longer than the Guinness one, comparing Zam-Buk with the liniments applied to Greek athletes and Roman gladiators and also mentioning the ceremonial anointing oil used in the Coronation of King George VI that year. People often speak of the loosening of standards; here is an area where they have been so tightened as to remove much romance from our daily lives.

Note that in this first Guinness advertisement, the drink is presented as restorative, not recreational. There is no hint that it might be fun to drink it, let alone that it might make you tiddly. Good for you, like Filboid Studge; but its dose of alcohol neatly reinforces the puritan message with a secret touch of the sybaritic.

During the first advertising years, the Press continued to carry notices in this wordy style. One gave 'seven reasons why Guinness is good for you'. The first posters all carried the slogan, with a glass or more of Guinness. The theme returned year after year: year as late as 1968 there was a bottle and glass of Guinness with just the slogan 'GOOD FOR YOU', and in 1983 Allen, Brady and Marsh revived the theme with the clever variant 'Guinnless isn't good for you'. But other slogans and ideas also derive from that first advertisement. The material about building muscles and enriching the blood becomes 'Guinness for Strength', which produced a series of posters including, in 1934, the most famous of all, the man with the girder. Like most of the best-known Guinness posters over thirty years, this was the work of John Gilroy who, though also a portrait painter, will always be mainly remembered for his posters; besides Guinness, he worked for other Benson clients, notably Bovril. The man with the girder is undoubtedly his *chef d'œuvre*. A workman in a flat cap is walking briskly with a 40-foot girder balanced (badly balanced if one looks, but never mind) on his head and one hand. He has just drunk a Guinness; his astonished workmate has just poured out another for himself. Many variations appeared in later years; there was a Father Christmas carrying an enormous Christmas tree; a workman in 1960 who had actually bent his girder into a figure 5 to represent the 5 million Guinnesses then being drunk every day; yet another one in 1976 who was brought up to date by being shown capless and wearing jeans and a donkey jacket. The political cartoonist Vicky made Harold Wilson carry the girder. Heineken pinched the idea, showing a man carrying a bent girder which after he has consumed half a glass of Heineken is straightened – it is, of course, one of 'the parts that other beers cannot reach'. Other 'Guinness for Strength' advertisements included one where a stalwart farmer is pulling a cart with an enormous carthorse sitting in it; another where a Guinness drinker lifts with one hand a manhole cover and a steamroller being driven over it; a third featuring an army bandsman whose breath is so powerful that it uncurls his tuba. But the man with the girder is the one people remember best.

The claim in the original advertisement to feed exhausted nerves begat another set of ideas based on the slogan 'Have a Guinness when you're tired'. Guinness drinkers were shown running up a down escalator on the London underground, or drawing white lines in the middle of a country road for mile upon mile. A variant was 'You'll feel *fresher* when you've had a Guinness', with a picture of a daisy.

However, had the advertising for Guinness referred only to doing you good, it might have turned into a 'niche product', which would not have done at all. Bensons produced many other ideas as well. There was 'Guinness Time', which began in 1931 with an illuminated clock in Piccadilly Circus. This was followed by Guinness clocks in other cities, and Guinness Time posters and parodies:

> *My grandfather's clock looked superb in the shop*
> *But at home it would never go right:*
> *Though we wound it and wound it it always used to stop*
> *At a quarter to eight every night.*

> *But my grandfather swore: 'That's exactly what it's for,*
> *I don't want it to tick or to chime,*
> *But I do want to look at the clock and see*
> *That it's GUINNESS TIME.*

Some messages dealt with how Guinness looks. If you pass a strong light through a glass of Guinness it looks reddish, at least to the eye of faith; this was called a 'ruby gleam' by the advertisers. Another feature was the tight and long-lived head on the top of a glass when it is carefully poured. Gilroy's first ever Guinness poster showed a glass of stout on a pedestal being grinned at by busts of Dante, Caesar, Nefertiti, Homer and Cleopatra, with the slogan 'Famous for its perfect head'. Soon the head began appearing with a cheerful moon face on it; in one poster the last few drops are being poured into the glass, and the mouth on the face is eagerly slurping them up.

Then there were the advertisements showing animals at the zoo with their keeper. This started with a sea-lion balancing a glass of Guinness on its snout, being chased by a keeper with a bottle in his hand. The slogan is 'My Goodness My Guinness': this not only expresses the keeper's feelings at losing his drink, but also refers back to 'Good for You'. More animals followed; there was an ostrich with the glass visibly descending its throat, a mother kangaroo with the Guinness in her pouch, a pelican with its beak full of bottles walking away from a table where several keepers are angrily accusing each other. The elephant is kindlier; the keeper is sitting on its head and smiling, being handed a full glass on the end of its trunk. But the most famous Guinness animal was a bird, the toucan. It first appeared in 1935 with two glasses of Guinness and this rhyme:

> *If he can say as you can*
> *Guinness is good for you*

> *How grand to be a Toucan*
> *Just think what Toucan do.*

The rhyme was by Dorothy Sayers, the detective story writer, who worked for Bensons. It was hugely successful. Randolph Churchill, trying in the 1935 General Election to join his father Winston Churchill in Parliament, plagiarized it:

> *If you agree as we do*
> *Churchills are good for you*
> *Just give your vote for Randolph*
> *And see what two can do.*

The toucan cropped up again and again, sometimes perching, sometimes flying. In one poster it is dressed as a Red Indian chief with feathers: 'Guinness – him strong', we are told, and 'See what Big Chief Toucan Do'. There have been toucan cruets, toucan lamps, toucans designed to be attached to a wall like flying ducks. One poster has a flight of toucans in formation, zooming along with two glasses of Guinness each, watched in surprise by two RAF pilots.

Altogether one is awestruck by the succession of ideas produced by Bensons in the 1930s and 1940s. Less well known than Dorothy Sayers, but in his own way equally brilliant, was a parodist called Stanley Penn. He was particularly good at Lewis Carroll pastiche and produced a series of wonderful imitations worthily accompanied by Gilroy's version of the Tenniel illustrations.

> *If seven men with seven tongues*
> *Talked on till all was blue,*
> *Could they give all the reasons why*
> *Guinness is good for you?*

> *I doubt it, said the Carpenter,*
> *But that it's good is true.*

When I did a six-week training course at Guinness in 1957 I met Stanley Penn, who was just coming up to retirement, and he showed me his well-thumbed copy of *Alice*. I looked at it with reverence. Brian Sibley expresses the view that 'the parodies not only helped boost sales of Guinness, but also of Lewis Carroll's books'.[8] This sounds almost an impertinence, but is perhaps not entirely far-fetched.

In due course the ideas dried up. After about 1960 there was less fun and originality, for which the Company and the agency share the blame. The chemistry between them began to fail, as in a stale marriage. The Company pushed for a hard sell, the agency promoted its own prestige with posters that won prizes but had little public appeal. Bensons was replaced by J. Walter Thompson in 1969, and the campaign did benefit by their new approach. The emphasis was now on the deliciousness of Guinness; it was shown with red and white wine as a third choice, compared with champagne and Irish coffee which, it was implied, was created in imitation of its appearance. Since then, Guinness advertising has had further ups and downs, some of which we shall be looking at. This earlier period is the important one, though, because it was then that a particular image for Guinness was embedded in the national consciousness; an image that was cosy, funny and wholesome. If Guinness under Ernest Saunders was in 1985 to seem a congenial 'white knight' to the desperate men who were trying to preserve the Distillers Company as a club for old-fashioned business gentlemen, this image had a lot to do with it. Never has wolf donned so reassuring a sheepskin.

FOUR

Symbiosis and Growth

From the very start the advertising campaign proved a stunning success; the sales figures show this clearly. The pilot scheme, it will be recalled, was in Scotland; it started on 1 April 1928. Scottish sales for the calendar year 1928 were 7.3 per cent above the 1927 figure, whereas sales in the whole of Britain were 8.8 per cent down. The campaign went national in February 1929; for that calendar year sales in Britain increased by 8 per cent, whereas sales by British breweries fell slightly. In 1930, the first complete calendar year of the campaign, Guinness's British sales growth accelerated to 13.8 per cent, whereas British brewers' sales declined by 3 per cent, this being the time of the Great Depression. In Ireland, where there was no advertising, Guinness sales also went down by around 3 per cent. The responsibility of advertising for the sales improvements in the late 1920s is further indicated by the fact that the effect was once for all; during the recovery of the late 1930s, Guinness sales rose less than those of other brewers, some of whom, in the meantime, had boosted their own advertising campaigns.

The decision to launch the campaign can be seen as the last stroke of Edward Cecil's business genius; but the continuing success of the business after his death can also be attributed to him, for he laid down the lines on which it was to develop. At the top, in particular, he perfected a system of symbiosis between his descendants as controlling shareholders and directors, and a professional management emerging from the Brewers' career structure described above. The family played a part that had something in common initially with that of Britain's elected Government, and latterly came more and more to resemble – I fear one might easily say to caricature – that of the Royal Family. Already, in Edward Cecil's own youth, Purser and his family did much of the practical management while Edward Cecil made the major decisions and, with his brother, drew the profits. As we have seen, Edward Cecil himself brought the arrangements up to date in such a way that they continued well into the third generation of his descendants, beyond the age of the managerial revolution into a time when such arrangements came to look more and more odd.

There was nothing remotely unique to Guinness about this symbiosis. It was a version of the normal relationship, in the early days of industrial capitalism, between proprietor and management. It did last a long time, but there have been other cases where such a pattern has lasted even longer, some even where they persist to this day. There are many examples in brewing, with families like the Whitbreads, Greenes, Youngers and Fullers, and others in banking: Rothschilds springs to mind, as does Barclays Bank with its numerous founding families. The continuing triumphs of the Sainsburys in retailing show that even now, with the right family, such arrangements can continue. In Guinness the system lasted until about a century after the issue and sixty years after Edward Cecil's death.

Edward Cecil organized the management hierarchy in the way already described. On the family side, as we have seen, he left his controlling shareholding equally between his three sons. This meant that after his death his supervisory role was mainly divided between Rupert as Chairman and Ernest as Vice-Chairman. Walter had his own political career and other interests to consider and could not be so closely involved. Even so, he was called in to participate in at least one major decision that was arrived at outside a normal Board Meeting, namely, to build the brewery at Park Royal. This joint role of the three brothers could only work because they were exceptionally close, but work it most certainly did, until Walter's death in 1944 and Ernest's in 1950. Sir Hugh Beaver, a future Managing Director, once told Owen Williams that any proposal on which Ernest and Rupert did not agree was dropped immediately.

The splitting of the controlling shareholding between the three brothers was in one sense a conservative move; it harked back to the days when the business had been a partnership. But a partner is more easily bought out than a large shareholder in a quoted company, so it became in practice impossible that one person would ever again come to concentrate control on himself personally, as the second Arthur, Sir Benjamin and Edward Cecil himself had all done in their day. Future family Chairmen would always have to reckon with the rest of the family because the family holding providing *de facto* control would be split between the brothers and later between their descendants, making it important that no holder of any substantial part of the controlling interest should ever turn against the family directors. This in fact never happened, probably because at nearly all times the Company did well; and in the late 1970s when problems appeared that could have been terminal, these never reached the stage where outside family members became sufficiently worried to complain. Even non-executive directors could always hope that things would come right. Obviously it was also important, for the maintenance of family control, that sales of Guinness shares by the family to outsiders should be kept as low as possible. Here too family solidarity was remarkable; there were indeed sales, but right up to the time when Ernest Saunders diluted the family holding by issuing shares for his massive bids the family still held between 20 per cent and 25 per cent of the company. (The exact figure is hard to arrive at.) The sales came disproportionately from the Ernest Guinness descendants. Rupert's branch was kept in line by moral pressure first from Rupert himself, then from his grandson Benjamin; Walter's branch was similarly disciplined, gently but effectively, by his elder son Bryan. As a rule, shares that had to be sold within each branch were taken up by other members of that branch.

So as to preserve an attractive career structure within the business, it was thought better that members of the family should not try to run the Brewery as executives. Using the word family in the strictest sense, namely descendants of Edward Cecil and inheritors of parts of his controlling shareholding, this principle was adhered to. Edward Guinness and Peter Guinness, who were later to be executive directors, came from other branches of the family, as in their day had Claude and Reginald Guinness; Viscount Boyd, Managing Director in the sixties, was perhaps the nearest to being a true exception because he was married to Rupert's daughter Patricia. Diarmid Guinness, Bryan Guinness's third son and the author's brother, was making his career in the Brewery but died unexpectedly in 1977 at the age of thirty-nine. That this policy of separating career management from the family was deliberate is indicated by the fact that Ernest Guinness was never made Managing Director, even though he not only knew the business inside and out but was also genuinely useful to it with his innovative suggestions on the production line. (But possibly Edward Cecil sensed that his second son, though good at engineering, was not likely to be able to cope with sales, management or marketing. Had his talents been more general, might his father have taken a different view?)

One reason why the family and the professionals got on so well was certainly that the executives, being public school men and graduates of the older universities, came from the same social background as the family directors. In two instances, Sir Richard Levinge and Mark Hely-Hutchinson, they were from the Anglo-Irish landed gentry; most of the rest came from the professional classes that the major public schools welded with the landed gentry to form one cultural group. They became, often, close friends of long standing with the family; the young Brewers who frequented for instance Ernest Guinness's house near Dublin became in due course, as executives, Board colleagues of his daughter Maureen. Bryan Guinness, Walter's elder son, who despite being a man of high culture and literary gifts was perhaps the least businesslike of all the family directors including the women, played a crucial part here in the days of the family's decline, his special charm helping to keep the executives on side.

Owen Williams, later to become Head Brewer in Dublin, has left an account of his own recruitment which gives a hint of how family and top management fitted together in 1929, two years after Edward Cecil's death. Williams was an undergraduate at Merton College, Oxford, busily preparing for Part II of his Natural Science Tripos. His tutor said to him: 'You'd better get your hair cut. There is a man looking for a new Brewer in Guinness's Brewery in Dublin. It's a pity you're not going to get a better degree; this job would have suited you down to the ground. Guinness is more like a club than a commercial firm.'

The man from the Brewery was the Managing Director, Thomas Bennett Case, whom we have already met; he was the son of the University's Professor of Moral and Metaphysical Philosophy and had been educated at Winchester and Magdalen, Oxford. Case took Owen Williams for a walk in the Parks. First they talked about cricket, something for which Williams was prepared because he knew that Case had played cricket for the University. Then the subject switched to music. Here Williams was well informed because he was very musical himself.

Case asked: 'Do you prefer Bach or Handel?'

Something prompted Williams to reply 'Handel'; when afterwards he discovered that Case's maternal grandfather had been Sterndale Bennett he felt this must have been the right answer, because Bennett was a musicologist and a well-known expert on Handel.

Soon afterwards Williams was invited by Ernest Guinness to his London house in Grosvenor Place. In due course he was appointed, having done well in his finals despite his tutor's misgivings. More than twenty years later he came across a note in Case's handwriting: 'I have seen Williams at Oxford. He is not up to our standards but Ernest seems to like him so perhaps we'd better get him over to Dublin to look at.'

He himself thinks he got the job 'largely because Launce McMullen (whose father was then second Brewer) had been in the same form at [Rugby] and spoke well of me, also because the only other candidate . . . retired into a lunatic asylum . . .' Yet the throwaway line 'Ernest seems to like him' points to the non-executive Ernest. Is there a faint note of impatience? If so, certainly only a faint one, with no suggestion that Ernest was putting any pressure on. Still, there he was, his views were a factor.

The faint note of impatience – it always did remain faint, but it was there – is something with which I was to become familiar. The executive directors, just because they had come through a process of rigorous selection both before joining and during their careers, were much brighter than the family, and must have known it. The difference rarely caused problems and was covered over by invariable politeness on both sides, but it had always to be borne in mind.

The first truly professional and non-family Managing Director was C. D. La Touche, who succeeded Sir Reginald Guinness in 1902 and had been the first Brewer to be appointed to the Board. He came from a Dublin banking family of Huguenot descent and became an apprentice Brewer in 1874. There was no room for him in the family bank, so his father recommended him to Edward Cecil. He was both brilliant and industrious; during his first four years at the Brewery he combined his full-time job with a course of study at Trinity College, being awarded his BA in

1878. La Touche resigned in 1913 and died shortly afterwards. He spotted the talents and promoted the career of Thomas Case, who became Managing Director in 1919 and ran the Company for most of the very successful period between the wars. C. J. Newbold, an assistant Managing Director, succeeded Case on his death in 1942. Then when Newbold died in 1947, Rupert went right outside the brewing industry for his next appointment. But this is to anticipate.

The next development after the start of advertising was the establishment of a large brewery in Britain. The extra sales generated by the campaign certainly helped to make this viable, but the immediate reason for building it was political; Dublin was not short of brewing capacity. The decision was made in 1932, in the depths of the slump, at the time of what became known as the Economic War between Britain and the Irish Free State. Eamonn de Valera had been elected Irish Prime Minister in March 1932 and proposed to repudiate annual repayments by Irish farmers to the British Treasury of sums lent them to purchase their farms; the British retaliated by imposing duties on certain agricultural products. The possibility that this might have been extended to beer worried Guinness seriously. British beer duty had already risen by 30 per cent in the Emergency Budget of September 1931, which was thought likely to reduce sales by about one-fifth; the addition of a protective tariff would have been devastating, because exports to Britain comprised more than half of the Company's sales. As an Irish Brewery, the Company would have been put back to the time before 1795. Guinness had already envisaged this possibility and asked de Valera's predecessor, William Cosgrave, to intervene on its behalf should there be any suggestion of such a tariff. Now, with de Valera quarrelling with London, it became vanishingly unlikely that any such intervention from the Irish would do any good. Preliminary arrangements were put in place to construct a British brewery.

The decision to go ahead was made following a meeting on 3 October 1932, between Rupert Iveagh and J.H. Thomas, Dominions Secretary in the National Government, who was conducting the British side of the Economic War. Thomas told Rupert bluntly that unless Guinness undertook to build a Brewery in England his government would impose an import duty on beer from Ireland. Rupert prevaricated at first, sending the minister a reasoned case against imposing such a tariff; all the same, after consultations over the following months of which no records were kept, he and his colleagues came to be sure that they had to comply. Exactly when this occurred cannot be pinpointed, but the decision to buy the land for the Brewery was made at an informal meeting on 27 March 1933 of what might be called the inner committee of the Board, consisting of Edward Cecil's three sons, Rupert, Ernest and Walter, and the Managing Director with his deputy, Thomas Case, and C. J. Newbold.

Following a previous project to brew in England, which had been actively planned just before the First World War but was abandoned because of the war, the Company possessed a site at Trafford Park near Manchester. The project had been seriously looked at again in the twenties, but again shelved. The new plans envisaged a brewery in the south of England, but the ownership of the land at Trafford Park proved useful in putting off inquisitive journalists without actually telling lies. The Company told them with perfect truth that there was no plan for a Brewery at Trafford Park, and this was as a rule accepted. The land purchased was in the event at Park Royal in outer London. A solicitor called Owen Howell found the site; his father had acted for Guinness in purchasing the land at Trafford Park, which was why Thomas Case approached his firm. As so often in the Guinness story, we find a family succession. Howell called in Sir Alexander Gibb and Partners, civil engineers, and their partner Hugh Beaver both helped in choosing the site and masterminded the construction. The search for a site was subject to a number of requirements. A very large amount of water had to be constantly available of which a good proportion – that required for the beer itself – had to be of excellent drinkable quality. The site had to be capable of taking heavy buildings containing massive equipment. Transport facilities and communications had to be excellent. Neighbours had to be what Case delicately called 'desirable', that is, there should be no sewage farms, cement works or similar under-takings anywhere near. At least forty acres were required, to allow for possible expansion.

Considering all these requirements, the site at Park Royal was found fairly quickly. Britain was, of course, only just beginning to come out of deep slump, which must have made the task easier and certainly reduced the price, which at less than £1,000 an acre was very low, even in those days, for industrial land. (The Traf-ford Park land had cost £1,500 an acre in 1913.) In the event far more land was bought than was required for the Brewery itself; the Company paid £132,000 for 134 acres, providing room for employees' housing, ample playing fields, a model farm and an entire industrial estate. It was apparently Beaver who urged the Company to buy so much more land than originally envisaged; his advice was to prove extremely profitable. The purchase and subsequent construction were carried out in conditions of secrecy so dark as to seem paranoic in retrospect. Walter was one Board member who thought the secrecy quite unnecessary, at least fol-lowing the original land purchase which obviously might have been more expensive had it been known who was buying. There were, however, two reasons for continuing discretion which seemed strong at the time. One was that it might offend the Irish Government; Guinness was at that time the largest industrial exporter from the Free State (as it then was), and a British brewery would inevitably take much of this trade – as, indeed, was the idea when J. H. Thomas thumped the table at his meeting with Rupert. To present the Irish with a *fait accompli* would at least avoid wearisome representations being made and refused, giving offence to de Valera's new and possibly touchy Government. In the event the Irish made no difficulties, and relations with de Valera were as cordial as they had been with Cosgrave. This can be seen as justifying the policy of secrecy, or as proving it unnecessary; one of those delightful alternatives where the choice can be left to the historian's whim.

The other reason for secrecy had to do with the Guinness mystique. The Dublin origin of Guinness, the mysterious Hibernian magic that was supposed to go into its production, the legend of the Liffey water, all contributed to its glamour. Would the consumer be happy with Guinness that had been brewed in a London suburb? Would the very fact that it could be produced elsewhere ruin the image? A great part of this danger might be averted if, in the beginning, British Guinness drinkers were under the impression that their tipple came as usual from Dublin.

What was impossible to conceal was that a huge red-brick construction of some sort was going up within full view of the A40 to Oxford and South Wales. Naturally people wondered what it was, and all sorts of theories circulated. The wildest was that it was a secret Government installation to make explosives out of potatoes. In any case the secret was kept.

The possession of a large Brewery in Britain did not make Guinness in all respects a British brewer. For one thing, a large proportion (usually about a third) of Guinness consumed in the United Kingdom was still imported from Dublin. More importantly, Guinness had never taken part in the development of the 'tied-house' system under which most public houses were owned by brewers, and all brewers, certainly all important ones, owned chains of pubs. Here, Guinness was the great exception. The situation had come about quite naturally; since Guinness was sold in virtually all British pubs anyway, and was an imported product, the Company had no particular reason to enter the retail licensed trade. A typical British brewery, on the other hand, had strong reasons to acquire pubs. It needed secure outlets for its beer; and somewhat naturally, as more houses became tied to a particular brewery, excluding the products of rivals, the motive became ever stronger. By the time Park Royal was constructed it was already much too late for Guinness to enter this particular contest. Without pubs, Guinness was in the delicate position whereby its most important customers were the other brewers who bottled the product for sale in theirs. To keep them happy, they were encouraged to charge a very considerable margin on the Guinness they sold. About 1960 a banking colleague of mine who had worked in the accounts department of a major brewer told me that his former firm made more money out of its Guinness sales than out of any single one of its own lines. If Guinness had started buying pubs it would have needed to stock every single beer brewed in the United Kingdom; failure to stock any beer would have invited that brewer to exclude Guinness from its pubs. When in due course, as the owner of a large hop farm at Bodiam in Sussex, Guinness did come to own a pub, it stocked virtually every bottled beer of every brewery from Land's End to John o'Groats, and an exceptional number of draught beers as well. The place became something of a curiosity, but never paid.

The other big brewers used to refer to Guinness, only fairly good-humouredly, as the 'cuckoo in the nest', and the fear was always at the back of every Board member's mind that they might stop selling the product. In some ways this was salutary; it kept the Company on its toes and ensured that it was always acutely cost-conscious as regards stout production. It also kept everyone conscious of Guinness's image in marketing and sales; for at the end of the day it was public demand for Guinness that made it dangerous for brewers to stop stocking it. It also encouraged the Company, following the Second World War, to cultivate friendship with the other brewers through assiduous attention to the Brewers' Society; a friendship that was to pay well. But this dependence on others for sales also put a constraint on the management which became more unhealthy as management became less confident. All new moves were considered in the light of not upsetting this particular applecart, which I shall refer to from now on as the Cuckoo Factor.

During the time when the Park Royal Brewery was being planned and constructed, Hugh Beaver became very close to Rupert and especially to C. J. Newbold, future Managing Director, who was the executive who dealt with Beaver most frequently. Both men learned to admire Beaver, and Newbold is said to have suggested to Rupert that when he himself retired Rupert should try to recruit Beaver.[1] Rupert needed no persuading and, when Newbold died in harness in 1947, made Beaver an offer he could not refuse. He was now Sir Hugh, having been knighted for his performance at the Ministry of Works during the war. His appointment was an extremely shrewd choice, for Beaver was to prove one of the brightest of all Chief Executives of Guinness. He had faults, to be sure; his energy could sometimes manifest itself in unnecessary restlessness. He also tended, rather dangerously, to expect others to show the same flair that he possessed himself. In these ways he sowed the seeds of future failures as well as of future successes.

Born in 1890, Hugh Beaver distinguished himself at Wellington but unexpectedly failed to get a scholarship to Oxford, his only recorded setback in a life which was to bring success in amazingly varied fields. Since his widowed mother could not afford to keep him at university unsupported, he went in for the Indian Police, coming top in the entrance examination. In the police he worked primarily in Intelligence. His superiors must have valued him highly, for when he returned to England in 1914, to enlist he was called back to India. He left the police in 1922 and began studying law, but the engineer Sir Alexander Gibb, a Buckinghamshire neighbour, 'spotted in the restless returned officer of police a talent he thought he must harness' and made him his personal assistant.[2] The choice of the epithet 'restless' is apt, as I have indicated. After building the Park Royal Brewery he went to Turkey where he constructed harbours. During the Second World War he became Director General of the Ministry of Works under Lord Reith, the formidable Scotsman who had created the BBC.

Sir Hugh was quickwitted, industrious, charming, highly dominant; the word dictator recurs in talks with those who remember him, although it is agreed he was a benevolent one. I repeat, however: he was also restless. In the hearing of Dr Arthur Hughes, later an Assistant Managing Director, someone suggested to Sir Hugh leaving well alone. 'The trouble is, well won't leave itself alone,' he said. He was always open to suggestions, always willing to go for it, always one for 'a sacred affirmation' (*ein heiliges Ja-sagen*) as celebrated by Nietzsche. His galvanic effect on the rather conservative hierarchy at Guinness can be compared with the later irruption of Ernest Saunders, except that Beaver made himself liked as well as respected. Working with rather than against the grain of the system, he found plenty of bright and efficient people to carry out his plans, which can be divided into three parts: internal reorganization, defensive moves, and strategy for progress.

Internally, Sir Hugh split Dublin and Park Royal into two separate Companies, both wholly-owned subsidiaries of the parent Company. This was tax-efficient at the time and also gave recognition to the fact that the political and economic conditions in the two countries were distinct, as well as ensuring that neither Brewery would suffer from neglect. The Dublin Brewery, in particular, was important to Ireland, and good relationships with the authorities were even more important to the Company. The parent had always been registered in London; now that there was not just a registered office there but an important production centre as well, Dublin could have felt itself becoming a backwater, with all sorts of unfortunate consequences. Britain, too, held its own particular problems for Guinness, notably that of the tied houses. The product had to be sold aggressively in Britain, so as to keep popular demand rising; whereas in Ireland, where Guinness consumption already hovered between 80 and 90 per cent of the market, salesmanship had to be defensive only, to avoid the possibility of a politically dangerous monopoly. The Company did not advertise in Ireland until much later. It was clearly sensible to have a properly constituted Board of Directors in each country, with a Managing Director for each, both reporting to the parent Board.

Sir Hugh built on the position already established by his predecessor, C. J. Newbold, in the Brewers' Society. He also gave Company money to a number of worthy causes: scientific and medical research, education, care of the aged, youth welfare. He became President of the Federation of British Industries, Chairman of the British Institute of Management, Chairman of the Advisory Council of the Department of Scientific and Industrial Research. All this consolidated the image of the Company in the public mind as an enlightened employer and a good neighbour. The Guinness Poetry Prize, given annually for five years, produced a great deal of goodwill and favourable publicity for very little outlay. It was once won by Robert Lowell, who was much later to marry Maureen Dufferin's daughter Caroline. In Ireland he backed the Peat Board and the Dublin Docks Board and helped fishery research both with money and by seconding some of his colleagues to work on it. The charitable element in these good works was encouraged by the family directors who were aware of the Guinness tradition of open-handedness, but who were personally restricted by the fact that at the time the top rate of income tax was $97\frac{1}{2}$ per cent. (Large personal benefactions did continue from the family, however, the Moyne Institute for Biology in Trinity College, Dublin, being the most conspicuous at this time; Walter's daughter Grania provided most of the funds for this, with Bryan contributing.)

Sir Hugh Beaver's positive strategy for the business was diversification. At the beginning of his time as Chief Executive

Guinness was a one-product company; the product came in different strengths, but that was about all. This was a risky position to be in if only because it left the Company at the mercy of fashion. When I was a junior reporter for Reuters in Bonn in 1955 it was brought home to me just how dangerous this might be. In the course of researching an article on the German beer industry, I discovered that in the early years of the twentieth century the proportion of dark beer to light consumed in Germany was about 85:15; by the 1950s the position had been neatly reversed. The graphs had been fairly steady – downwards for dark and upwards for light – through both World Wars and all the turmoil in between. Suppose the same thing happened in the British Isles; where would that leave Guinness? Some such reasoning may have occurred to Sir Hugh, prompting him to start Guinness on the road to brewing ale and lager. The ale in particular could clearly not be sold in Britain because it would compete directly with the products of the major brewers who would certainly regard it as an additional cuckoo's egg; but there was always Ireland, and Sir Hugh took over some small breweries there which became nice little earners. He also initiated the brewing of both ale and stout in the United States. This was a failure, despite the Irish population there. Guinness could not afford the gigantic promotional effort that would have been required to achieve a worthwhile market penetration. Lager was clearly going to grow in popularity, although at the time it represented only about 3 per cent of British beer consumption. The development of Guinness's lager trade, in particular the Harp brand, came after Sir Hugh's time, but it was he who sowed the seed.

To brew different kinds of beer obviously made sense for a brewer, and these moves have paid off well. But Sir Hugh's restlessness did not allow him to stop there. The most brilliant and imaginative of his ideas was the *Guinness Book of Records*, which over the years has given the Company an immeasurable amount of good publicity. It has become known in countries where the product has not penetrated, and must have helped to blaze the trail for exports. The germ of the idea came to Beaver in September 1954 when he shot at a plover and missed; it was flying at speed, and he wondered if it was the fastest game-bird. After searching in vain in an encyclopaedia, he thought, why should there not be an encyclopaedia devoted to superlatives? Why should Guinness not publish it? On returning to Park Royal he discussed the idea over breakfast with Christopher Chataway, who had run a four-minute mile, was later to become a minister, and worked at the time for Guinness. Using the athletes' network, Chataway rang a firm called McWhirter Twins Ltd which dealt in facts and figures; it had been set up by the fleet-footed identical twins Norris and Ross McWhirter. Beaver invited the twins to lunch. They turned out to be as energetic as he was; with the help of two others they wrote the book in sixteen weeks and it was published less than a year after the lunch with Sir Hugh. (But it never listed the fastest game-bird.)

For the rest, William Nuttall was a group of confectionery companies, best known for Callard & Bowser butterscotch, Nuttalls' Mintoes and the Lavells chain of CTN (confectioner-tobacconist-newsagent) shops. One of the group's factories was at Park Royal, and Major Allnatt, the chairman of William Nuttall, called on Sir Hugh and offered to sell Guinness his group. Allnatt was also chairman of Slough Estates, a company in which Guinness held shares, and this probably helped persuade Sir Hugh to do the deal. For many years the sweets made a steady if modest contribution to Group results. Years later this investment went bad and had to be sold for a song, but Sir Hugh can hardly be blamed for this.

Beaver's venture into pharmaceuticals went more seriously wrong, and more quickly. He reasoned that the presence in the organization of skill in biochemistry might make this a suitable field for Guinness to invest in, and part of his motive may have been humanitarian. He established a Guinness subsidiary, Twyford Laboratories Ltd, to conduct research near Park Royal; he also took over, jointly with Philips of Eindhoven, a quoted pharmaceutical company called Crookes. These shares were bought at a grossly inflated price giving an earnings yield of about 5 per cent, and the Company, with Philips, proceeded to pour more money into it. The venture lost money steadily until it was finally brought to an end in 1971.

This first set of Guinness diversifications outside brewing, though on balance unfortunate, did not seriously harm the business. All the same, a warning bell should have sounded. Guinness was a closed culture; its managers were expert at what they did, and they were also civilized and intelligent men, rounded human beings. But they were sheltered. Not for nothing was the system compared with the Civil Service. Even Sir Hugh Beaver did not shake it up to any radical extent; he found it worked well for him and left it alone. To let such people loose in the outside world and expect them to manage small businesses as sharply as a hungry entrepreneur was asking for trouble; and trouble, eventually, came.

FIVE

The Fading of the Family

Two family directors were killed in the war. Walter was one, assassinated in Cairo as we saw in Chapter 3. His survival might have made quite a difference to Rupert's dispositions in his old age, for Walter was respected by Rupert as Bryan, Walter's son, would never be. Walter's influence would have been salutary, since he was cool-headed and tough-minded as well as eminently fair. More obviously damaging than the loss of Walter was the death in action of Rupert's only son, Arthur Viscount Elveden, who would have been his natural successor as Chairman and might have been expected to take over in 1949 when his father turned seventy-five. He was by all accounts a sensible and decent man, who had been brought up to know the business; born in 1912, he had been a director since 1935. He left a son, Benjamin, who was born in 1938. Rupert hung on as Chairman until 1962 when he was eighty-eight and Benjamin could take over at the age of twenty-four. He was determined that the Chairmanship should remain the prerogative of his own descendants. It did not look good, and it was not good, but to do Rupert justice, if a family is to control a company in the way the Guinness family did, a system of primogeniture is probably the best way to cut out dissension.

When Ernest died in 1949, his Vice-Chairmanship went to Walter's son Bryan, now Lord Moyne. Bryan had joined the Board in 1935 at the same time as Arthur Elveden. Born in 1906, he was called to the Bar as a young man but found that he was given far fewer briefs than the other young barristers in his chambers. This was because he was rich; quite understandably, the clerk preferred to give work to those who really needed it. It was deeply discouraging, however, and Bryan's heart was not really in the profession anyway. He gave up the law and settled down in the country to be a writer and farmer. As the latter he was nothing like as scientific as, say, Rupert; he was more concerned than anything with keeping alive traditional crafts such as hurdle-making. He made a name for himself as a writer, producing novels, reviews, poetry and children's books. He was at various times a friend of Lytton Strachey, Evelyn Waugh, John Betjeman, Harold Acton, Robert Byron and Laurie Lee, and he knew the Sitwells, Virginia Woolf, James Stephens and V. S. Pritchett among others. His poetry had its admirers and he figures in some anthologies; he wrote especially well for children. His novels for adults were pleasantly written and well reviewed, but were thought to lack incisiveness. This was related to a personal characteristic of his, namely a hatred of gossip, a shrinking from conversational sharpness; I sometimes wonder how he put up with the Bloomsbury Group, who were not like that at all. It is hard for a novel to have much impact if its characters are never sharp about each other. Yet at times, for those who knew him, his writings show a subtle and enjoyable self-caricature which is certainly deliberate. People waltz around each other in continual dread of hurting each other's feelings.

Bryan did not just lack incisiveness, he disapproved of it. He avoided it, or smothered it with a cloud of waffle in the way a squid puffs ink at its pursuer. He also disliked competitiveness and encouraged his eleven children to keep this to a minimum, to the occasional exasperation of those of them who were born with a competitive spirit. I believe this trait goes back to Bryan's relationship with his brilliant and worldly father. This was not, I should make clear, a cruel relationship such as the one portrayed in *The Way of All Flesh*. Walter was coolly critical, not unkind; he was also a scrupulously fair man and fond in his way of Bryan. But Bryan, born thin-skinned, could be badly hurt by even the most moderate criticism of the kind all fathers have to come out with. This is indicated by the way he suffered when he later had occasion to reprove one of his own children; he would have to walk us halfway round the garden before saying in hurt tones what another father might have brought out in one harsh bark. Also, Walter's brilliance, his success in all that he did, gave Bryan a feeling of inadequacy. A bout of polio at Eton set him back intellectually and prevented any sort of athletic success. Nobody blamed him, obviously, but he was deprived of the sort of triumph that might have let him feel he could look his father in the face. He began to make a virtue of inferiority, to Walter's irritation. When he was about eighteen it came to his father's ears that he had shot rather badly at some house-party and then made a joke of his own incompetence. Walter wrote him a cutting letter to the effect that field sports were something it was necessary to be good at, and that if Bryan shot badly he should at least not be proud of it.

Perhaps Bryan rebelled against this at some deep level. His imprecision annoyed his father; very well, he would cultivate it. This strategy was not a conscious one; if it had been, Bryan could never have kept it up under Walter's laser eyes. But just because it was unconscious, it became a habit. Walter seems ultimately to have been affected rather little by it. When made a peer he chose the motto *Noli Judicare*, do not judge; and he did not judge Bryan. He was not one of those fathers who expect unfailing brilliance, and he appreciated the qualities Bryan had. These included a native shrewdness that he could not always obscure, and which may have had something to do with his poetic gift.

He revered all the arts and was, in a quiet way, a patron of them; he had perhaps the finest private collection of the paintings of Henry Lamb and of Jack Yeats, who were both friends of his.

Sir Hugh Beaver respected Bryan's gifts and his connoisseurship. In this area he even allowed Bryan to influence his own taste, for after some years during which Beaver mocked Jack Yeats's paintings as incomprehensible daubs, Bryan was amused to see that one had appeared on the wall of his office. After that Sir Hugh bought several, both for the Brewery and for himself. As regards the running of the Company, though, Beaver kept Bryan firmly in his place. Once there was some minor emergency in the Dublin Brewery, and Bryan, who happened to be the only director present, coped with it perfectly well; but there followed a ukase from Sir Hugh to the effect that there must at all times be an executive director on duty, the clear implication being that Bryan could not be trusted. Bryan was rather offended at this, though less than some might have been; he possessed the Christian virtue of humility. However, the incident shows how the influence of the family was insensibly fading. Bryan simply did not enjoy the respect accorded to his father or his uncles. Nor, *a fortiori*, did his first cousins who also came on the Board, all of whom were women.

Bryan's relationship with Rupert was even less easy than that with his father. Bryan was in awe of his uncle; Rupert regarded Bryan with a certain irritated affection, but often thought him a nuisance, and sometimes showed it. Yet his dominance over Bryan was not complete; there was a certain element of give and take. If a needle on a gauge between 0 and 100 were to represent Rupert's dominance and Bryan's subordination, it would certainly have rested well Rupert's side of 50 but it would not have reached anywhere near 100. Talking to Rupert's descendants, and making due allowance for their politeness, I have the impression that Bryan was not as underestimated in that branch of the family as I had assumed. He seems to have been regarded as unusual, even odd, but also as distinctly bright. Much more important, though, was the fact that if really badly treated, Bryan could have blown the whole position of the family. As head of Walter's branch, he represented a third of the family holding; his brother Murtogh, his sister Grania with her family, and his own children, would all follow his lead. He had to be kept on-side, and his support needed to be active, not merely passive. Specifically, his influence on all his branch was needed to stop shares being sold outside the family.

Ernest's branch of the family was at first equally important, since Ernest too inherited a third of the family holding. When he died his middle daughter Maureen, Marchioness of Dufferin and Ava, was made a director; he had no son. Maureen, however, did not have the same authority over her branch as Bryan did over his, and estate duty hit Ernest's fortune hard. His descendants gradually sold most of their shares.

The other family directors at the time of Ernest's death were both effectively from Rupert's branch: his sons-in-law, both Conservative Members of Parliament. Alan Lennox-Boyd was married to Rupert's daughter Patricia; the diarist Henry ('Chips') Channon had been the husband of her sister Honor, although they were now divorced and Honor had married František Švejdar, a Czech air force officer whom she met during the war. When Patricia and Honor were themselves later appointed to the Board, Sir Hugh was heard to growl, 'There are too many fur coats on this Board.' None the less, he always loyally supported the family, and never resisted measures to help perpetuate its position in the Company. It was part of his implied contract with Rupert to do this, and anyway the family had effective shareholder control (though already less than 50 per cent). He had also become the family's personal friend.

Beaver's successor was Alan Lennox-Boyd. In 1958, after resigning from the Government, he became Joint Managing Director with Sir Hugh, taking over altogether in 1960, having meanwhile been raised to the peerage as Viscount Boyd. The appointment may have looked like a violation of the unspoken rule that the family kept out of running the business. But then

Boyd was a very special case. As an ex-Minister he would have been regarded as a catch by many other businesses. He was in fact accepted very well and his years with the Company were successful ones; the management selection system, still in place, ensured that there was plenty of first-class talent to back him up, and he himself brought to the business knowledge and ability that were entirely his own. In particular, his contacts from his time as Colonial Secretary were helpful in his big push to brew Guinness in Commonwealth countries, the most important results of which were the profitable operations in Nigeria and Malaysia. Boyd was also an exceptionally charming man and inspired among his colleagues not only respect but, in some cases, warm affection, a fact which has become clear to me during my researches. I myself liked him for his warmth, but sometimes found his charm a touch professional; though a good listener, he seemed now and then to be trying to please me rather than to take in what I was saying. This may have been my fault more than his. He was guilty of one important extravagance, namely the acquisition by the Company of a quite unnecessary aircraft. He arranged this because he hated spending the night in hotels, and in his travels around the country always wanted to reach one of his homes, either in London or in Cornwall, by nightfall. Although the aircraft was available to other members of the Board who might wish to hire it either personally or on other business, it was grossly under-used; we were fairly effectively deterred by the fact that a trip in it was costed at about three times the commercial fare. I myself used it twice. Boyd, to be sure, at least had a reason for wanting this aircraft; but unfortunately it was kept, through inertia, for years after he retired, replaced three times and only finally got rid of in 1974. The cost to the Company over the years hardly bears thinking about.

My cousin Paul Channon and I were made non-executive directors in 1961, a year after Boyd had taken over as Managing Director and a year before Benjamin took over as Chairman.

However, unlike Benjamin, we were appointed only to the parent Company Board, not to the Dublin and Park Royal Companies. The significance was clear; we were to be strictly non-executive. To me, this was a matter for private regret. When I did my six-week course at the Brewery in 1957, I saw at once how much more rewarding a proper career with the Company would have been than the work I was then doing in a merchant bank. However, it was much too late, for by this time I was already twenty-seven. My father had made it clear to me when I was at Eton that in order to become a Brewer I would need a science degree, and my schoolmasters were insistent that my mathematics were not strong enough for me to have any hope of this. My performance in School Certificate indicates that I might have proved them wrong, but to have done so would have been to take a hard option. Without clearly realizing what I was giving up, I went in for history and modern languages, which was where my talents seemed to be best suited. After Oxford I spent three years as a journalist with Reuters, then switched to merchant banking. The die was cast; I could only go into the Brewery at the top, at the ceremonial level. Essentially, I was on the Board as my father's eldest son and for no other reason. It was an honour and a pleasure, of course, but I never felt that my role was particularly well defined.

Paul Channon had become a Conservative Member of Parliament in 1959, at the age of twenty-three. His father, Henry, had died the year before, and the Southend West Conservative Association had chosen Paul to represent the rock-solid seat, which he still does to this day. Central Office seethed with fury when he was chosen; this was exactly the kind of nepotism that they thought gave the Party a bad name. They produced a bright researcher of theirs and did their best to induce the constituency party to choose him. The Association paid not the smallest attention, however; Paul's father had always made himself pleasant to them and they had known Paul himself from childhood. If the constituency officials were typical, they probably rather enjoyed defying Central Office and the media. In any case, Paul was in no way an irresponsible choice, being a competent speaker and well versed in current affairs. The seat had been represented in turn by Rupert, then on his succeeding to the Iveagh peerage by his wife Gwendolin, then on her retirement in 1935 by her son-in-law, Henry Channon.

Paul was to vindicate his constituency association by proving a better than average Member of Parliament. He has a good mind, logical and exact; he loves timetables. His taste for planning unusual journeys with their connections may have been useful to him as Mrs Thatcher's Minister of Transport. He has been at least as effective, over the years, as many who have come up a harder way. He had a career handed to him on a plate, to the derision of much of the Press, but he has had the last laugh.

If only the same could be said of his cousin Benjamin. He came on to the Board in 1958 at the age of twenty-two, at the same time being appointed to both the Dublin and Park Royal subsidiaries as an Assistant Managing Director. Three years later, in 1961, he became Chairman. Benjamin had great virtues. He was conscientious and a trier; he had the family fairmindedness; he was quite sufficiently intelligent and possessed an unforced dignity, a 'presence'. In the management of his own affairs he was always shrewd; for example, his divorce was a model of discretion and hardly noticed in the Press, who would have made a meal of it given half a chance. He also had immense reserves of quiet courage. But he had two crucial failings. One was that he was painfully shy, to the point of acute introversion; the other was his appalling health.

Shyness was as bad a fault in him as chronic seasickness in a professional sailor. A good part of his job involved pressing the flesh, making little speeches as if he meant them, and jollying people along. An icy coldness emanated from him when, for instance, he had to make a presentation for long service. His shyness kept all human feeling out of his remarks: this in spite of the fact that, deep down, he may well have meant them, being thoroughly benevolent and considerate. He loathed the Annual General Meeting, with its crowd of several hundred shareholders, mostly friendly but including one or two who would be good-humouredly stroppy. To the rest of us, this was all part of the fun; but Benjamin dreaded addressing that assembly. It made no difference that every word of his speech was written for him, every answer to every foreseeable question carefully scripted. As to fielding the spontaneous questions from shareholders, he was surrounded by a praetorian guard of expert executives. He still dreaded it.

Strangely, he gave the performance of his life on what should have been a genuinely difficult occasion, to which we shall come in due course: the Extraordinary General Meeting of September 1986. Perhaps it was because he knew this was the last general meeting he would ever have to chair, also, it was a genuinely exciting occasion for all of us, and nothing helps with shyness so much as a flow of adrenalin. But on most of the occasions when Benjamin failed to chair the Annual General Meeting on 'grounds of health' these grounds were all too genuine. He suffered chronically from Krohn's Disease, undergoing thirteen operations altogether, and the recurring pain from this trouble drove him to alcoholism. Where his courage showed itself was in the way he would often take a Board Meeting, or attend some other function, when very ill; and on these occasions he kept up an iron front. I never once saw him give way. I always admired Benjamin's courage and appreciated his decency; all the same, I was unkind enough to christen him King Log, referring to Aesop's fable in which a community of frogs choose a log as their first king. The comparison turned out to be more apt than I had thought at the time. Aesop's frogs get bored with King Log and replace him with King Stork, who gobbles them up. Benjamin's successor as Chairman was Ernest Saunders.

What of myself? After university and my spell at Reuters, in 1956 I was offered a job which seemed to have better prospects, with the merchant bank, Erlangers. The firm was taken over by Philip Hill in 1959 and was later to merge again and become Hill Samuel. I then took part with some colleagues in buying a controlling interest in Leopold Joseph, where I was an executive director from 1962 to 1968. After this I took up politics, writing, farming and other things, retaining a toehold in Leopold Joseph as a non-executive until 1990.

The only job I was ever to have in Guinness was given me by Alan Boyd, not by Benjamin. This was to chair the Park Royal Development Company, a subsidiary which collected the rents from the Park Royal trading estate and also, with Boyd's encouragement, went in for a small amount of property development for the Company, fairly successfully. However, PRD, as it was always known, was soon caught in a dilemma. On the one hand the parent would not let it borrow in the open market because this would be more expensive than borrowing from the parent; on the other hand the parent would not lend to it, because projected returns on property development always looked lower than on equipment for the business. In due course PRD lost its director responsible for development, and I saw his point; property development with no borrowing facility is impossible. My job came to consist mainly of signing minutes at meetings where nothing concrete was done. In retrospect, property development was yet another diversification without real relevance.

About a year after Paul Channon and I joined the Board, something happened which caused a fair amount of embarrassment. My then wife, Ingrid, became attached to Paul and it became clear that the only satisfactory course of action was for her to divorce me and marry him. I was offended, I suppose, but not intolerably so; over the previous ten years my wife and I had slipped into a mode of resigned incompatibility. The marriage looked solid enough; but so does a chair when termites have hollowed it. Well-meaning friends did their best to make us quarrel, but we all kept our nerve rather well, and achieved the switch with remarkably little trouble. I had to explain, in particular to my father and Alan Boyd, that I was quite happy to sit on the same Board as Paul and that our relations remained perfectly cordial. It was lucky that the tabloid newspapers had not yet taken to behaving in the way they do now, because they might have made the position impossible. As it was, the episode had the effect of launching Emma Tennant on her literary career, because a recognizable version of it formed the central event in the novella *The Colour of Rain* which was her first published work.

In any case, however, the family directors of my generation were even more peripheral than those of my father's. A great deal of this was due to the attitude of Benjamin, who identified himself with the management, not with his cousins, whom he could have used much more than he did to do various odd jobs. He liked us, I think; he had a warm relationship with Bryan in particular. But he never confided in us, not even in Alan Boyd's son Simon when he became Vice-Chairman of the Company, although he depended on him to stand in for him at Annual General Meetings. It was understandable that Benjamin should lean on the executive directors rather than on us. All we could do was make comments and ask questions, at best superfluous, at worst awkward. It was the management who provided him with well-researched briefs, who knew the facts and figures. To go along with them was to avoid problems. He also knew them personally better than he knew us, since he spent quite a lot of time with the Company. He depended on them, and found them dependable. They on their part did all they could to prop him up and make things easy for him. At the beginning, when as Assistant Managing Director he was pushed unprepared into top management, there was some minor friction. He was put in charge of metal containers at Park Royal. Paul Clift, later head of Guinness Overseas, complained to Edward Guinness at having to get Benjamin's signature on some documents when he did not know anything about it. But none of this passed beyond the trivial. There were no serious murmurs against Benjamin or against the family in general, even when as years went by the evolution of the business world made the arrangements seem more and more unusual.

Frogs who knew they were well off with King Log? A kinder and more accurate way of putting it would be that Benjamin as head of the family symbolized something that still lingered from the time when the Guinness family and business pioneered in pensions and medical care for workers. He himself organized an important gift to the nation from the Guinness family, namely the chandeliers in Westminster Abbey. A family like this could still seem to the executive directors like a shelter against the jostling world outside.

However, in a changing world even the Guinness management could not stand still; it required the occasional shake-up from outside itself. This had always been the case, and an important function of the family, over the years, was to provide this shake-up. Edward Cecil did so in the 1880s by making the Company public, and again in the 1890s when he backed Alexander Watson; Rupert did so in the late 1940s by introducing Sir Hugh Beaver, and in the early 1960s by bringing in Alan Boyd. Benjamin could never initiate anything of the sort when it became necessary; he was too much the creature of the existing management and too isolated from the other family directors to be able to form an outside view.

Nor, *a fortiori*, did he encourage initiatives of this sort from any of us family directors; if he was a log, our role in backing him was to be sticks. He was to remark to the DTI inspectors at the time of the Affair, on the subject of Tony Purssell, Saunders' predecessor: 'I had in place a Managing Director, A. J. R. Purssell, whom I had never related to very well because he did not feed back enough information to me as Chairman.' One might have thought that if Benjamin felt like this we, the other family directors, would be aware of it, for we could have been an important resource in helping to control the Board. He never dreamed of using us as such. He was management's man, through and through. A shake-up did come, it is true, with the appointment of Ernest Saunders, who not only saved the Company but pushed it into world class. However, it was not Benjamin's doing.

Peter Guinness was one of two members of the Guinness family who came on the Board without being descendants of Edward Cecil. The other was Edward. Peter and Edward could be thought of as 'outer family'; that is, they did not belong to the phalanx of family directors who represented the controlling block of shares, but were there as part of the management, largely on their merits but also owing something – it is difficult to disentangle how much – to the family connection. Although they identified themselves, and were identified by the rest of us, with the family, their management role meant that they obtained more hearing for their views than the members of the inner family.

This was particularly true of Peter. He was an active family director of Guinness Mahon, the bank founded by Robert Rundell Guinness, Adelaide Iveagh's uncle. Guinness *and* Mahon – the Dublin arm of the bank kept the 'and', which the London parent had discarded – had always acted as the Brewery's bankers in Ireland, and the families remained close. The cousinship was reinforced by intermarriage between the two branches, notably when Edward Cecil married Adelaide. Benjamin Guinness, a member of the banking family who had made his own fortune in Australia and America, was for a time between the wars a non-executive director of the Company; his granddaughter was to marry Sheridan, Marquess of Dufferin and Ava, later to succeed his mother Maureen, *née* Guinness, as a family director.

Peter originally came to the Brewery as a merchant banking adviser on behalf of Guinness Mahon; in this capacity he went with Arthur Hughes, Dublin Managing Director, to Ikeja in

Nigeria to prepare the way for the first Nigerian brewery, and later helped to establish Guinness Malaysia. Both these operations were to be very important to the Company's growth. He joined the Dublin Board in 1964 and the parent Board a little later. In his own words he 'held Alan [Boyd's] hand' on finance, an area where Boyd lacked any experience. This made Peter *de facto* Finance Director; an appointment which at that time did not exist in the Company and which, when it was created, corresponded more to what in other companies would be the company accountant. In the pre-Saunders days, the Finance Director was not part of the group that made the really important decisions; he was charged with administering the financial aspects of what the management decreed. The general attitude of Guinness's top executives to money was allowed to become rather cavalier. Will Phillips, the director in charge of advertising, once said to Edward Guinness after Edward had wondered about the cost of promotional activities: 'Don't worry, we employ clever people called accountants.' The attitude was not profligate, just relaxed.

Peter Guinness came in due course to devote all his time to the Company. He became a financial troubleshooter; it was he, for instance, who masterminded the disentanglement from the loss-making diversification into pharmaceuticals. As troubles increased from the late 1970s onwards, so his troubleshooting function became more important, though his effectiveness in the role varied. He also played a prominent part, though not the leading one, in recruiting Ernest Saunders and working out with him his conditions of employment. He then helped Ernest Saunders to put through his internal reorganization, before retiring himself.

Edward, too, is by birth a 'banking Guinness', descended from Arthur's brother Samuel, but related more closely to the descendants of Edward Cecil through Adelaide; he is her great-nephew. He made his entire career in Guinness, forty-five years of it. Demobilized from the army after the war, he was invited by

Rupert to his house at Pyrford in Surrey; Ernest was there too. All three got on well, and as a result he was offered a job which he accepted. The brothers may have invited him in order to strengthen the family presence following the death of Arthur Elveden. He went in as an Under-Brewer and worked his way up. Sometimes his membership of the family certainly helped him; he was made Personnel Manager at Park Royal in 1951 when he was twenty-six, and it was explained to him that he was appointed so as to give status to the post, the implication being that he already had status. In any case the appointment was a suitable one, for Edward has always been particularly good with people, possessing the human touch that Benjamin lacked. During the years immediately before the arrival of Ernest Saunders he also filled a gap in this respect among the executive directors, who at that period were all rather introverted. Then, during the Saunders years, his presence helped to reassure those who were worried about the future. Finally, it was he who in January 1987 delivered the 'black spot' to Ernest Saunders on behalf of both family and management.

Alan Boyd became joint Vice-Chairman with Bryan when he relinquished his post as Managing Director in 1967. It seems to have been thought that in so far as Benjamin needed backing up in speaking for the Company Alan would be more effective than Bryan, and that for this purpose he needed to be more than just an ordinary non-executive director. Thought by whom I am not sure, but probably the prime mover was the aged Rupert Iveagh. Bryan told me about it, as a *fait accompli*, not long before it was announced. Boyd was succeeded as Managing Director by his deputy Norman Smiley. This was a reversion to normal after the interruption represented by Beaver and Boyd. Smiley was a very typical Brewer of the best sort, cultured, intelligent and enlightened. He had been with the firm all his working life. At Oxford he had been captain of the cross-country team, and he obtained a first-class degree in natural sciences. He had been Assistant

Managing Director with a seat on the Board since 1942, when he was only thirty-three. More than anyone it was C. H. Newbold, Beaver's predecessor, who brought him on; he was Newbold's 'right-hand man', according to an obituary written by Bryan for *Guinness Time*, and Beaver made him Managing Director of the Park Royal company. Outside Guinness he did a great deal of public work, especially for the brewing industry, and had a number of appointments in what was then the FBI (now the CBI). He succumbed to a heart attack in 1968, the year following his appointment, at the age of fifty-nine. Possibly the long-distance running in his youth had strained his heart.

This unexpected death posed a problem for the Board because there were two good candidates for the job whose status was equal: Dr Arthur Hughes, Managing Director in Dublin, and Robert McNeile, his opposite number in Park Royal. Strict seniority would probably have pointed to Hughes, but most decision-making in the firm had now moved to London, and it may well have been his presence at the Company's effective centre that made the Board, after some hesitation, choose McNeile. He was an Old Etonian engineer with a first-class mind and great charm and presence, rather like the best sort of schoolmaster. McNeile ran the Company until 1975 when he was succeeded by A. J. R. Purssell, whom we shall meet again in the next chapter. But a distinctly odd arrangement followed McNeile's retirement; he was made Joint Chairman with Benjamin. This was because for tax reasons Benjamin felt that he should become an Irish resident. He had in any case by then become an Irish Senator, and since he also sat in the House of Lords this meant he was a legislator in two countries, an unusual distinction. The move to Irish residence meant that Benjamin, certainly to his relief, could now leave the Company's Annual General Meeting in the hands of McNeile. The arrangement came to an end in 1978 when McNeile ceased to be Joint Chairman and became Deputy

Chairman; at the same time Alan Boyd stepped down from the Board.

The last members of the 'inner family' to reach the Board, one from each of the three branches, were Alan Boyd's eldest son Simon Lennox-Boyd, Maureen Dufferin's son, Sheridan, Marquis of Dufferin and Ava, and Bryan's third surviving son, Dr Finn Guinness. All joined in 1979, and each was appointed in succession to a parent retiring. Simon Lennox-Boyd replaced his father. Trained as an accountant, he was already managing some family business affairs. Bryan would certainly have been replaced by Diarmid, who had made his career in the Company and in nearly twenty years reached a senior position, but had suddenly died of cancer two years before. Finn, our next brother, was chosen. A biologist with a doctorate in animal genetics, he runs a stud of Arab horses, which Bryan had started as a hobby, and has converted it into a serious enterprise. Sheridan presented more of a difficulty. He was a collector of and dealer in modern painting with no connection to the business world. This would not have mattered, except that the family were well aware that members of Ernest's branch had sold most of their shares; what, in reality, was he representing? There was some worry too about Sheridan's open homosexuality; he was to die of AIDS. But Maureen flatly refused to retire unless Sheridan was accepted; also he was liked by all of us, so the appointment was made.

On Bryan's retirement somebody needed to become Vice-Chairman. By seniority the office should have come to me; but I had annoyed the management by having been Chairman of the Monday Club. When I attained that office in 1970 Benjamin wrote to me to get me to resign as a director, in a letter presumably drafted by Robert McNeile. I refused. The fear was that my presence on the Board might damage Guinness's image in New Commonwealth countries because the Monday Club opposed immigration from those countries. However, any trouble that might have arisen from this was nothing to the rumpus that I could (and would) have raised if the point had been pressed, so no more was heard of it. This incident from nine years before had left an aftertaste, though, and a consensus emerged in favour of Simon Lennox-Boyd as Vice-Chairman. His mother, too, was still on the Board, though she would soon retire. Thus when Ernest Saunders was recruited in 1981, the family directors were:

Inner family
Benjamin Earl of Iveagh, Chairman
Simon Lennox-Boyd, Vice-Chairman
Patricia, Viscountess Boyd
Jonathan Guinness
Sheridan, Marquis of Dufferin and Ava
Dr Finn Guinness
Outer family
Edward Guinness
Peter Guinness

How did this collection look to a thrusting new member of the international executive elite coming fresh to the Company and to the British business establishment? He told his son James that it helped to increase his anxiety about the Company. 'The family behaved as if it was still their private business, rather than being a public company with a Stock Exchange listing.'[1] He also said much the same thing, in almost the same words, at his trial. Judging from the number of inner family members on the Board, this may have seemed to be the case; but the reader who has followed me this far will agree that it was an illusion. For many years the inner family directors had been kept well away from any management function; Benjamin was only a partial exception. Apart from him we drew very modest fees and we had virtually no perquisites. To say we behaved like proprietors is laughable; we were much more like a collection of mascots. My brother Finn once remarked to me, 'We may not do much good, but at least we don't do any harm.' Yet however passive we were, our presence still helped to give the Company a certain distinctiveness. It is almost certain that it disarmed the Distillers board and made them think they would get a better deal from Guinness than from Argyll. It is even possible, despite Saunders' opinion quoted above, that it had some effect in persuading him to take on the job. But that is to anticipate.

SIX

The Brewers' Last Spurt

The twenty-one years between the retirement of Sir Hugh Beaver in 1960 and the arrival of Ernest Saunders in 1981 can be divided into four unequal parts. During the early 1960s the Company made good progress in several directions and the general feeling was optimistic, although profits marked time. During the late 1960s and up to 1972 continued progress did feed through into profits. Then came a time – say from 1973 to 1979 – when an apparently respectable record of progress in profits disguised a real decline. The management was becoming more out of touch and inward-looking, and cash flow was channelled into new diversifications for which the management ability was not available in the Company. Yet the figures showed what looked like progress, although since it was a time of high inflation, this was less solid than it looked. Even allowing for this, however, there did not seem to be reason to worry.

Then came nemesis. The results for 1980 and the interim figures for 1981 led to the desperate search for a Company doctor and the rather haphazard appointment of Ernest Saunders. The Company's enduring successes were on the brewing side, especially from the traditional black stout; there were successes too in ale and lager, but these were not so profitable. Attempts to diversify out of brewing secured transient and deceptive success, but ended as dull at best, at worst as disastrous. The most important exception here was the *Guinness Book of Records*, but this was a small-scale victory and in any case a spin-off from the Guinness brand.

It was only to be expected that Brewers would be best at brewing. Yet it can also be observed that clever people can often turn their hands to many different things, and the Brewers were certainly clever. The idea that they might be able to mastermind the change from a one-product company to a conglomerate did not in the 1970s look as absurd as it does now; the figures seemed to endorse it.

The core business was still stout-brewing in the British Isles. This always benefited from the enormous, though intangible, strength of the brand name; but at the same time it suffered from what I have nicknamed the Cuckoo Factor, the fact that most Guinness had to be sold in other companies' pubs. The way this affected Company decisions varied according to whether the Managing Directors were feeling confident or worried. When they were confident it was regarded as if anything an asset; Guinness, after all, got by without the need to run thousands of small catering businesses that tied up capital, required constant new injections for renovation and wasted management time. I have heard this opinion often enough over the years. But when management were worried they concentrated more on the dangers, the fact that the Company was to an important extent in the hands of its rivals, that every time it put up the price of its product, the other breweries which were its main customers could add more on for bottling and selling it. In theory there was also the nightmare that one of the bigger brewers might take it into its head to brew its own stout and push it in its pubs at the expense of Guinness, even exclude Guinness completely. Top secret calculations used to be made as to the effect such an operation would have on the profits of such a brewer. It never seemed that it would be a sensible policy, and sure enough it never happened during the period we are talking about.

All the same, the other brewers were steadily swallowing each other and creating much larger groups; this inevitably increased their bargaining strength relative to Guinness which had to concede ever larger bulk discounts. Today's giant brewing companies mostly originate through mergers carried out during the 1960s and 1970s; large groups amalgamated with each other and smaller breweries were continually swallowed up. The list of major mergers and acquisitions between 1960 and 1978 is impressive. It was a time when the brewing industry resembled nothing so much as a lake stocked with various sizes of hungry pike:

1960	Scottish Brewers + Newcastle Breweries = Scottish and Newcastle Courage + Barclay Perkins + Simonds = Courage Barclay Simonds (CBS, later Courage)
	Joshua Tetley + Walker Cain = Tetley Walker
	Watney Mann acquires Ushers and Wilson and Walker
1961	Tetley Walker + Ind Coope + Ansells = Ind Coope Tetley Ansell (ICTA, later Allied Breweries)
	Whitbread acquires Flowers
	Courage (CBS) acquires Bristol United Breweries
	Bass + Mitchells and Butler = Bass Mitchells and Butler
1962	Charrington + United Breweries = Charrington United Breweries
1963	Charrington United Breweries acquires Tennents
1965	Whitbread acquires Lacons
1966	Charrington United Breweries acquires United Caledonian Breweries
	Watney Mann acquires Drybrough
1967	Whitbread acquires Threllfall Chesters, also Fremlins
	Bass Mitchells and Butler + Charrington United = Bass Charrington
1968	Whitbread acquires Bentleys Yorkshire Brewery
	Bass Charrington acquires Stones, also Hancocks
1969	Whitbread acquires Strong & Co.
1970	Courage (CBS) acquires Plymouth Breweries
1971	Whitbread acquires Brickwoods
	Courage acquires John Smiths
	Watney Mann + Truman = Watney Mann Truman
1972	Courage bought by Imperial Tobacco
	Watney Mann Truman acquires Websters
	Watney Mann Truman bought by Grand Metropolitan Hotels
1978	Allied Breweries + J. Lyons = Allied Lyons

Sir Hugh Beaver foresaw this development as early as 1950; Gourvish and Wilson quote him as telling the Board: 'We shall have to prepare for greater competition from the larger groups.'[1] From Guinness's point of view perhaps the most dangerous aspect of this development in the long term was that three giant groups, all themselves resulting from numerous mergers and acquisitions, became part of conglomerates which were outside the brewing industry altogether. These were Courage, bought by Imperial Tobacco in 1972; Watneys, bought by Grand Metropolitan Hotels in the same year; and Allied Breweries which merged with J. Lyons in 1978. In effect, the brewing trade – known formerly to friends and enemies as 'The Trade' – was no longer master in its own house.

The start of the 1960s, under Alan Boyd, was not as I remember it an unhappy time at Guinness. It ought perhaps to have been unhappier than it was, for profits for some years were rather worse than static. Profit after tax attributable to the holding company for 1961 fell by 8 per cent as compared with the previous year, then was stationary for three years, and only nosed above the 1960 figure in 1964. The figures were:

1960	£4.61m
1961	£4.24m
1962	£4.23m
1963	£4.23m
1964	£4.79m

Gross profits looked a little better than this, but not much. Sales in the same period went ahead by almost exactly 25 per cent, which with its implication for margins might well have been seen as sinister, but in fact contributed to the 'feel-good factor' which radiated from Boyd himself. The hopeful mood seemed to be endorsed when profits did begin to move upwards, modestly but noticeably, in the late 1960s (again these are post-tax-attributable profits):

1965	£5.52m
1966	£5.66m
1967	£6.73m
1968	£7.05m
1969	£7.25m

Even in this second period, though, sales still rose faster than profits; by 70 per cent against 50 per cent between 1964 and 1969.

An important new move at this time was to start serious and effective promotion of Guinness on draught; despite the Cuckoo Factor, the Company scored a success with this both in the short and the long term. At first draught Guinness was mostly sold in free houses – those not owned by brewers – but growing demand made it also appear in selected houses of some other brewers. There was then a large increase in the number of outlets because those brewers who became allies of Guinness in the Harp Lager trade also accepted draught Guinness into most of their houses. Draught Guinness is important because, being rather less bitter than the bottled product, it appeals more to those who come new to the product; it acts as an introduction to it. Those who begin with draught Guinness often go on to the bottled variety later. At the start of the 1960s, the proportion of stout sold in the United Kingdom was about 85 per cent bottled to 15 per cent draught. The margin on draught stout was appreciably lower than that on the bottled product, which is one reason why profits did not respond properly to higher sales. Even so, the success in volume terms was dramatic. Draught Guinness sales in the United Kingdom were sixteen times higher in 1970 than in 1956, and outlets selling the product had risen from a few hundred to 40,000.[2]

The promotion of draught Guinness was greatly helped by the invention of the Easy Serve cask with a gas compartment inside it, because previously Guinness had been neither quick nor easy to dispense and overstretched barmen were reluctant to serve it. The Easy Serve cask has been improved over the years but it is essentially the invention of Michael Ash who introduced it in the late 1950s.

Ash, an outstandingly clever Brewer, experienced triumph followed by disaster in a way that epitomizes Guinness at this period. Easy Serve has earned many million pounds' profit for the Company, and though Ash's prototype has of course been improved upon, the benefit of it can be considered to continue today. After this brilliant success, Ash was put in charge of Crookes. As Managing Director of that company, and its representative on the main Board, he became excited by the long-term potential of some of its products and infected by a fatal disdain for immediate profits that fitted in all too well with the general Guinness culture. Crookes, before being taken over, was best known for manufacturing old-fashioned products such as halibut liver oil capsules, making a modest living. Guinness and Philips moved it closer to the frontiers of research, turning out more glamorous items such as snake-venom extract and various sorts of serum. Crookes sent glossy and high-minded circulars to doctors and vets detailing its new high-tech specialities. However, it still continued to make its halibut liver oil capsules; when Paul Channon and I went along to visit its seriously under-used new factory in Hampshire, the production line from which the capsules emerged seemed the only important centre of present activity. At a Board Meeting shortly afterwards I made the suggestion that perhaps there should be a little more publicity for the capsules, which did after all make a bit of money, to mitigate the performance of the rest of the company. I was told that this would not do at all; doctors now considered halibut liver oil obsolete, and any attempt to promote it would damage Crookes's image in their eyes. As a new and junior director, lucky to be there at all, I did not argue very much; but this reasoning seems to me even more aberrant now than it did then. I may have made a reference at the time to Beechams, a company which continued happily to promote its traditional pills and powders yet also turned out some of the newest and most glamorous antibiotics. No doctor failed to prescribe these just because the same company also produced an old-fashioned cold cure. As we have seen, the whole pharmaceutical operation was to end in tears, losing millions.

This might be the place to mention a similar intervention I made on the Board, equally coolly received, about the *Guinness Book of Records*. This was at the time regarded purely as an advertising operation, and was sold at a low price which did no more than cover its costs. It was, however, already every schoolboy's favourite Christmas present. I suggested that the price should be increased so as to contribute to Group profits. Many years later this was indeed done, and Guinness Superlatives became a flourishing profit centre adding all sorts of *Guinness Books of This and That* to the *Records*. At the time I was made to feel that my suggestion of raising the price was superficial, even faintly vulgar. The *Guinness Book of Records*, it was made clear, was for advertising the Company and the product, not to make money itself. I do not claim any merit for making either of these rather obvious suggestions; had I been listened to on both of them the *Guinness Book of Records* would have added a little to Group profits while Crookes reduced Group losses by another modest amount, perhaps improving Group results by a couple of percentage points. But on both subjects the attitude shown seems to me now to have been symptomatic of a deep-seated indifference to profitability.

Ale in Ireland was another brewing success. It was clear that simply because of its domination of the Irish brewing market Guinness was on the defensive in that country – it had over 90 per cent of the stout market in the Republic in 1968.

As regards stout the Company had a monopoly, with the exception of two independent Cork breweries, Murphy and Beamish and Crawford. Beamish, as we have seen, was the largest brewer in Ireland in the early nineteenth century. Since then it had neither grown significantly nor disappeared. Guinness refrained from aggressive competition to keep it alive, with Murphy, so as not to be seen as a monopolist. But either or both of these breweries could be taken over by a well-heeled international group and present a real challenge to Guinness's stout trade. Expansion, modernization and publicity would cost millions, but it could be done, though the Guinness management always calculated that it would not be a rational investment. Investment is not always entirely rational, however. An acquisitive Canadian brewer E. P. Taylor, backed by the Royal Bank of Canada, had built up a group called United Breweries, and he bid for Beamish. Guinness reacted strongly. With sufficient finance, United Breweries could not only create a threat in Ireland but – the ultimate nightmare – replace Guinness with Beamish in its own pubs in Britain. Gossip had it that Taylor, not a modest man, was saying he would break Guinness. Guinness bid for Beamish itself and there was a bid battle in which the winners were the Beamish shareholders. From 5s a share the price was bid up to 20s at which Taylor finally secured the prize, such as it was; from the pure investment point of view it was considered expensive at 5s, so at this level Guinness was certainly right to let go of the rope. Murphy was in due course also acquired by Watneys, now part of Grand Metropolitan. No serious competition came from either until very much later when Guinness had ceased to be a one-brand firm anyway. Taylor's United Breweries, including Beamish, is now part of Bass Charrington, and Murphy's is part of Grand Metropolitan.

The 1960s saw the first serious attempt by the Company to diversify out of stout since the time, a century and a half earlier, when it had come to concentrate exclusively on black beer. Stout had long established itself as overwhelmingly the most popular beer in Ireland, accounting for around 90 per cent of consumption. This obsession with stout was quite unique; it is hard to think of a parallel to it in any other product in any other country.

It was clear that with more people travelling, and markets all over the world becoming more homogeneous, it could not continue in this extreme form. It was equally clear that both ale in the British style and lager as drunk internationally would increase their modest shares of the Irish beer trade, although no one could tell when or at what rate, and that in Britain lager, by then overwhelmingly the most popular type of beer in the rest of the world, would increase its percentage from 3 per cent.

As regards ale, Sir Hugh Beaver had already begun purchasing some of the small ale breweries in Ireland. Boyd continued this with the purchase of Smithwicks, perhaps the best known of them. More important was the Company's entry into the lager market. At the end of Sir Hugh Beaver's time Guinness created a new brand which was christened Harp. A harp had always been the Guinness trademark, so the new product followed on the Company's tradition; but it was given a pale blue and gold livery that deliberately differentiated it from stout. A secret public opinion poll conducted by Guinness among the general public and innkeepers, as to which brewery they would expect to be best at brewing lager, produced a confusing result with Guinness coming top among the innkeepers and bottom with the general public. This meant that the Guinness connection needed to be emphasized in the trade and underplayed outside it; the old trademark with a new colour scheme neatly achieved this.

Harp was first brewed at Dundalk in 1959 under the direction of Dr Hermann Muender, a German brewer brought over from Hamburg. It quickly became the dominant brand in Ireland, but this trade was small. The real prize to go for was the British lager trade. The obstacle here was the Cuckoo Factor; the difficulty of getting any further Guinness product into the tied pubs to compete with the lagers being marketed by the other brewers. The answer was, by a series of skilful negotiations, to establish Harp Lager Ltd as a joint venture with some of the pub-owning brewers so that it would qualify as their own in-house lager. From their point of view the arrangement made considerable sense as long as lager remained only a modest part of British beer sales; it came apart in the late 1970s when the lager trade became too large and lucrative. The proportion of lager in the UK beer trade was 1 per cent in 1960, 7 per cent in 1970, and 31 per cent in 1980. In the late 1960s Harp attained the status of top-selling British lager with about 25 per cent of the lager market. It was brewed in Manchester and at Alton, in Hampshire, as well as at Dundalk. The main partners of Guinness in the Harp business were Courage and Bass Charrington in the South, Scottish and Newcastle in the North; lesser stakes were taken by Greene King and others.

Guinness also expanded overseas, mostly in the former British Empire. A certain amount of Guinness had always been sold in the various Dominions and Colonies: like other trade, stout followed the flag. Nor was it only drunk by the colonizers; the indigenous peoples liked it too, even in the tropics. This seems odd, because in England Guinness is thought of as a winter drink; the statistics showed this clearly in my day, and I expect they still do. All UK brewers showed two main peaks of consumption, one around August Bank Holiday, the other at Christmas. Except in the case of Guinness, the August peak was the higher; Guinness, and only Guinness, showed its higher peak at Christmas. So why do the inhabitants of hot countries like it? Partly because some of them perceive it as an aphrodisiac; Bruce Chatwin came across this attitude to Guinness in the Cameroon Republic. The slogan 'Guinness for Strength' – in Nigeria 'Guinness for Power' – apparently translates in some languages into a word that implies *sexual* strength. The Chinese, too, may have regarded it as an alternative to rhinoceros horn; export figures for Hong Kong used to be taken to indicate that a lot of Guinness was smuggled into Communist China.

The first overseas venture was into Nigeria, first established in 1964. It was successful from the outset, but just as the Cuckoo

Factor compelled Guinness to give away the lion's share of Harp, so economic nationalism made it dispose of most of Guinness Nigeria to Nigerian shareholders. None the less the venture was a great success. By the early 1980s Guinness Nigeria was operating four breweries. To be sure, it has caused headaches over the years in two ways, both rather typical of developing countries. First, there were problems in repatriating dividends. In the end this was always achieved, though sometimes at an unfavourable exchange rate. In addition, it was at one time very difficult for Guinness Nigeria to obtain the dollars to buy the imported barley which was needed to keep production going. The parent Company could have bought the barley and sent it in, but this would have been wholly irresponsible; it might have amounted to throwing good money after bad on behalf of a company which was in any case only partly owned. The problem was to arise in acute form in the early 1980s; Thomas Ward, through his law firm, arranged for its solution and may have saved Guinness Nigeria from ruin. Ward was a close associate of Ernest Saunders whom we shall meet again.

Then came Guinness Malaysia. Considering that the Malays are a Muslim people this may seem an odd choice, but the country contains a very large minority of Chinese, as well as Tamils from South India and other non-Muslims, and neighbouring Singapore is in fact predominantly Chinese. Here again the parent had to dispose of most of its shares; but the Malaysian venture was highly successful. Further breweries were established in due course in Cameroun, Ghana and Jamaica, all of which did well; by 1979 they were providing a quarter of Group profits. The trouble was that owing to the uncertainties of operating in Third World countries these profits could not necessarily be counted on, a fact of which investment analysts were very much aware and which led them to lower the earnings multiple at which they would recommend the shares. This was especially true before the ideological collapse of Communism. Any of these countries might have been taken over by a Marxist government which would have been delighted to expropriate all capitalist ventures without compensation.

Guinness advertising became much more serious in the early 1960s. Frivolity was out; it was replaced by the hard sell. Did it therefore become more effective? People can still argue about this, but the probability is that it did. Sir Hugh Beaver commissioned the first serious sociological research with a view to answering the question: who drinks Guinness? The answer came loud and clear, identifying the typical Guinness drinker by sex, class and age; apparently he was male, working-class and getting on in years. The conclusion drawn at the time was very clear, namely, that the main thrust of Guinness advertising should be aimed at people of this sort and, more generally, should be sociologically driven rather than springing from flair and intuition.

The Guinness animals were dropped; their appeal was too general, too diffuse, insufficiently connected with any direct encouragement to drink the product. In addition, in the late 1950s there had been a tendency, fostered by T. L. Marks as advertising manager and abetted by Bensons, to make the campaign rather highbrow, with subtle drawings by Edward Ardizzone and avant-garde ones by Abram Games. It was Marks, too, who was largely responsible for the five years of the Guinness Poetry Prize. This sort of thing was swept away. Hard as it is to prove, the reason why the new seriousness is likely to have paid off is that it was a variation of the message of the very earliest campaigns based on 'Guinness is Good for You'. The first campaigns, after all, had also been based on research of a sort, even though this consisted only of Bensons' people going round the pubs, and it confirmed the general perception that Guinness was indeed good for you; the Filboid Studge Factor. The first campaigns on these lines had been provably and spectacularly successful. This time the message was naturally shorn of the pseudo-medical verbiage, which would have got Guinness into trouble with the new health puritans while remaining largely unread by a public which the television habit was making allergic to chunks of didactic prose. Even 'Good for You' was not on the whole used explicitly. The direct thrust of the new message was based on the observation of Dr F. E. Emery, a psychiatrist, who divided drinkers and their drinks into three categories: social, indulgent and reparative. Guinness falls neatly into the reparative slot; which merely put a verbal label on what Philip Benson and Oswald Greene had discovered in the 1920s, and Ernest Guinness had always known. Putting this Filboid Studge image together with the sociological profile of the Guinness drinker added up to identifying Guinness as the reward for the steady, senior workman after a day's toil. 'After work – Guinness'. Then, in a concession to sixties' slang: 'Man! You've earned that Guinness.' The earliest television commercials from the 1950s had been animated cartoons featuring the animals; they were succeeded by ones that showed workers going into pubs at the end of their stint.

The change was rather unpopular with that part of the public which consciously notices advertising – which is, of course, not the same as that part of the public likely to be persuaded by advertising to drink Guinness. The Guinness family directors were doubtful, though when Marks's successor, Alan Wood, had a meeting with some of them to explain the new policy, it went better than he had expected. The only reaction came from Lady Honor Svejdar (Rupert's daughter and Paul Channon's mother) who said, 'Everything I've heard seems common sense.' At Board meetings and in private family members did agitate from time to time to restore some humour to the advertising. This had some effect, notably in the form of a poster in 1966 which imitated the Bayeux Tapestry and carried the slogan 'Battle of Hastings 1066 – Bottle of Guinness 1966'. This poster was the last to be thought up by the great parodist Stanley Penn. It helped to counter murmurs that Guinness advertisements were becoming boring; had these become louder, they would have damaged the Company's image. By the 1960s the public had become accustomed to regard Guinness advertising as free entertainment; to disappoint it would have been dangerous for the perception might have spread that the Company was going downhill.

Was it? By the 1970s, the view that perhaps this was so began to spread like a slow-growing mildew among management. It had something to do with the question of the brand image in Britain. Around 1970 the perception began to arise that the pulling power of the male working-class image was declining; Edward Heath's unexpected election victory for the Conservatives in that year was thought to be a straw in the wind. There was certainly a view that Guinness needed to recruit women, young people and the upwardly mobile. The advertising began to thrust in all these directions and also, rather effectively, to use a tempting glass of Guinness by itself, without a drinker. The new aim was sexlessness, agelessness, above all classlessness. Draught Guinness did break out of the traditional category of Guinness drinker to become popular with some young people, but bottled Guinness, still the major product and the one on which the profit margin was highest, seemed trapped.

Non-brewing activities during the 1960s and early 1970s were not very significant. Confectionery turned in a steady profit of six figures, though on the whole a diminishing one. More management attention of the right sort might well have turned it round; there were some decent and well-established brands in the group. Callard & Bowser's butterscotch, Nuttalls' Mintoes, Riley's toffees; all or any of these could have been pushed, and a blitz on costs would certainly have been possible. If Ernest Saunders could do this with Guinness in the 1980s, it could have been done on a smaller scale with the confectionery companies earlier on. There were strong arguments against trying this; there always are. The confectionery trade had become dominated by a few large groups, notably Cadbury Schweppes, Rowntree Mackintosh and United Biscuits, and to break into the big time against them would have required both money and flair. A determined management could probably have done it, but at that time Guinness did not have the drive and was unwilling to spare the money, so the confectionery group was allowed to vegetate.

The plastics group arose originally from a company formed to give employment to redundant coopers in Dublin, but by 1971, through acquisition, it had become a mainly British concern. In that year it earned over £500,000, and it was to be further expanded during the seventies.

Pharmaceuticals went on losing money. Twyford Laboratories, the wholly-owned research organization, could be expected to lose until it hit the jackpot with some product or other, which never happened. It was closed in 1971. Crookes, still 60 per cent owned by Guinness with Philips holding 40 per cent, was supposed to be profitable, but continued to be a drain on both groups. It was sold to Boots, also in 1971, for £2 million. However, also counted in with pharmaceuticals was a more recent acquisition that was to take on a certain importance: J. Morison Son and Jones Holdings Ltd. This was acquired in stages from 1964 with its management in place; its main proprietor, Michael Ogle, stayed as Joint Managing Director. It manufactured and sold, among other things, various pharmaceutical products, and owned a chain of pharmacists, mostly in New Commonwealth countries. During the late 1960s its profits mitigated the losses of the rest of the pharmaceutical group, and on the whole it did well; but the annual report for 1971 states:

> We still retain, and are increasing, our holding in J. L. Morison Son & Jones Holdings Ltd, which company continues to expand in a satisfactory way. This year exceptional losses due to civil disturbances in one of that company's major overseas trading areas made it necessary to write off a substantial sum.

But for this the pharmaceutical group as a whole would have made a positive contribution to group profit this year.

Guinness, then, was quite happily increasing its investment in an enterprise which obviously involved thrills and spills. Because it was on a small scale, this departure from its normal solidity did not attract attention at the time; but it was a sign of much worse to come.

SEVEN

Heading for the Weir

In the final years before the arrival of Ernest Saunders the directors lost faith in the magic of the Guinness brand name, and
hence in the future of the Company. That, at least, is how it looks
now, although at the time none of us saw it in those terms.
Indeed, if we had been accused at the time of having lost faith we
should all have denied it. We may have seen ourselves as having
become objective, as accepting the real world; rather as Siegfried,
in *Götterdämmerung*, says he no longer bothers to listen to the
language of the birds which in youth he was magically enabled to
understand. Loss of faith is always accompanied by a reasoned
case, whether the loss occurs because of that case or whether
the case is just an excuse. Saunders, the outsider, was to show us
how to believe in our own brand again. Our pessimism stemmed
from the change in taste from dark beer to light; this change,
which I had noted so long before when looking into the German
beer industry, had finally reached the British Isles, though it was
gradual and erratic. Harp Lager was a help here, but the actual
profit from Harp was limited (£3.477 million in 1977 or about 12
per cent of brewing profits). The worst effect of the decline in
confidence was not so much direct as indirect. Whatever the
doubts of the management, the Company continued to brew
the product, promote it and sell it at a profit. However, those
doubts made management obsessed with the need to diversify –

it hardly seemed to matter into what – when it did not possess the skills to do so successfully.

Anthony J. R. Purssell became Managing Director of the parent Company in September 1975, the last Guinness Brewer of the old regime to run it. He was twenty years younger than his predecessor, Robert McNeile; a new generation – my generation – was now in charge. A tall, bonily good-looking man whose floppy and poetic fringe untouched with grey made him at forty-nine still look like a star undergraduate, Purssell had been an athlete in his youth and secured a first-class degree in chemistry. He was also – and remains – a man of goodwill, culture and charm. He certainly charmed the authors of *The Guinness Affair*, Nick Kochan and Hugh Pym; they listened to what he said respectfully and uncritically. He struck them as a 'rather unworldly, gentle character'.[1] The epithet 'gentle' surprised me, though much had happened by the time they interviewed him. In his heyday he seemed, by Guinness standards, rather brusque. He enjoyed an argument and conducted it vigorously, though pleasantly; he did not particularly welcome suggestions. 'Unworldly' is a more interesting description. What Kochan and Pym sensed in Purssell seems to have been the Guinness donnishness. This is the quality that emerges when bright people become isolated and make themselves a comfortable nest; Oxford colleges are the prototype, and we may recall here the episode with Alexander Forbes Watson (see Chapter 2). After McNeile, what the Guinness management required was another shake-up from outside the charmed circle, and the family ought to have provided it. If either of the first two Earls of Iveagh had been in charge they would have done so, whether by galvanizing Purssell or by replacing him with another Hugh Beaver. But they were gone.

It would be unfair to blame Purssell for the Company's decline in the late 1970s, because this was under way before he took over. He was the product of a culture, and the best person available within it. But as the leader of the team running the

Company he saw no remedy for the long-term decline in the value of the brand, but harboured the illusion that the Company could divert its resources successfully into other activities under the existing management.

We, the family, shared this illusion to some extent, but not entirely; our confidence had its limits. Although none of us possessed the authority to initiate the required shake-up, we did still, collectively, prevent the fading management from taking action that would have made matters worse.

It looked to Purssell as if the Company was running out of money. Backed by the other executive directors and by his predecessor Robert McNeile, he proposed that it should raise money by a rights issue, and obtained advice from merchant bankers Samuel Montagu as to how this should be done. A rights issue, not normally a very attractive proposition for shareholders, used sometimes to be referred to as a 'forced levy'. If a shareholder takes up his rights, he is paying liquid cash for merely maintaining his proportion of the company. If he sells some or all of the rights he will be reducing his proportion of the company at a price which will be depressed by the fact that those holders who are short of cash will be selling simply for that reason. Members of the family who held Guinness shares would have been hit particularly hard because their holdings were often a high proportion of their assets.

The family directors vetoed Purssell's proposal. In doing so we did the right thing, though to a great extent for the wrong reason. The right thing, because to allow the management, in the condition it then was, to raise extra funds from the market would have postponed the drastic change which would sooner or later be needed, and provided more good money to be thrown after the bad. The wrong reason, because we were concerned less for the prosperity of the Company than for maintaining the family's proportion of it and avoiding the forced sale of rights. Samuel Montagu proposed to arrange for rights sold by the family to be placed in the market at 10 per cent below the quoted price, an offer we found wholly devoid of charm. If in taking this line we might have been accused of self-seeking, the executive directors for their part were by no means guiltless of this; one point put to us was that the Company would not progress unless it could pay salaries high enough to retain high-quality people.

The proposal was put to the Board in Purssell's absence by McNeile, as 'Co-Chairman' of the Company, at a Board Meeting on 25 November 1975. The minutes of this meeting show that the executive directors knew that the Company, if not exactly in trouble, was heading for it. Their mistake was to think that an injection of equity capital would solve the problems. Their main point was that more and more money was having to be borrowed; re-equipment and diversification were exceeding cash flow, and in McNeile's words (as recorded in the minutes), 'the position might well be reached where it was impossible to borrow more money at acceptable rates'. Samuel Montagu had recommended the raising of £19 million by a rights issue on a two for nine basis. Several of the executive directors spoke at the Board Meeting of identifying new fields for investment (*absit omen*, one may remark with hindsight); one, according to the minutes, 'commented that the work of the strategic planning staff so far indicated that the Guinness Group had reached a static situation and without additional funds no growth could be foreseen'. But if the management was achieving static profits with the resources then at its disposal, why should it achieve growth with additional funds?

I found the proposal profoundly depressing, but had learnt enough in my years on the Board to realize that it had to be opposed obliquely, at first at any rate. In particular I made a hypocritical show of accepting the bit about the need for high salaries. I quote from the minutes: '[Mr Jonathan Guinness] accepted . . . that if opportunities for worthwhile careers were not available within the group the most able staff would leave.' But 'in the general economic climate with rising unemployment [he] felt it wise to pause before seeking further growth'. My allusion to the family position was cautious and not very clear, to the effect that a diminution of the family's percentage holding 'could affect the Company's position'. I was very relieved to find myself backed by a far more influential figure, Alan Boyd, who went into more detail about the difficulties the family would be caused, and described Samuel Montagu's offer of a 10 per cent discount for family rights as 'most unsatisfactory'.

The meeting came to no decision. I wrote to Purssell two days later:

> It would be interesting to know the exact terms of reference given to Samuel Montagu . . . Was the figure for capital requirements, notably, given them as an unalterable 'fact of life?' . . . On some assumptions one might think Montagu had somewhat skimped their assignment, but another possibility is that the general urgency . . . made us ask partial questions, and then forget, in our evaluation of the answers to them, that they were only partial.

Purssell, on 28 November, took exception to what I had written but implicitly admitted that it was true:

> I think it is dangerous if every director were to ask private questions to check up so to speak on Samuel Montagu. I believe these questions should be asked at a Board Meeting . . . The terms of reference given to Samuel Montagu were on the lines that, given our capital structure and capital requirements for 1975/1976, did they agree with . . . feelings of the executive directors at Albemarle Street that some form of refinancing of the Company would soon be required. As such the capital requirements were given to them as an 'unalterable fact of life' to quote your phrase, and they were neither asked, nor did I

consider it their function, to consider changes in the figure for capital expenditure. This is for the Board to decide.

Quite so; Samuel Montagu were not management consultants.

Purssell went on to admit that the matter had been rushed, but kept to his view that 'we shall have to go to the market within the next twelve months or run a very real danger of severely contracting our operations in the future'. If the Board agreed with this, they would have to agree to the refinancing. As to the problems of major shareholders, the Board should consider them, and give those concerned plenty of time to overcome these problems. 'I feel sure that we must examine this whole subject very much more in the coming weeks.'

My reply (2 December) was unyielding:

> I am delighted to ask my questions at the next Board Meeting, and shall do so. My purpose in asking them by letter was not to keep them 'private' – what good would that do? – but to start working on them ten days earlier ... You yourself agree that time is, and has been, a factor ... What I am asking you to do ... is to help in retracing for all the Board (your) reasoning ... If nobody has 'seriously questioned' the analysis, perhaps it is because not all the elements of the analysis are available ... With more open terms of reference, (Samuel Montagu) would no doubt also have looked on a rights issue ... as money that has to be serviced ... Major shareholders are only different from others in degree. All would suffer from any equity issue that was inadequately serviced ...

The proposal was killed off at an unofficial meeting, such as was always held every year not long before the December Board Meeting, between Purssell as Managing Director and the inner-family directors, that is, Bryan, Alan Boyd, Patricia Boyd, Honor Svejdar, Maureen Dufferin, Paul Channon and myself. Benjamin

Iveagh was not present since he was establishing Irish residence, but I feel that if he had been there he would have said nothing on either side of the argument. He normally identified himself with the management which sustained and protected him; all the same, it is certain that any rights issue would have been inconvenient to him as a very large shareholder, and probable that our veto came as a relief to him. I remember Purssell saying, rather plaintively, 'Then I take it the family doesn't trust the management with more of its money.' I had not quite seen it in these terms but his remark struck me at the time like a ray of light through the fog; yes, that *was* the position, and I saw from the embarrassed faces of the others that they, too, felt that Purssell had hit target.

This was the last time that the family, acting as such, decisively influenced the policy of the Company. Its action certainly helped the Company, and may have saved it. This should weigh a certain amount in the balance against the anomaly, pointed out by all commentators, that a family which held no more than about 23 per cent of the Company should appoint eight directors to the Board. For in this case, had it not been for the family directors, the rights issue would certainly have gone ahead. It is inconceivable that the institutions, which were the largest of the other shareholders, would have prevented Purssell's plan from going through.

An example of what might then have happened is provided by the collapse of the hotel group Queens Moat Houses in 1993 with a negative net worth of £389 million. An unnamed banker told Patrick Weever of the *Sunday Telegraph*: 'For several years the cash generated to pay dividends and interest came from rights issues.' This would not, of course, have happened by design at Guinness, any more than it did at Queens Moat Houses. 'Financial controls were inadequate,' admitted former Chairman John Bairstow to Weever, and the new Chief Executive, Andrew Coppel, said, 'We had to rebuild the financial database from scratch. The company did not even know how many banks it had.'[2] This implies management far slacker than ever existed at Guinness; yet Ernest Saunders was to discover much muddle and ineffectiveness, and it would have been more imprudent than any of us suspected for shareholders to provide Purssell's management with extra money. The proceeds of any issue would partly have been lost in further unsuitable ventures, partly used to 'smooth out' dividend payments when profits fell, under the illusion that the fall was temporary. When it turned out to be permanent, the cash would have been a convenient resource to keep shareholders happy – until it ran out. Certainly the management would not have felt the need to recruit Ernest Saunders for a couple of years more, by which time the Company would have slid further down the slippery slope. Shareholders would certainly have ended worse off. In its muddled, self-interested way the family succeeded in defending all the shareholders.

One argument put by the management for a rights issue was that more cash might be required because of inflation. This argument was both inherently specious, and rather a giveaway as regards the true feelings of management as to the Company's prospects. The 1970s were certainly a decade of high inflation; the cost of living in Britain multiplied 3.6 times between 1970 and 1980, and at a progressively more rapid pace after the tripling of the price of oil in 1973. However, the proposition that this meant Guinness needed an injection of capital was only stated, not argued at all rigorously. One management document says that 'capital expenditure and working capital tend to rise at about the same rate, if not faster than the inflation assumed'. This is obvious, but it need not mean that the business needs more capital introduced. If capital expenditure and working capital requirement rise at the same rate as inflation there is only a problem if profits do not keep pace but fall in real terms. Working capital requirements should not rise faster than inflation if a company's finances are sensibly managed; current assets – stock, work in progress and debtors – should rise in nominal value in line with inflation. If cash and bank balances are kept at a negative figure, the company should actually benefit. Had there been anything in the argument that inflation purely as such was a reason for the need to increase the equity base, the problems which surfaced from 1980 onwards would have been problems of liquidity, which was not the case. On balance it looks as if inflation actually helped the Company, because it seemed to be making very respectable progress until as late as 1979.

This was in fact a watershed year. Let us forget for a moment everything that has happened since the publication of the 1979 report and imagine that it is early in 1980 and we are looking at the five-year review shown in that report. What we see looks very like the beginning of a success story. Here is a mature brewery, reliable, unable to grow very fast, yet showing respectable progress in its traditional business, investing some of its cash flow into other areas and doing pretty well. The non-brewing concerns, taken as a whole, have outstripped the core business over the period. In 1977 a slight setback in brewing profits was more than made up by an excellent advance on the non-brewing side, so that Group profits continued their smooth progress; during 1978 the non-brewing side advanced further, both absolutely and relatively; and the last year, 1979, showed the diversifications still improving, though more slowly and eclipsed by a leap forward in the brewing business.

Net profit attributable to the parent Company, and dividends, performed as follows:

	1975	1976	1977	1978	1979
Attributable net profits (£m)	16.8	20.2	22.3	23.2	31.7
Dividends (pence per 25p unit)	5.7	6.3	7.0	7.8	9.8

This gives a rise of about 72 per cent in shareholders' income, which compares well with the increase in the cost of living over the same period: about 65 per cent. Book value of net assets employed rose by 62 per cent in the same period, just less than inflation, but the more significant figure of net current assets went up by no less than 245 per cent, beating inflation by a considerable multiple. From the standpoint of 1979, it could have been argued that the management was pretty successful and that the family had been unfair to tie its hands. This becomes clear when we break down the above results between brewing and the various non-brewing activities.

	1975	1976	1977	1978	1979
			(£ million)		
Brewing	24.5	31.3	29.2	31.0	39.6
General trading	3.0	3.5	6.3	8.4	7.9
Plastics, etc.	0.8	1.0	2.5	4.6	5.3
Leisure	—	-0.2	0.6	0.7	1.3
Confectionery	0.3	0.5	0.3	0.4	0.7
Property	0.1	0.2	0.1	—	—
Total non-brewing	4.4	5.0	9.8	14.1	15.2
Total	28.9	36.3	39.0	45.1	54.8
Non-brewing (%)	15%	14%	25%	31%	28%

Financial commentators were rather impressed; the *Investors' Chronicle* for 19 January 1979 commented on the 1978 report using the headline 'Diversification is good for Guinness'. That was how it looked, and the piece was optimistic: 'For the current year an increase in earnings of 20 per cent is not an impossible target.' It certainly was not; it was virtually achieved. The main lesson of this exercise is the rather obvious one that it is foolish to extrapolate into the future using figures alone.

Yet it is also useful in another way, because it puts into perspective the rather glib comments that have been made about the old Guinness management to the effect that the business had 'lost its way' and stagnated for twenty years or so. The fact is that up to 1979 there was apparent progress. There were then two bad years during which the diversifications virtually collapsed, although the brewing business did not. The Board cannot be accused of letting things drift once the bad results came through, for Ernest Saunders was recruited in 1981.

What were the diversifications? Easily the most important was the 'General Trading' group centred on J. L. Morison Son and Jones Holdings, now no longer counted as pharmaceutical. General trading is in fact a better description of its activity, even though pharmacies and medicines played a considerable part. Its former proprietor, Michael Ogle, was now a Joint Deputy Managing Director of the Guinness Group. Ogle, a tall, genial, bespectacled figure, fitted well into the quasi-academic style of the old Guinness management. By background a Devon farmer, he had discovered a talent as a wheeler-dealer and put together the Morison business which traded over much of the world, notably in the Commonwealth countries of Africa and Asia where it owned a good many retail outlets; the goods it dealt in included 'auto engineering and fire prevention equipment, confectionery and food manufacture, branded baby products, toiletries and sunglasses, photographic equipment, lighting and heating products', to quote the Guinness report for 1979. Ogle was an example of how difficult it is, in real life, to typecast people. From his business record one would expect him to be rather brash; in fact he comes over as scholarly and quietly spoken, which was probably to his great advantage because it must have inspired confidence. By 1979 his responsibilities at Guinness covered not only his own former business but also Guinness Retail Holdings, of which he was Chairman, part at least of the 'leisure' group, and other activities which he introduced. The most controversial of these was film finance. Morison Son and Jones was now split between Guinness Morison International Ltd and MSJ Overseas Ltd. It engaged in general trading over much of the world, notably in Africa and Asia, where it owned a good many retail outlets; the list given above from the 1979 report of the goods in which the General Trading Group dealt is certainly not exhaustive.

Apart from this there was the plastics group; the results here are flattered by the purchase during 1977 and 1978 of White Child and Beney which was about the same size as the existing GPG (Guinness Plastics Group) which had descended from the small concern started to employ the former coopers. The confectionery group bought by Sir Hugh Beaver with its old-established brands still carried on, turning in modest profits. There was a new leisure group with camping sites and boat hire which, though it looked progressive, was still on a modest scale. Bearing all this in mind, it is clear that the creditable performance of non-brewing profits was essentially due to Michael Ogle's operations. He was the hero of the hour. There was even vague talk of his eventually replacing Purssell as Managing Director.

The brewing business itself performed very respectably throughout the 1970s and continued, as we shall see, to hold up after the collapse of the diversifications, although how long that would have continued without Ernest Saunders can never be known. An important factor affecting each individual year was the incidence of the price rises in Britain and Ireland. Again, in overseas trade profits were sometimes held back by political and economic difficulties in the countries concerned, Nigeria being the most important. The 1977 report, to take an example, says that in Nigeria 'the demand for our products is persistent, but the breweries are at present caught between rapidly rising costs and firm control of ex-brewery prices'. In Ghana 'our development is cramped by insufficient allocations of foreign exchange for essential raw materials'. However, the same report tells of a good year for Guinness Malaysia, expansion in Cameroun, and new arrangements to brew Guinness under contract in Gambia, Togo and Reunion.

The Harp Lager consortium finally came apart in 1979. The major pub-owning partners of Guinness, Courage and Scottish and Newcastle had become increasingly restive because of the ever-increasing popularity of lager in Britain; it now represented 29 per cent of the whole beer market, and they felt that too much of the profit generated in their pubs by Harp was finding its way to Guinness. The smaller partners, Greene King and Wolverhampton and Dudley, were still content, and joined with Guinness in a reduced operation brewing Harp at Park Royal. Courage and Scottish and Newcastle continued to brew and sell Harp, but as franchisees, and were not obliged to promote it. The negotiations were conducted on the Guinness side by Purssell, who is accused by some of using his astuteness to help the partners through their legal and practical difficulties rather than putting obstacles in their way. There can clearly be two views on this, and I have heard both expressed. Perhaps a stronger personality might have done better for Guinness through dominance and bluff. All the same, Guinness did not have a strong hand to play, and it is likely that in the circumstances the outcome was as good as could reasonably be expected. This is certainly the view of the Company Secretary, Alan Scrine. As a matter of fact the profit contribution by Harp to Guinness, though useful, was never decisive; in 1979 it was just under 10 per cent of brewing profits. A great deal of its importance was psychological, in that it gave Guinness a visible stake in the fastest-growing sort of beer.

All was changed by the results for 1980. They were catastrophic, for non-brewing profits collapsed from £15.2 million to £5.4 million. This broke down as follows, with the 1979 figures repeated for comparison:

	1979	1980
	(£ million)	
Confectionery	0.7	−0.3
General trading	7.9	1.8
Plastics	5.3	3.1
Leisure	1.3	0.8

As will be seen, every one of the non-brewing activities suffered a slump. Confectionery even went into loss. The disintegration of profits from general trading, taking it well below its level of 1975, accounted for more of the fall than all the others put together. The situation of the Group as a whole would have been worse than it was but for a rise in trading profits on the brewing side from £39.6m to £44.1m.; despite this, net profit attributable to stockholders slumped by nearly a third, from £31.7m to £22.4m.

Michael Ogle had to go; the decencies were preserved, despite murmured recriminations. After giving six months' notice, he left the Company at the end of December 1981. Many harsh things were said about him, and still are. Probably the fairest comment is that there was a fundamental clash of business cultures between him and the Company. To an individual entrepreneur, all opportunities are there to be taken, even where there is a certain risk involved. Obviously the odds must be right, and risks must be limited to what can be afforded; nevertheless some ventures will always go wrong and some spectacular fluctuations in performance must be expected. But to a quoted company, and especially an old-established company of Guinness's type which is a 'blue chip' on the Stock Exchange, this approach is quite alien. Part of its stock in trade is reliability; institutions such as pension funds and unit trusts that hold its shares must be able to count on a steady income. It must be, as the saying goes, 'suitable for widows and orphans'. In a time of inflation this is particularly the case. Shares in solid companies, which can be relied upon at least to keep pace with inflation, are in a sense to contemporary investors what Consols were to the Victorians.

Ogle was especially blamed for involving the Company in film finance. When this was first proposed I remember an uneasy feeling that things were somehow slipping out of control, and I was one of several directors who asked for an assurance that no more would be at risk than the modest amount which we had invested. Ogle always gave the impression that this was the case. Unfortunately it was not; guarantees had been given on the Company's behalf for further amounts, some of which were then called. To be fair to Ogle, it seems that had the Company kept its nerve and hung on to these film rights, the temporary losses would eventually have been recouped and a useful income earned over the years. This is not only maintained by Ogle himself, it is also borne out by an impartial Company source.

However, this fact, though interesting, is quite academic. In a company like Guinness with pretensions to be suitable for widows, orphans and investment managers, it is not true that 'a profit is a profit'. Profits are by no means all alike, and losses even less so. Profits only really count to the extent that they are repeatable; in Guinness's case, brewing profits were the best because the concern had been making them since 1759 and it therefore looked very much as if they would continue in future years. At the other extreme, 'exceptional' profits mean little because by definition they are unrepeatable. Profits made in any given activity are only properly validated when a steady record has proved that they are likely to recur.

As for losses, when a blue chip company takes an obvious risk, a loss is by no means simply the converse of a profit. When Guinness went into films, any profits that might arise could not bring credit corresponding even remotely to the catastrophic loss of reputation attached to making losses. This was why the decision to go into films was so aberrant. The Company could lose money in brewing from time to time without suffering serious harm, as long as it did not become a habit. In the 1950s a brewery was established on Long Island to break into the US market. It failed, but few blamed the management, then or later. Similarly, temporary losses in plastics or retailing or even in caravan sites could be excused; even the long-running haemorrhage of money in Guinness's pharmaceutical group during the

1960s was tolerated. As a colleague of mine on another Board once remarked, the only way to avoid all risk is to do no business. But if money was lost in films, everyone would at once say, 'I could have told them that.' Not that this would have mattered as much as it did if Ogle's other ventures had not turned sour. As it was, the same reasoning was applied to the whole non-brewing spectrum; what was a company like Guinness *doing*, for heaven's sake, messing about with holiday villages and babies' potties?

Ogle, with his entrepreneurial background, could not be expected to think like this. To him, you win some and you lose some; he could 'meet with triumph and disaster/And treat those two impostors just the same', which is exactly what a blue chip company cannot do. So why did Purssell not keep Ogle under control? Partly because of his lack of a general business background outside Guinness; but partly also because of the performance of Ogle's businesses up to 1979. The prestige this gave Ogle was a pale anticipation of the moral ascendancy which was to enable Ernest Saunders, a few years later, to get virtually anything past the Board. Ogle's manner, his quiet, gentlemanly way of putting things, may also have had something to do with it. Whatever the reason, Purssell did not control Ogle as he should have; although, if he had tried, Ogle could well have countered, 'If orchids and snake venom, then why not films?' Anyway, it was not only Ogle himself whose judgement was discredited in the 1980 results. Inevitably a shadow also fell on Purssell.

All the same, it was Purssell who saw the need for a radical shake-up and who decided to do something about it. He must be given credit for this decision, although he may not have seen how severely, in the circumstances, it would endanger his personal position. It was his last service to the Company, and by no means his least. Had he simply resigned, the position would have been much worse. As it was, the comparison of Ernest Saunders' appointment in 1981 with that of Sir Hugh Beaver in 1947 is a sad one. In 1947 the management was in all essentials doing well; Rupert, with the connivance of Newbold, simply saw the opportunity of recruiting a near-genius to lead the Company into the post-war world. The purpose in 1947 was to reinforce success. In 1980 the task was, urgently, to stem failure.

The family was no longer of the remotest use for the purpose. It had shot its bolt. Rupert Iveagh, the last family Chairman with the personal authority to achieve anything of the sort, was long gone. His grandson Benjamin was both in poor health and accustomed to follow the management line in all matters. Unable to thump the table himself, it would never occur to him, either, to mobilize the rest of us. Alan Boyd had retired and was out of touch; his son Simon, my brother Finn and Maureen Dufferin's son Sheridan were new to the Board. Could I have intervened? It would have been highly unwelcome had I done so, and probably not much use, since I did not have the contact with top management circles in industry that could have enabled me to put forward a sensible candidate. In any case I did not feel any great sense of urgency; more a mild long-term gloom. The Board papers still showed optimistic forecasts for the future, especially for several years ahead. They had been doing this for years, and as the future approached, the forecast prosperity faded. The notion that this trend might be due to bad management never occurred to me, nor that better management could improve matters. I saw the trouble through the eyes of the executive directors as reflected in the Board papers, in which it seemed to be entirely caused from outside. It was beginning to look as if the best that Guinness shareholders could hope for was for the Company to be taken over; perhaps a much larger concern might be able to make use of the brand and the name. Unilever was sometimes mentioned, because it was the main original partner in Guinness Nigeria. My relations and I still refrained from selling stock outside the family, though we would complain among ourselves; I remember referring to it as 'mouldy old Guinness stock'.

My recollection is that the other family directors took much the same view as I did. Decline looked likely, but catastrophe did not seem imminent. Purssell, who was actually in charge, not only had a clearer and starker vision of the Company's troubles than the rest of us, but also knew that there was scope to improve management at the top and that for this purpose no one within the organization would do; a first-class man from the outside was needed. What he did not at first see was that in the circumstances no first-class man would risk being merely a reinforcement. Leaving aside entirely the fact that, normally, a first-class man is ambitious for himself, it was certain that the new man would have to demand an absolutely free hand. Without this, he would certainly fail to make the necessary changes and be dragged down with everyone else. Effectively, anyone of top quality would insist on being not a reinforcement but a replacement.

It has been suggested that the City institutions which were large shareholders gave Purssell some sort of an ultimatum. There is no evidence of this, and it is unlikely; they had not at that time developed the habit of acting in this way. James Saunders tells us that several of them met Saunders soon after he took over and advised a 'total shake-up, and fast',[3] but to give a pep talk to the new man is very different from twisting the arm of the existing Managing Director. They were certainly voting with their feet by selling shares, which consequently fell fairly steadily. Peter Guinness, as Joint Deputy Managing Director, encouraged Purssell to recruit someone, as did Benjamin, but the original initiative was his own. He looked for a 'marketing man', and Peter Guinness for one was under the impression that the new man was to be of equal status to Purssell; not senior to him but not junior either, a situation which was bound to be unstable. It also seems rather odd to have looked for a marketing man when profits from selling Guinness were still progressive. It is true that further progress there was by no means assured, also that the existing management knew more about production than selling;

but help with marketing as such was not of direct relevance to those problems of the Company that were most immediately pressing. What was needed was a radical streamlining and revitalizing of the management, and on the non-brewing side a completely new corporate strategy. Marketing could certainly do with improvement, but this was less urgent. What was also true was that – with whatever face-saving formula this was achieved – Purssell had to cease to run the Company. But he himself, in the circumstances, could hardly be expected to see this, while the rest of the management – and, I am afraid, the Board as well – were befogged by habit and loyalty and could see it only dimly, if at all. When the beam of hindsight is turned on the confused thinking in the Company at the time, it seems clear that whoever was appointed would have to engage in a sharp struggle to establish his supremacy. To omit this, or to lose the battle, would simply make the Company drift ever faster down towards the weir.

EIGHT

Ernest Saunders

My feelings were mixed as I arrived at the Albemarle Street offices for the first meeting of the directors attended by Ernest Saunders, on Tuesday, 6 October 1981. Apprehension was combined with curiosity. The last few Board Meetings had been depressing. Now there was this new Managing Director who was to be present. My respect for Purssell did not prevent me from seeing this new appointment as a hopeful development. What would he be like?

I saw a tall, silver-haired, elegant figure with a slight stoop. He was clearly a man of considerable self-confidence, yet his manner was relaxed and modest. There was nothing aggressive or abrasive about him, though he clearly knew exactly what he was about. He made a good impression on me, not least because he showed something of the donnishness that I was used to in top Guinness executives. Altogether he seemed well suited to the Board and to the Company. This good impression was strengthened at subsequent meetings. In fact, over the next few months, he struck me more and more as a breath of fresh air. I used this phrase to the DTI inspectors when they questioned me later and it perhaps surprised them, yet it accurately describes the impression I had at the time.

Alan Scrine, the Company Secretary, told me that his first impression of Ernest Saunders was that he was 'a listener'. That was how he struck me, too. He seemed to give some weight to us ordinary family Board members, both when we intervened at meetings and when we made approaches outside them. We had over the years become accustomed to be consistently, if politely, disregarded. This was not always because we talked nonsense. I was once told that points we made at Board Meetings had sometimes been made by executives beforehand at Executive Committee meetings and turned down there. Executives who had raised such points invariably kept silent when they were raised at the full Board by one of us, making the Executive Committee the equivalent of a political caucus and depriving the Board of proper discussion. I cannot remember who told me about this, and I can quote no specific suggestions to which it may have applied. However, I find it entirely credible.

It cannot be claimed that Ernest Saunders was any more open with his fellow Directors than his predecessors; this was especially the case towards the end of his time. His superiority was not in informativeness but in receptivity, apparent or real. This willingness to listen was particularly conspicuous by comparison with Purssell, who seemed to welcome our opinions less than any of those who had come before him during my Directorship. I was not in the least surprised to read in *Nightmare* that Purssell 'had no time for the family as directors, and said so.' Our refusal to countenance his proposed rights issue must have sharpened this feeling, though there is no reason to suppose that it was its only cause. Saunders' private opinion was rather similar to that of Purssell. He, however, was more diplomatic because as a newcomer he had to be assured of Board support. This may have been why Saunders listened to us. It still felt like an improvement.

How had he been found? Virtually by chance. The executive directors at Guinness had little personal contact with the new high-flyers in international business. In character they were, as business executives go, rather introverted, and as such they were not 'networkers', to use the current term. Purssell's predecessors – Sir Hugh Beaver, Alan Boyd, Norman Smiley, Robert McNeile –

had all been clubbable people, and as such had been reasonably familiar with their peers in other businesses. Purssell was not, nor was Peter Guinness who was by background a banker, not an industrialist. True, contact with the Brewers' Society and in general with other brewers was still close and cordial; the Harp Lager consortium, though it was brought amicably to an end shortly before this time, was both the result of this relationship and a help in furthering it. Edward Guinness, who was Chairman of Harp and represented Guinness in the Brewers' Society, was certainly an extrovert and a networker, but he was outside the central group. As Saunders was to put it scornfully in *Nightmare*, Edward 'sat alone in our Jermyn Street office, looking after what was supposed to represent PR'.[2] Edward sat on the main Board, but as a simple director, not a Joint Deputy Managing Director. Also, the brewing industry, with which Edward dealt and within which he had his network, was not a promising place to look for the right man; it was still, like Guinness itself, in many ways sheltered and old-fashioned. So whereas Sir Hugh Beaver could very likely have found whoever he was looking for by a couple of telephone calls, Purssell and Peter Guinness were obliged to consult that very grand and discreet variety of employment agent known as a headhunter. Three candidates were produced, of whom the 'least unimpressive', in Purssell's phrase, was Ernest Saunders.

He was the son of an Austrian Jewish gynaecologist, Dr Emanuel Schleyer, who had settled in London just before the Second World War as a refugee from Hitler. Dr Schleyer built up a practice that prospered sufficiently to afford his sons a public school education. Ernest's brother, Dr Peter Saunders, has successfully followed in his father's profession. Ernest was two when the family moved to London; his accent is entirely English. His German is good, though, and so is his French. He belongs to that new breed of British European businessman who is at home in other languages and countries. In religion he is a member of the

Church of England, which means that to describe him as Jewish is only possible to the extent that Jews are regarded as a race rather than a religion. He read law at Cambridge, achieving a lower second-class degree.

His first job was at the American office products company 3M. It was there that he first became interested in the technique of marketing. In due course he joined the advertising agency J. Walter Thompson, where he gravitated to the market research side; a client for whom he did a lot of work was Unilever (Lux, Persil, Surf, and so on.) After a short time with Schweppes, he went to Beechams, another company where he could learn more about brands (Brylcreem, Silvikrin, Lucozade . . .) Beechams was also an international business, and Saunders' years there gave him experience of controlling operations in other countries. He also proved, to his own satisfaction, that brands do not really age; or that if they do, that hormone replacement therapy can make them as good as new. Brylcreem was a good example. Changing hair fashions were causing its decline in Europe, but an effective advertising campaign made its sales surge in the Far East against Japanese competition. This lesson was not to be lost on Ernest Saunders when he ran Guinness, whose brand name was similarly thought to be ageing. After Beechams, Saunders moved to Great Universal Stores where he ran the European mail-order business under Leonard Wolfson. Then he moved for a short time to Eutectic, a Swiss engineering company.

At the time of the offer from Guinness, Saunders was working in Geneva for Nestlé, the world's largest food company. As a product manager he was an important executive just below the very top level. Nestlé had been caught up in a worldwide controversy about its marketing of baby foods, which some salesmen in Third World countries had been pushing with too much enthusiasm. Some mothers were said to have taken their babies off the breast and put them on Nestlé's formula mixed with infected water. A left-wing campaign followed which used the World Health Organization to boycott Nestlé; this made some headway in the United States.

Saunders masterminded the company's response to this campaign, and by common consent did it well. He arranged for some doctors to write articles favourable to the Nestlé case. One who refused Saunders' request to take part in this campaign emphasized to me that he was not asked to do anything that was not 'squeaky clean', but he felt that he was being 'led down a path where I preferred not to go'. Those who did take part were very effective, and my informant underlined a quality in Saunders that we shall come across again; namely, a talent for picking exactly the right people. Saunders was essentially conducting a holding operation, because the food industry, including Nestlé, did soon clean up its act. At Nestlé's initiative it introduced a new code of practice which satisfied most of the complainers. The time was to come when Saunders could never be admitted by the media of any political shade to have done anything right, and the baby-food episode is sometimes brought up against him. Yet Nestlé could hardly have been expected not to defend its corner while deciding how to change its practices, and the campaign against it was in many respects unfair.

How much, if at all, has Saunders' Jewish origin affected him? To anticipate a little, my view is that it has had rather little direct effect. When it became known to the general public, initially through *Private Eye*, he was put out, but this need only have been because he thought that it would affect the attitude of others to him; as indeed it probably did, though less than he now thinks. Speaking to me, he speculated that some of his opponents in the Press have been motivated by anti-Semitism. There is probably no real truth in this, but it is the kind of thinking that can result when someone suffers a reverse as spectacular as that of Saunders. Were he not of Jewish origin, he could just as easily blame the hidden hand of Jewry. I suspect that in the days of his prosperity, his reaction to the revelation went no further than mild irritation. As an international, free-ranging businessman, he had been able to feel free from origins of any sort. To be pigeon-holed was a come-down. Yet is this the whole truth? Probably not. He had been educated as a member of the British Christian upper middle class. His wife, Carole, was English, and his two eldest children went to boarding school in Britain. One of the attractions of the job at Guinness was that Carole, in particular, wanted to move back to her own country from Switzerland, and James Saunders is clear that he and his siblings, also thoroughly English, were pleased at the move.[3] Saunders wanted to be not just a top businessman, but a top British businessman. He wanted to be part of the mainstream Establishment, not of a minority offshoot.

Saunders, in short, was ambitious. Was he also greedy? The word greed has been prominent in the immense coverage of the Guinness Affair, and certainly it motivated many of the participants. Yet in the case of Saunders I think it was at most secondary. Money was important to him not so much in itself as because it helped him attain what he was really after, which was prestige. If he made money for Guinness he would make his name; his own fortune would follow. In the meantime he was surprisingly neglectful, even sloppy, in managing his own finances.

This is neither an exoneration nor an accusation, simply an assessment. I make it because it helps with a question which, though important, has been rarely asked. What was the attraction to Saunders of the job at Guinness? Why should he want to risk his career, which was developing nicely, in playing Company doctor to a declining brewery?

Probably the idea appealed both to his reason and to his emotions. As regards his reason, the attraction was the brand. His skill was in marketing, including the use of images and brand names; he was particularly conscious of the value of a successful brand. This had nothing to do with liking the product; it is doubtful whether in his previous jobs he had used much Surf or Brylcreem, and as to Guinness, it was with difficulty that he could get himself to swallow it. After being photographed with a glass of the stuff, he would often empty it into the nearest plant pot. But the image did impress him; what, one can almost hear him thinking, could I not do with a brand like that? A brand universally known even before the days of advertising, a brand which had then been boosted for half a century by one of the most famous campaigns in the world, a brand which had gained the ultimate glory of displacing the name of its own product! If he could not pull this company round, his name was not Ernest Saunders.

As to his emotions, we can be cynical or kind; neither interpretation excludes the other. The cynical view points to social ambition. Saunders probably quite liked the prospect of working with Benjamin, in particular. Here was a Chairman who as a belted Earl and Irish Senator was a conspicuous grandee; some of his cousins, on and off the Board, looked interesting as well. In return for rescuing their business, these people would accept Saunders, boost him, introduce him into all sorts of charmed circles. The family façade was imposing; he had yet to learn how little real power lay behind it. The kinder view points to his romantic streak – he certainly had one. Once when I had occasion to see him after hours in his office at Portman Square he was watching on television the opening ceremony of the Commonwealth Games at Edinburgh, with the military ceremonial, the soldiers with their kilts and bagpipes. 'Don't you love all this, Jonathan?' he said. It is likely that the idea of running Guinness and restoring its fortunes appealed to this side of him. Here, after all, was an old company with traditions, a family concern with the family still there. 'Please regard me as a son,' he once remarked to my father; coals to Newcastle, this, because Bryan already had five sons living, but it was a kind thought.

In *Nightmare* we are told that the headhunters first approached Saunders in early 1981, that is, not long after the appearance of the 1980 results which were the first bad ones. They met him in London in March of that year. After a rundown on Guinness they said that the Company was looking for 'a more professional marketing approach', and talked of the difficulties in the non-brewing businesses. Saunders got the impression that Guinness was looking for a high-powered Marketing Director rather than a Managing Director, 'which was the level he was now aiming at'.[4] Whether or not his ambitions were at the time so clear-cut as this implies, he was interested enough to indicate his wish to negotiate. Purssell then met him in Zurich, and more or less repeated what the headhunters had offered. Saunders said that if he were to move he would require the Managing Directorship and a free hand. This was not forthcoming, yet he left the door ajar.

A couple of months later Saunders was again telephoned by the headhunting firm. Circumstances had changed; the Company's need for a new man had become more obviously acute. The interim results to be published in June were bad, and there was no sign of an upturn. The mere addition of a new Marketing Director to the present management was hardly going to reassure the City, or indeed pull the Company round. Purssell and his colleagues were now prepared to offer something much closer to what Saunders wanted.

The interim results were certainly dreadful. As compared with the same half-year in 1980, and adjusting to compare like with like, the figures were as follows:

Trading Profits (£m)

	1981	1980
Brewing	19.2	19.1
General trading	0.8	1.8
Plastics, materials handling	0.9	2.4
Leisure	0.7	0.8
Confectionery	−0.5	0.1

Share of profits of associated companies, mostly overseas brewing, was up from £3.8 million to £5.2 million, but central management costs, interest and tax were also up and the net profit attributable to stockholders for the half-year fell heavily from £12.4 million to £8.9 million. The trend from 1979 continued, as will be seen; brewing profits were still marginally improving but non-brewing profits were plummeting, even without potential losses on the film business which were not mentioned in these interim results.

What hit the stock market like a bombshell, though, was a warning that the final dividend might not be maintained. This meant a drastic downgrading in Guinness stock. Hitherto it had been regarded as safe, if rather dull; dividends might not keep pace with inflation, but at least their nominal level was regarded as secure. A dividend warning made the stock unsuitable for any shareholder such as a pension fund, dependent on maintaining a guaranteed income, and many shareholders were in this category. The shares were immediately marked down by 8p to 66p, where their historic yield was about 11 per cent; a clear sign that the market took seriously the danger of a dividend reduction at the year-end. In Ireland Mark Hely-Hutchinson, chairman of the Dublin end of the brewing business, managed to put a more optimistic spin on the results, telling the Irish weekly *Business and Finance* that he expected an upturn in the second half of the year, his Irish profits having fallen in the first half. This had little if any effect.

In the event the full year's results, though not brilliant, proved better than some of the gloomier forecasts, and the final dividend was maintained. In the light of this, admittedly with hindsight, it is rather hard to see the reason for giving the warning with the interim results. If the worst fears had been realized and the final dividend had been cut without the warning having been given, how much additional criticism would there have been? Some, perhaps, but not much. The market might claim to have been misled, yet in the event it *was* misled. It is true, if illogical, that few seriously object to being misled that way round; any annoyance there may be, for instance, among shareholders who have sold at a price depressed by the warning, is washed away in the general relief. Perhaps the management felt that, given that it might want to cut the dividend, the fall-out would be less if markets were given time to get used to it. The warning seems now to have been over-scrupulous in a way rather typical of the clumsy, old-fashioned honesty one associates with the Company at the time.

What the dividend warning certainly did was to weaken Purssell's bargaining position in his negotiations with Saunders. A first compromise was hammered out between the two men and Peter Guinness; though not immediately giving Saunders quite what he wanted, the compromise afforded him the opportunity to get it, given the circumstances.

Saunders joined Guinness as from 1 October 1981, at a salary of £73,000, which matched his pay at Nestlé; but arguments as to his exact status and function continued right into November. When he was first appointed, the announcement stated that he would be Managing Director and Purssell would be 'promoted' to Chief Executive, as the *Daily Telegraph* tactfully, or more likely naïvely, put it. Purssell was to be responsible for the strategic direction of the Group; Saunders to undertake day-to-day management.

A comment that was not made at the time, although it easily could have been, was that it did not seem particularly sensible to leave the strategic direction of the Group in the same hands that had allowed such a mess to be made of the non-brewing side of the business. For this practical reason, quite apart from personal ambition, Saunders could not be content with this arrangement. As he saw it, he had to be in sole charge. Purssell, still believing that Saunders was there to support him rather than to supplant him, put up a stubborn resistance. Various proposals were made; at one time the two men were to be Joint Managing Directors. This would have produced a two-headed monster and been inferior even to the Chief Executive–Managing Director idea, which at least divided responsibilities.

Saunders took up his post at Guinness a few days before the appointment officially took effect, on Saturday, 26 September 1981, and moved with his wife straight into the flat above the head office of the Company which was then at 10 Albermarle Street in Mayfair, off Piccadilly: a tall, narrow town house of six storeys with possibly the slowest lift in London. During the previous three weeks, which he had spent on holiday with his family, Saunders had taken time to study a mass of documents. Guinness sent him a suitcase full of them; he says he found them singularly lacking in up-to-date detail. What did worry him were some brokers' reports, which he got hold of separately; notably a sinister one from David Campbell of Wood Mackenzie. This certainly did contain detail, most of it damning. The doubtful quality of the non-brewing interests was shown, as was the lack of management grip. Saunders was to find that Campbell had guessed very shrewdly and perhaps had a clearer view of what was going on than the Company's management. On the strength of the circular, this medium-sized firm was eventually to be appointed official broker to Guinness in succession to James

Capel; an action which exemplified the alert and imaginative way in which, at his best, Saunders picked his advisers. 'You have got it right,' he told senior partner John Chiene, 'no one else has.'

Saunders also followed the share price which was headed consistently downwards. The task he would face was not only big, but urgent. In the short term, some of this urgency was brought on by the dividend warning; but Saunders was not to know that this would prove unnecessary, and the brokers' opinions rather implied the reverse. He devoted much of the Sunday, the day following his arrival, to examining another pile of documents that had been left for him, but found them as patternless and confused as those in the first suitcase.

His mood was not improved by what seemed a distinctly lackadaisical approach in confronting the Company's problems; the following day, Monday, he found that Purssell was not in his office. On the Tuesday there was the Board Meeting at which he was introduced to those of us he had not met; I have described my thoughts on this occasion. Saunders conveyed his impressions of that meeting to his son James: 'What struck me most forcefully ... was the absence of any facts and any sense of urgency, despite the picture painted by the brokers' reports. There was lots of chat ... But there was no real feeling of concern that they had to take a grip of the situation.'[5]

Inevitably Saunders won his tussle with Purssell, and by the time the 1981 results were published in December it was clear that he had done so. When it came to the point, both Benjamin and Peter Guinness realized that the Company needed Saunders more than he needed it; certainly, if the question had reached the full Board it would have taken the same view. Saunders was confirmed as sole Managing Director and Purssell was made Joint Deputy Chairman. His last throw was a request to be described as Executive Deputy Chairman, but this would have still left it dangerously unclear who was really in charge. As it was, no doubt could remain on this score, for Purssell's appointment, in

Guinness terms, was non-executive. The fact that his colleague as Joint Deputy Chairman was Simon Lennox-Boyd, an entirely non-executive family director, makes this clear. Purssell and he were appointed simultaneously to replace Robert McNeile, who retired; McNeile, too had been non-executive in that post. The hard fact was that Purssell was no longer, as of right, part of the management. This was glossed over in the 1981 Chairman's statement, presumably in a confused attempt to save Purssell's face, so that it seemed as if Simon was executive: 'Mr Simon Lennox-Boyd and Mr Tony Purssell have been appointed Deputy Chairmen and Mr Ernest Saunders has joined Guinness from the Nestlé headquarters in Switzerland as our new Group Managing Director. It is to this strong management team that we are now turning . . .' Management team forsooth! Nobody who knew the form could be taken in by this. Purssell was clearly being kicked upstairs.

He nevertheless continued to work full-time for the Company, introducing Saunders to everyone and showing him the ropes. The two men managed to perform in tandem most of the time, although inevitably the relationship was not easy. Saunders did not always bother to keep Purssell informed of what he was doing. Purssell once asked Margaret McGrath, Saunders' secretary and later his personal assistant, to show him her boss's engagement book. Since Saunders had instructed her to keep this confidential, Mrs McGrath refused. Purssell tried to snatch the book, but Mrs McGrath managed to hang on to it in a tug of war until Purssell desisted.

In public, appearances were kept up. The *Financial Times* of 16 December 1981 shows the two men in harmonious mood when presenting the preliminary results for the year to September 1981. They both agreed 'rather disarmingly' that Saunders represented 'an injection of professional management'. Saunders struck exactly the right note: 'Guinness has always been an institution. If we can turn it into a professional commercial organization as well, then watch this space.' This was the first example of Saunders' convincing way with the media, a talent which was to help the Company greatly over the next few years, then become a trap when he came to rely on it exclusively. The philosopher William James said: 'Faking a fact can help create the fact.' This is true, but to grasp what it means we must underline the word *help*. Faking works when it is embellishment, not, in the end, when it is sheer invention. In the world of company reporting as of political spin-doctoring, embellishment can transform a situation; but it needs to be an embellishment of something. As long as Saunders had a good case, he could play on the media like a virtuoso.

The 1981 results for the full year came as a relief to the market. Not only was the dividend not cut, but profits were several million pounds above most of the estimates. They showed a continuation of the same trends; brewing was again higher – Hely-Hutchinson's expectations of a much better second half in Ireland were duly fulfilled – but the non-brewing activities were even worse than indicated at half-time, showing an overall loss. The films were mainly to blame for this, but every single non-brewing activity showed a deterioration. The whole diversification programme was in ruins.

Trading Profits (£ million)

	1980	1981
Brewing	44.1	48.0
General trading	2.9	2.7
Plastics, materials handling	3.1	1.2
Leisure	0.1	−1.6
Confectionery	−0.3	−1.3
Film finance, distribution	−0.4	−3.9
Total	49.5	45.1

The Company also had to write off £9.8 million for 'terminal costs and provisions relating to non-brewing activities', that is, essentially in respect of the films; as a result of this the dividend was left uncovered. On the 'current cost' basis discounting for inflation, which was just then becoming fashionable, the accounts looked even worse; they showed a Group loss. The financial Press noted that the diversifications had done disastrously, as it could hardly fail to do; but on the whole its reaction was surprisingly favourable, mainly perhaps out of relief that the dividend was maintained. The *Guardian* even carried the headline 'City Drinks to Guinness Results'. The market also took the results well, but only marked the shares up 5p to 66p – the price to which the shares fell after the dividend warning. This might imply that the dividend was still not thought safe.

All the same, it is not necessary to take quite literally the lurid estimates given much later by Saunders to his son James of the disaster that would have been suffered by the Company if he had not appeared. He exaggerates the trouble in which the Company found itself in 1981, and on this matter his detractors as well as his supporters accept his line.[6] James Saunders describes the Company as 'near collapse';[7] Kochan and Pym talk of 'chaos';[8] Peter Pugh quotes Saunders as making the bizarre claim that it had been 'badly managed for 100 years', which means ever since becoming a quoted company: a claim which Pugh seems to accept.[9] Saunders denies saying this. All the same, one statement he certainly did make, to James Saunders, is almost as reckless: 'From profits of £41 million in 1980–81, sales projections suggested as little as half that for the current year unless drastic steps were immediately taken.'[10] It is neither possible to establish what might have been, nor profitable to try to do so; nevertheless this claim that profits without Saunders would have halved is ridiculous. It is said to be based on a 'crude canvass' of estimated results obtained largely on the telephone from executives around the world. Crude, it would seem, is the right word. In the event there was a small but noticeable improvement in profits for the first half-year of 1982, from £18.4 million to £20 million. Little of this can have been due to Saunders' efforts; common sense tells us that a newcomer, however brilliant, can only have a limited effect during his first half-year. If Saunders is right to claim that profits for the whole year would have been halved, this means that for the second half-year, without him, there would have been virtually no profits at all. This is altogether too apocalyptic. Saunders did indeed rescue Guinness, but he rescued it from gradual decline, not from sudden collapse.

There remained important strengths in the Company. One was the continued and steady increase in the brewing profits, up again by nearly 9 per cent in 1981, a performance which, as the *Daily Telegraph* noted,[11] bucked the industry trend for that year. Another was the net current assets, which rose that year by 16 per cent to £87.9 million, though the increase was rather more than offset by a rise in long-term loans. The Company was still financially sound and could face the enormous sum which was to be written off in the 1982 accounts without being in any danger of going under. It is true that the management in the late 1970s was 'not good' in the words of Peter Guinness, who was part of it. It was old-fashioned; those who ran Guinness had little idea of modern management techniques, in fact they may not have seen management as a technique at all. Worse, they were pleased with themselves; they believed that their ability to run a brewery with its familiar technology and ample finance could be applied in the world outside. On several occasions they took over a reasonably prosperous business and turned it into a dud within a few years. In particular, they were a great deal too impressed by Michael Ogle and his businesses.

Yet, all in all, the prognosis for the Company in 1982 did not look hopeless. Its financial strength and the continued, though endangered, prosperity of its basic brewing business gave every reason to hope that a new Managing Director might turn the Company round, provided the useless diversifications were disposed of and the management of the whole was tightened.

NINE

Resurgence

Ernest Saunders soon became convinced that he could not solve the Group's problems without reinforcement. Back-up resources were nil, he was to tell James. 'There may have been accountants floating around, but no one was producing monthly management figures, overheads were not being properly allocated to subsidiaries . . .' Further, 'there wasn't a lawyer in the place. The personnel and secretarial functions were out of the way at Park Royal, and Edward Guinness sat alone in our Jermyn Street office, looking after what was supposed to represent PR.'[1]

He paints too stark a picture. If it was entirely correct, the Company would scarcely have managed to maintain every appearance of prospering until as late as 1979. The description needs to be put into perspective. Some of the deficiencies Saunders complains of were tolerable in a one-product concern which had grown organically. In the old Guinness business people knew each other and did not need rigid systems and written rules; there was trust because there was mutual knowledge. It was the fact that the Company had turned into a conglomerate, put together by takeover and full of strangers, that rendered these laid-back habits unacceptable. Take the lack of in-house lawyers. Guinness as an old-established brewer of stout would hardly need these; Guinness as a diversified company was rash to do without them. There were now numerous directors of subsidiaries, not personally known to management, with profit-sharing service contracts, options, and so on. For instance, we read in the 1981 Annual Report on page 8, under the heading Transactions requiring disclosure under The Stock Exchange Listing Agreement: 'Island Sailing Ltd. Acquisition from the minority shareholders of their 49 per cent minority interest for a cash consideration of £48,500. At the time of the acquisition the net assets attributable to the minority shareholders were negative at £193,000. As a result of the acquisition any further claims to severance payments have been waived.' There are a number of similar transactions listed in the same Report, unwinding options previously accepted. Did the Company get the best possible deal in all these arrangements? Perhaps, but perhaps not.

The crisis of confidence with the film business induced Saunders, early on, to make two new professional appointments from outside. He appointed Price Waterhouse as auditors; initially they were made joint auditors with the existing firm, Ernst and Whinney, who were dropped at the end of 1982. Saunders blamed Ernst and Whinney for not keeping the directors sufficiently informed of the film situation; it may be doubted whether this was entirely fair, but when blame is flying around it is often the auditors who get landed with it. Since much of the action on the film business had to take place in America under US law, he also appointed his old contact Thomas Ward, and his Washington firm Ward Lazarus Grow and Cihlar. Ward had worked with Saunders on the trouble at Nestlé about baby food. He was to become ever closer to the Company and to play a leading part in the drama as it developed, although I did not meet him until he joined the Board of Guinness in 1984.

But Saunders felt that the mere appointment of new professional advisers in certain areas was not enough. There was a new world out there, and its practices had to be introduced into Guinness. The only quick way to do this was to bring in management consultants. Saunders' first choice was McKinsey, who had worked for Guinness Ireland, but they were already working for another brewer. They recommended Bain and Co. Saunders went to see John Theroux, Bain's Vice-President. Theroux's first concern was that Guinness might not be able to afford his services. Reassured on this score, he laid down that the people he seconded to Guinness must at all times have access to the Managing Director.

Theroux introduced Saunders to Bain's London consultant, Sir Jack Lyons. Lyons was loosely attached to Bain as an adviser and as landlord of their London office. He had been a director of the clothing chain United Drapery Stores (John Collier, Richard Shops) of which his brother, Sir Bernard Lyons, was chairman, but had resigned in 1980 after allegations, never substantiated, of insider trading. Lyons, an indefatigable contact man, impressed Saunders from the first, and this was increasingly the case as Saunders came to realize that members of the Guinness family had fewer powerful contacts than he had expected, and sometimes scrupled to use those contacts they did have. Lyons was known, in particular, for his charitable work, for which he had been knighted.

Just as important as the appointment of Bain was Saunders' recruitment of Shaun Dowling. Saunders had known Dowling when they had both worked for J. Walter Thompson, in which firm Dowling had been senior to Saunders. They had not, it seems, been particularly friendly, but Saunders remembered Dowling as a man of formidable efficiency and talent. Purssell approached him on Saunders' instructions and recruited him as Special Projects Manager. At first he was an independent consultant, then in due course he was made a director at a fee second only to Saunders himself; he was very much aware of his own value. He worked very closely with the Bain team, mainly on rationalizing the non-brewing businesses, with a view to selling them at the best price.

Saunders said in an interview with the author that one reason why he appointed Bain was that his Chairman, Benjamin Iveagh, was insatiable in his desire for detailed information about the Company. About once a week Benjamin, who had the habit of staying in the blandly luxurious Churchill Hotel in Portman Square, would call Saunders over and quiz him, politely but insistently, for hours. The hotel was little more than a hundred yards from Guinness's new offices, also in Portman Square. As a means of clarifying Saunders' mind and making him discover facts he might otherwise have overlooked, these sessions with Benjamin had their value. They were, however, time-consuming; Bain's people were needed not only to provide information asked for by Benjamin, but also to make up for the expenditure of so much of Saunders' own time. Benjamin never imparted anything he learned on these occasions, even informally, to me or any of the other family directors; I did not even know they had taken place until Saunders told me in interview. This information made me respect Benjamin rather more than I had in his lifetime. He was not unaware of the emergency. But he never took us into his confidence.

One can certainly see why the arrangement with Bain was disliked by the existing Guinness management. The events following the Distillers bid have enabled some people to present it in retrospect as a sign of Saunders' inability to do his own management, even as an early indication of 'villainy'. Kochan and Pym say that Bain 'were instructed to divide the loyalties of the staff and thus undermine the authority of the Deputy Chairman, Tony Purssell'.[2] This must be nonsense. As we have seen, Purssell no longer had an executive post; he had no authority to be undermined. Saunders was in the saddle already, he did not need to intrigue to get there.

All the same, one can see why something of the sort came to be believed. For a man with a strong personality, Saunders was oddly diffident when it came to personal confrontation. He disliked sacking people, or rather, he was squeamish about interviewing them personally with this in view. He left it either to

Peter Guinness or to Maurice Freeman, the Personnel Manager, or, later, to Thomas Ward. This made him seem devious when he had no reason to be so, an impression which was strengthened by his engagement of Bain with direct access to himself, doing no one quite knew what. And can his personality really be called a strong one? There are a number of signs that in this area he had a tendency to punch above his weight. What he did have was an almost uncanny knack of finding, picking and using people of the very highest ability, whether as employees or as advisers. He recruited them, but they never became his men. He cast no psychological spell in the style of Napoleon or Robert Maxwell. They remained clear-eyed and objective; two in particular, Shaun Dowling whom we have mentioned, and Olivier Roux whom we shall meet, both turned against Saunders without qualms. His attempt to 'psych' the jury at his trial did not work at all; sometimes its members yawned, sometimes they tittered.

In fact Saunders, with all his gifts, was not in the first rank as an inspirational leader; and this contributed to a certain malaise among middle management. The necessity for sweeping changes was not quite so obvious to them as it was to Saunders. Nor, to be sure, had they quite the same personal motivation. If Guinness failed or was taken over, this might have been a setback to them personally, but need have been no more. To Saunders, the international high-flyer who had taken personal responsibility for the whole Company, failure would have been disastrous. So the middle managers saw the reasons for the arrangement with Bain less clearly than they saw its abnormality. Saunders, they reasoned, was Managing Director; he was top of the heap. All reporting channels led to him; surely all he needed to do was to make use of them, perhaps improve them in due course. To bypass the channels in this way seemed to the middle managers to be a reflection on them.

But Saunders saw that the 'usual channels' were not accustomed to produce information of the quality he needed.

Something like fifteen Bain employees were immediately seconded to Guinness to provide management help in depth; this number grew as the years went on reaching a maximum, some say, of eighty. What is more, the Bain involvement continued, on a diminishing scale, long after Saunders' departure from the Company; a sure sign that the firm was still considered useful.

Some of the criticisms of Bain by the Guinness 'old guard' are cogent. Alan Scrine pointed out in interview with the author that none of their people had ever run anything much; they were business school graduates who had had little to do with the hard graft of production or sales. He admitted that their analysis of the various businesses they looked at was good, but said that in every case their conclusion was always to close it or sell it, never to improve it. However, as regards the inessential businesses this was in line with the brief they were given: how, not whether, to get rid of everything which did not fit with the plans for the future. The fact that some of the businesses might have potential was not important; the best that could be hoped for was that some of this potential might be reflected in the sale price. Scrine also felt that men from Bain insulated Saunders from some of the negative feedback within the organization of which he as Managing Director ought to have been aware. Insensibly the top 'Bainies', together with two or three picked Guinness employees, came to constitute a sort of court. Saunders saw too much of them, too little of many others.

Did Saunders suffer from not hearing a sufficient variety of views? Perhaps, yet there is another side to this. He could hardly listen to everybody; the time available to him for listening to suggestions was limited, considering the size and urgency of his task. Scrine himself, and the Company Secretary's department, were banished to the Park Royal Brewery – 'to get rid of me', Scrine thinks; perhaps unfairly, for Saunders' new arrangements were creating a shortage of space at the London office, even at the new and larger premises in Portman Square, acquired in 1985. When the crisis blew up a few years later Scrine was brought back to the centre. Saunders had learnt to rely on his clear mind and unobtrusive competence.

Dowling, who saw Saunders' 'court' from the inside, criticized his performance to me in a way I had not expected. He accused him of being insufficiently organized. Evidently he had the habit of staying very late at the office without actually doing very much – he would discuss problems discursively and repetitively. At one time, it seems, this habit of staying late even endangered Saunders' marriage; Carole became fed up because he was never at home. Dowling himself has an absolute rule of never staying in his office after 7 p.m. at the very latest, and when that hour was reached he would leave abruptly even if Saunders was in mid-sentence. Sometimes he would point out that the same subject had been gone over five or six times. Saunders put up with this; if he respected someone's ability as he respected Dowling's, he would put up with a great deal from them.

The most important Bain employee to be seconded to Guinness was Olivier Roux, a thirty-one-year-old Frenchman with a background in sales and computers who had worked in France, Germany and South Africa after graduating from the Rouen business school. Although he had no formal training in accountancy, he was brilliant with figures. Howard Hughes, the Price Waterhouse partner who dealt with Guinness, told the DTI inspectors that Roux was 'one of the most naturally numerate and effective people I have dealt with'. His English was excellent, but he seemed Gallic to his fingertips; Jacques Delors gives a similar impression. Much of the unusual relationship with Bain over the years can be put down to an obstinate personal tussle between Saunders and Roux. Saunders wanted Roux as a full-time Guinness man, specifically as Finance Director. Roux always insisted that he worked not for Guinness but for Bain, that Guinness was just a client. He was quite willing to do the work, but insisted on being, essentially, an outsider. The result was an eccentric compromise under which Roux became in form a non-executive director, but performed the function of Finance Director while continuing as a Bains employee. The City, and City journalists, tend to be unhappy with what they do not understand, and the arrangement contributed to the bad name the Company acquired during the Affair. It is an example of a trait in Ernest Saunders that has not, I think, been noticed; namely a curious, almost aristocratic, unconcern with formalities that fits strangely with his expertise in fostering the image of a brand.

Roux, at first working under another Bain man, David Hoare, was responsible for putting in the new computerized management accounting system that Saunders saw was so necessary if he was to know what was going on. The system was already in place and working by March 1982, that is, within three months. Saunders was deeply impressed. In August 1982, when Tony Spicer, the Guinness Finance Director, retired through ill-health, Roux was made Operations Controller under the new Finance Director, John O'Brien. O'Brien stayed until June 1983, and when he left Saunders asked Roux to act as caretaker Finance Director until a replacement could be found. He became Head of Finance on a part-time basis, helped by Alan Bailey who was an experienced Chief Accountant. In practice, whatever his title, Roux became Saunders' right-hand man on finance from this period. With Saunders, he interviewed merchant banks at the end of 1983 to choose one for a bid that was to be made. This was for Booker McConnell, and as we shall see it was abortive; the merchant bank chosen was Morgan Grenfell. It was at the end of July 1984 that Roux was finally appointed to the main Board, and described as 'non-executive'. All this time Roux was still based at Bain; he did not have his own desk at Guinness until late in 1985. According to his own account he was servicing another client for half his time; this is an indication of his ability, because his work at Guinness would have been a full-time job for most people.

Saunders' first and most urgent task was the rigorous cutting of costs. When he told us this at Board Meetings, I had a strong sense of *déjà vu*; under the old management we were always hearing how expenses were being cut to the bone, how nothing superfluous could be afforded. (Least of all any pet projects of family directors: Press comment to the effect that it had been the family that led Guinness into unsuitable areas read strangely in this respect.) This time, though, things really were different. Saunders, trained by Leonard Wolfson at Great Universal Stores and at Nestlé in Switzerland, was expert in this area. With the help of the systems installed by Roux, his cost-cutting was to the efforts of the previous management as a jet aircraft to a pennyfarthing bicycle. Targets were set, weekly control meetings were instituted with a weekly sales analysis. He told James: 'It must be recognized that the managements of the operating companies had never been expected to provide the sort of performance details to head office that were now demanded, and they were irritated at having to do so. But it was my view that it was not only those of us at HQ who needed the figures. How could the operating companies themselves be properly managed if their executives didn't have this sort of data at their fingertips?'[3] How indeed? Under the new regime expenses in both brewing and non-brewing businesses were squeezed more effectively than most of the executives would have believed possible. Despite the irritation at the new demands, and at Saunders' management methods, morale on the whole improved.

There was also the urgent task of stemming the losses from the non-brewing businesses, which meant getting rid of most of them. During the year to end-September 1982 the group disposed of the following:

The confectionery group except the Lavells shops
Holiday villages and inland cruising
Plastic containers and materials handling equipment
Horticultural services
Veterinary products
Decorative lighting products.

Some of the prices received were very disappointing. The confectionery group was sold for only £2 million, whereas earlier there had been expectations of at least £5 million; Scrine criticized this in interview. Pursell, talking to Kochan and Pym, blamed the family for stopping an earlier sale: 'It's a lovely product, butterscotch, super,' is the way we are said to have put it.[4] It is true that Bryan, in particular, always had a sentimental attachment to Callard & Bowser, which he probably expressed when a sale was mooted. To me, too, it always seemed that the brand names in the sweets group had potential: Callard & Bowser, Rileys, Nuttalls and the rest. However, it was clear that this potential, if it existed, was not being realized. I certainly never opposed a sale, and Bryan had a long record of giving way to management views when they were decisively expressed. Anyway, it is admitted that we yielded later, and that a sale was imminent when Saunders took over.

The film operation was wound up, at an appalling cost; it was by far the largest item in costs and provisions, totalling no less than £48.7 million. This amount was taken 'below the line'. The ordinary Profit and Loss Account showed a good recovery; profit before tax rose by 18 per cent. Despite the huge amount written off – about 18 per cent of the net assets of the entire Company – the results had quite a good press.

To an extent, this was independent of Saunders' efforts at public relations. The change in Managing Director was in itself a positive factor because it indicated that the Company knew of its troubles and was doing something to put them behind it. There is also, I think, a subtler reason. The Company's age, its good record for 230 years until 1979, its tremendous brand image, the affection in which it was held on account of its advertising, made it seem in the public mind more likely that two bad years were just a setback rather than the beginning of the end. Subliminally, people rather *wanted* the Company to revive; Guinness was part of the general background and would have been missed. Any Managing Director might have been given a fair wind for one year.

Even so, much of the favourable comment secured at this early stage can certainly be attributed to Saunders' talent with the Press. How much? This is one of those questions which are essentially unanswerable, yet need to be aired if the story is to be understood. For a time was to come when Saunders would seem like a pilot whose controls suddenly fail, or Sparky when his magic piano refuses to perform; we shall see him stabbing, first with confidence, then with increasing desperation, at accustomed levers which no longer function. Harold Wilson went through something like the same experience when the media turned against him in 1966. Probably Saunders' generation of good publicity for the Company felt to him like more of a personal success than it really was; this helped to foster the self-confidence that was later to turn into something like hubris. Yet his skill at public relations cannot be denied. He had the start of a recovery to report, true, but it was still at an early stage when it might have aborted. Smoothly, competently and entirely legitimately, Saunders put the right spin on the facts to induce City editors to look on the bright side.

He had genuine achievements to report. As Managing Director he was rising to the occasion superbly. He was helped, of course, by Bains, but his detractors are wrong to insinuate that most of the credit for the revival belongs to them. They provided information and advice, and assisted in the formulation of policy. All the same, they did not initiate it. There were occasions when Saunders overruled them, even slapped them down. There was also useful managerial talent within the existing Guinness organization which Saunders found and brought on. But as time went by most of the top people were neither from Bains nor from within Guinness but recruited by Saunders himself; Dowling was the first of these. As one of the new international jet-setting executives, Saunders knew many of the others, and could recruit among them from personal knowledge.

The advertising campaign was naturally one of the first things that Saunders looked at; advertising was, after all, one of his specialities. He found the campaign in an unsatisfactory state. His former employers, J. Walter Thompson, still had the account after replacing Bensons in 1969. They had produced some good ideas in their first years, including a poster with the anagram 'GENNIUSS' – the germ of the Guinness–Genius theme which was much later to be the main feature of Guinness advertising and which is still used. During the time of the Affair it caused a great deal of sarcastic comment. But it was others who were to elaborate on this theme; JWT did not use it for long. By 1981 the agency had gone stale.

Some of us on the Board had already noticed this nearly three years previously. I wrote a letter on 9 May 1978 to Michael Hatfield, Managing Director at Park Royal, which is as uncomplimentary about the agency as it is possible to imagine: 'Of recent years they have plumbed depths of forgettability undreamt of in the philosophy of poor old Bensons. . . . We certainly need a resurgence of the imagination, and probably another change of agency.' My father, Bryan, weighed in at about the same time, complaining to the head of the Advertising Department about the current poster and adding: 'I would only stress the URGENCY of getting a powerful poster up in Britain.' How much attention was paid to these strictures at the time I am not sure. Certainly there was no change of agency. In 1979 the Guinness toucan was recalled from its honourable retirement, and it may be that this was supposed to be some sort of a sop to us, but it can hardly have been called creative thinking.

When Saunders arrived, he took the same view as Bryan and I had done, only more strongly; and his mood was probably not helped by the fact that he had not left J. Walter Thompson on the best of terms. It seemed to him that the agency had gone to sleep on the job and that the marketing people at Park Royal were utterly complacent. The resurrection of the toucan particularly irritated him. (He gets a detail wrong in *Nightmare* when he implies that the toucan was revived after his arrival; this had happened about two years before.) By his account he gave his former employers three chances to brush up their performance. In September 1981, just before he moved into Guinness, he invited them to 'think about a wide-ranging and objective review of the brand's advertising and marketing'. A few weeks after installing himself in Albermarle Street he called in again, and this time, by his account, he was politely rebuffed: 'Their attitude was that this was something I shouldn't really concern myself with. They told me that their relations with Park Royal were excellent, and the people there thought they were doing a great job.'[5]

This seems a crazy response to a new Managing Director who had the power to clear out the whole Advertising Department and change the agency as well; and we may assume that in reality JWT were a good deal less cavalier with Saunders than he maintains. We know they were extremely keen to keep the account and dreaded getting the sack from Saunders; they well knew that his experience when he worked for them was not of the happiest, and felt he might bear a grudge. Shaun Dowling thinks he did. Shortly after he was recruited to Guinness, and after JWT were told they would have to go, former colleagues in the agency contacted Dowling and asked him to see whether Saunders would not change his mind. When Dowling made this approach, he was given such short shrift as to form the view that Saunders was determined to sack J. Walter Thompson from the start.

This may be so, but it is a superfluous postulate. The reason why JWT had to go was that it had fallen victim to the Guinness advertising culture. A view had grown up that Guinness advertising was a subject in itself that had to be studied, an expertise that had to be acquired, before any newcomer could validly criticize it. The Guinness campaign had, by allowing itself to develop established principles, insensibly declined into predictability. That which is predictable is on the way to being invisible, and visibility is the first duty of an advertisement. There was a mutual admiration society between client and agency, a closed feedback loop which had to be broken up. The British campaign in particular needed to get back into gear, for British sales were static or gently declining; the improvement in brewing profits came from Ireland and overseas.

Saunders reckoned that Guinness must try a direct appeal to younger drinkers. This was heresy. Received wisdom accepted that because of the drink's bitterness, as also because its attraction was partly to the health-conscious, it was not likely to appeal to the young directly; the hope was that they would grow into it. Past experience indicated that this did in fact happen; and the years during which this view had developed were years when the brand had done consistently well. Unfortunately the strategy was becoming as outdated as the skill in trench warfare of the Allies' armies at the start of the Second World War. Times and the beer market were changing. The mild and bitter drinkers of traditional Britain graduated easily with the passing years to Guinness, which if stronger and more bitter than what they were used to was nevertheless closely related. The new young beer drinkers liked lager, whose appearance and flavour are further away from Guinness than beer of the British type. There was a distinct danger that they might not make the necessary leap. The passing of the years could no longer be counted on; the young had to be wooed directly.

Naturally Saunders had his way; he was after all the man in

charge, and had the right to impose his views. His task was made easier by the fact that even in its own terms the existing campaign was falling flat. 'The latest batch of commercials failed their research tests, so JWT had to fall back on old material. One night that November I was sitting in the Albemarle Street flat watching TV, and up came an old toucan ad talking about April Fool's Day! I was livid.'[6] This was just the right mood for him to be in if he was to show the necessary ruthlessness. He thumped the table at Park Royal, sacked J. Walter Thompson, and gave the account to Allen Brady and Marsh who were already handling the advertising for Harp Lager.

One of the partners in the new agency, Mike Brady, had worked with Saunders at Beechams. Its guiding spirit, however, was Peter Marsh. Marsh was a prize card who stood out as such even in an industry where everyone is a card. In Max Beerbohm's *Poet's Corner* there is a cartoon of Rudyard Kipling, prancing along beside a calm helmeted Britannia and blowing a large trumpet. The caption is: 'Mr Rudyard Kipling takes a bloomin' day aht, on the blasted 'Eath, along wiv Britannia, 'is gurl.' Marsh lacked Kipling's aggressive moustache, but otherwise he was Beerbohm's Kipling. He was a showman, not to say a show-off; an advertising barker. Kipling's trumpet might easily have occurred to him as a way of amusing the Guinness Board when he invited it to see his presentation. As it was, he and one of his partners opened the proceedings by doing a soft-shoe shuffle in white suits, reminding me of the bespangled and portly pianist Liberace when he galumphed across the stage in soft shoes before observing: 'I ain't good – but I got guts.'

After this odd but promising start, Marsh opened his presentation by wasting everybody's time. He preened himself at interminable length about the past performance of his agency; I think one of the concerns it had worked for was British Rail, but I may be wrong because my mind wandered. What on earth, I wondered (and still do) was the point of talking about past performance when Saunders had already engaged Marsh? I longed for him to tell us what he intended to do for Guinness, and was not the only director to start fidgeting.

When he did get to the point my mood changed rapidly. It quickly became clear that there had indeed been some new thinking, of considerable quality. The new campaign still related to the past, but in contrast to J. Walter Thompson's warmed-up toucan it was not simply a repetition, it was a genuine reworking. It might or might not succeed, though I suspected it would; what cheered me was that the reasoning seemed right. The campaign was to be based on the oldest of all Guinness slogans. 'Guinness is Good for You' was embellished by a double negative: 'GuinnLess isN'T Good for You'. This was to appear on posters to familiarize the public with it, but that was to be only the start. It led to further concepts: of 'Guinnlessness' as a state to be remedied, of the 'Guinnless' as an unfortunate set of people who needed to be helped, of Guinness itself (as it appeared on one poster) as 'Relief for the Guinnless'. A spoof society was dreamed up called the Friends of the Guinnless, with a logo showing a glass of Guinness passing from one hand to another.

These ideas had two main merits, which Marsh explained. Firstly, the adapted slogan was a clever way of expressing the 'Good for You' message in an acceptable way. In its straight form the old slogan had become unsuitable in a time which had become more literal-minded about health claims. The new version put it over in a joky form to which if anyone objected (one or two did) they could be shrugged off as humourless and pedantic. Secondly, it addressed the problem of the younger generation. At the time, young people tended to regard Guinness as not for them; those who did drink Guinness were out of things, unsmart, old before their time. What the Guinnless campaign did was to suggest the reverse of this. Guinness drinkers were the insiders and it was the Guinnless who needed help and were given it, by the kindly mediation of the Friends of the Guinnless who could lead them to a cooperative barman. This attached Guinness drinking to the herd instinct at the same time as it made it seem smart and cool; no longer a drink for old farts, but an elixir for the streetwise.

To me, for one, it seemed that a campaign on these lines might very easily work. Of the other directors some liked the presentation more than others, but we were all interested and many of us were bursting with questions. The afternoon was drawing on, however; Marsh closed the meeting with a perfunctory apology to the effect that there was no more time. So the long initial rigmarole about the agency's other clients had not only been futile in itself, it had prevented any discussion, any input from us as individual directors. This irritated me; it even seemed rather insulting. The Guinness Board had, I observed to Saunders later, been treated like a class of schoolchildren. Saunders was only a little more apologetic than the advertiser. 'You must understand Peter Marsh,' he said. 'He has a large ego.' Quite so.

TEN

Towards the Big League

Saunders and his advisers from Bain devised a five-year plan from early in 1982. The first two years were to be a period of retrenchment, involving a sale of the superfluous businesses and a rigorous cost-cutting of the companies that remained. At the same time public relations, including the advertising campaign and relations with the financial press, would be transformed to meet Saunders' exacting requirements. After that, there was to be a period of expansion, both by organic development and by acquisition. Saunders, who was as ambitious as he was able, was never going to be content with running a company in the second rank, as Guinness had now become, simply because it was over-shadowed in size by the new giants resulting from the mergers in the brewing industry. He was aiming at the big league; and he was in more of a hurry than anyone knew – except possibly Benjamin, and he was not talking.

The five-year plan was carried out, the first four years of it at any rate. During the first two years Bain, on Saunders' instructions, researched the world market for consumer goods, and drinks in particular, with a view to finding businesses that might be acquired in the next period. In the meantime the management of the existing businesses, helped by Bain, was successfully carrying out the programme mentioned above. Profits, earnings and dividends rose, and this gave the necessary underpinning to the improvement in the Company's image being achieved by the new advertising campaign. The share price rose fast in 1982 and more slowly in 1983. The fact that the rise took place this way round may well reflect the solid Guinness reputation. It is more usual for a 'recovery stock' to start rising slowly, then for the rise to accelerate as good results come through. But as I have already suggested, Guinness was regarded, subliminally, as a stock that was somehow inherently solid, where a fall in profits was considered as likely to be exceptional until otherwise proved. Saunders' success seemed not a new departure but a return to normality. I am not talking here about investment analysts and other experts; it is not they, but the general public, who are affected by these subliminal feelings. But the general public affects markets.

In any case, over the two years the price more than doubled, from about 60p in December 1981 to 135p in January 1984, at which level the *Investors' Chronicle* recommended a purchase.[1] Crucially, this meant that the yield on the shares dropped, despite increased dividends. When the shares were yielding over 11 per cent, as they were in 1981, any takeover for shares would have been ruinously expensive for Guinness shareholders. It would have been impossible to find a decent business to yield as much, and to take over a company yielding very much less would have diluted the earnings and endangered the dividend. At the yield of 6.1 per cent shown at the beginning of 1984 an acquisition for shares was no longer out of the question.

So in January 1984 John Theroux of Bain made a presentation to the Board for what was intended to be the first major company for Guinness to acquire in the new era: Booker McConnell PLC. This was a conglomerate particularly well known for the growing and shipping of fruit from the Caribbean area; Guyana, formerly British Guiana, was at one time nicknamed 'Bookers' Guiana', especially on the political left. Morgan Grenfell was merchant banker to the deal. The idea seemed exciting. But the share price of Booker McConnell soared, proving at least to my satisfaction that the project had been leaked. It was dropped, and I for one felt not only disappointed but quite bitter.

The episode convinced me that everyone except those directly concerned had to be kept in the dark about any possible bid until the very last moment. This was by no means a complete safeguard against leaks. Even if right up to the last minute knowledge was confined to the so-called *force de frappe* of Saunders, Benjamin and Olivier Roux, there were also the advisers and everyone's secretaries and assistants, too many people for security to be complete. Years before, I learned that a merchant bank had quietly sacked a messenger because he had made himself a fortune through information gleaned from wastepaper baskets. This kind of thing is always hushed up where possible, for obvious reasons, even though the culprit then enjoys the swag. It can probably never be eliminated completely. But in order to reduce the danger as far as possible, it seemed quite clear that consultation had to be kept to a minimum, and I became all too relaxed about not being told until the last minute because the reasons seemed so clear.

Booker McConnell was the one that got away, but Guinness was now intent on acquiring other companies. With this in view, it took on new advisers. Morgan Grenfell became the regular merchant bankers to the Company. This firm, which in the 1950s had seemed rather sleepy, was now, under Christopher Reeves, one of the cleverest and most active in the acquisition field. The Company's stockbrokers, James Capel, were also replaced; Saunders thought they would not perform satisfactorily in the new, active phase, and after interviewing various firms he chose Wood Mackenzie, essentially on the strength of their circular that had impressed him on the eve of his appointment. They were told that if large-scale underwriting was required, as it would be for any large acquisition, Cazenoves would take charge of it. New solicitors were also appointed a little later in the year; Travers Smith Braithwaite, who had served the business since well before it went public – John Humphries, for long the senior partner, says the relationship goes back at least to Sir Benjamin Guinness's Chairmanship in the 1860s – were replaced by Freshfields. Freshfields were, as they had been since before the First World War, solicitors to the Bank of England, therefore at the heart of the Establishment; yet they were also a major player in corporate business, well used to masterminding takeovers. This combination of the respectable with the go-ahead exactly suited Guinness with Saunders in charge.

The first important acquisition to come off was in the field of retailing; Saunders, encouraged by Bains, thought that this was a good business to be in. To a modest extent the Company was already in it, with the Drummonds chain of pharmacists and the Lavells CTN (confectioners, tobacconists, newsagents) chain. Lavells had been part of the confectionery group, but Guinness retained it while selling the rest of that group. To increase its involvement in CTN, Guinness took over Martins the Newsagents in June 1984. Martins had a chain of just under 500 shops and, rather like Guinness, was a family company in which the Martin family had Board control and nearly 20 per cent of the shares; the recent profit record had not been progressive. At £3.44 million, pre-tax profits for the year to October 1983 were rather lower than the year before, and turnover at £141.6 million was up; margins, then, were being seriously squeezed.

Guinness was not the only business interested in Martins. W. H. Smith got in first with a bid of £34.4 million for the Company, or 260p per share, announced on 2 May 1984. The bid was rejected by the Martins' Board as inadequate. Left to themselves, Smiths would probably have gone up a certain amount; but on 17 May Guinness announced a bid more than a third higher at about £48.6 million. This was an offer that the shareholders, including the Martin family, could not refuse. Smiths began by saying they would consider their position, but no further was heard from them; clearly they considered, as indeed it seemed to me at the time, that Guinness was paying a very full price. At the Board Meeting on 5 June, the family directors made some comments about this operation, all rather typical of our several attitudes. Because the purchase had been made at nearly fourteen times pre-tax profits, I worried about the price, and asked for an assurance that if it had to be increased this would not take it above what it was prudent to pay; there was no point in being successful at any cost. Saunders naturally expressed agreement. Simon Boyd was concerned that there had not been enough consultation with non-executive directors, although he recognized the necessity for secrecy and speed of action; he was backed up by others, but I kept silent on this point, because I was still sore about Booker McConnell and felt that the need for secrecy was paramount. Saunders' case on this matter was expressed by Benjamin Iveagh; I am not sure if he mentioned the Booker leak specifically, but we all knew what he was referring to when he emphasized that secrecy and urgency were the essentials for success. No family director commented on the fact that close on 60 per cent of the consideration was for Guinness shares, whose issue reduced the family's proportion of the Company by something over 10 per cent. This nonchalant attitude persisted during the much larger bids for Bells and Distillers, which reduced the proportion far more dramatically. The contrast with the family's attitude at the time of the proposed rights issue could not be more complete. In the end, the absolute value of our holdings was more important to us than the proportion we had of the Company.

The Martins acquisition was followed by a much smaller purchase which none the less received plenty of attention. This was because the business acquired for about £3 million in November 1984 had a very high profile; it was Champneys health farm. Health was another area in which Saunders and his advisers at Bains felt the Company should have a serious involvement, and the acquisition was followed by another in the same field:

Nature's Best Health, which was bought for £2 million in January 1985.

The purchase of Martins in particular must have pleased the market, despite the high price, because during the autumn of 1984 the Guinness share price again moved ahead strongly. Too strongly in fact for the *Investors' Chronicle* when it announced the year's results in January 1985. Having recommended the shares at 113p in 1983 and 135p in 1984, the weekly jibbed at the price of 232p in 1985, commenting: 'It looks as though the recent run up in the shares has been overdone.' One can see the case for this view. The yield, despite dividend increases, had come down to 4 per cent, which for the first time for many years was below the brewing industry average, 'lower than the return on Allied-Lyons, Scottish and Newcastle, Grand Metropolitan and Whitbread, on all of whom Guinness relies for pub sales of its products . . .' Quite so; the Cuckoo Factor had never been a secret, and 'for all its much-publicized recent acquisitions in retail and health . . . Guinness remains overwhelmingly a one-product company', with brewing accounting for 92 per cent of trading profits. The unspoken question was, why should Ernest Saunders make quite such a difference in the shares' rating?

Well, he did. The results themselves were very respectable, showing growth in all important areas and earnings per share, even after the purchase of Martins, up by about 22 per cent. The new acquisitions seemed sensible, although the earlier diversifications had also seemed sensible in their day, not least to the *Investors' Chronicle*. But the good figures themselves only explain a part of the transformation in the Company's image. They were necessary, but they were not sufficient. It was what Saunders and Roux made of them that counted, in endless Press briefings on and off the record, in continual meetings with City firms.

Late in 1984 Guinness recruited Sir Jack Lyons to advise on retailing and retail property, subjects that had become more important to the Group following the acquisition of Martins. Sir

Jack was retained at £3,000 a month. The appointment was logical because his background was in retailing. His activity with Bain, and now with Guinness, gave him a new and interesting business career as he entered his seventies.

Sir Jack's significance to the Guinness Affair as it was to develop arises from his business and political links. He was a superb contact man, who knew everyone, from the Queen Mother downwards. Since he was a respected member of the Jewish community his business connections were predominantly with that community. Sir Jack was a particular admirer of Mrs Thatcher, and not too shy to write to her when he had something to ask. The fact that he was a prominent Jew certainly presented no problem with the Prime Minister, who had learnt to like Jews during her dealings with her Constituency Association in Finchley. In the first Guinness trial all the defendants without exception were either Jews or, in Ernest Saunders' case, of Jewish extraction, and other Jewish businessmen and their families were also involved in various ways. It was Sir Jack who introduced Saunders to these people, directly or indirectly, beginning with Anthony Parnes who became the Company's 'eyes and ears' in the stock market during the bid for Bells. At about the same time, and also through Sir Jack, Saunders met Gerald Ronson, chairman of the large, privately owned Heron Group.

In itself the Jewish connection does not mean much; Sir Jack, through Bain, happened to be the contact man and his contacts happened to be Jewish. Had he been Armenian, no doubt he would have introduced Armenians. To give this significance in the light of Saunders' own Jewish origin is to transgress the rule known as Occam's Razor; namely, that in seeking explanations one should not introduce postulates that are unnecessary. There is no evidence in this affair that anyone behaved differently because of being Jewish. Yet to Saunders himself there may have been significance in the renewal of his Jewish links. There are indications that the time when he felt it possible, and worthwhile, to be an 'honorary Guinness' was drawing to a close. By 1984, Saunders was beginning to know the Guinness family a bit better and to realize that our real influence was a good deal less than a gossip columnist or other superficial observer might have supposed. We rarely acted as a group; the gift in 1965 of new chandeliers to Westminster Abbey, organized by Benjamin, was the last time we were ever to do so. Also we neither had, nor could procure, nor would we have been likely to want to procure, large quantities of liquid funds to help in a City operation. Essentially all we did was to sit there, draw our dividends and pursue our own activities; those of us who sat on the Board had long become accustomed to being treated by the management as little more substantial than decoration. Benjamin in particular was pleasant and pliable, but as regards any positive action he was – well, King Log.

In addition, Saunders began to feel that we were excluding him socially. *Nightmare* strikes a sour note: 'While his official position in the Company strengthened, he was left in no doubt about his personal status in the eyes of the family.'[2] How true is this? In the only concrete instance quoted in James's book, Saunders gets it absurdly wrong. In July 1984 he and his wife Carole came to the wedding of my daughter Catherine to Lord Neidpath. This took place at Bryan's house, Biddesden, on a blazing July day, and was followed by a dinner and dance in a marquee on the lawn. According to *Nightmare*, 'Ernest was introduced as "the new brewery manager" and they were seated at a table with the Company Secretary and the Moyne estate manager. They were gradually promoted to more important seats . . .'[3] What Saunders clearly did not take in was that on that occasion there were no important or unimportant seats; everyone settled down where they happened to find themselves. In this context it emerges that in fact we seem to have looked after Saunders and Carole rather well; if he was 'promoted to more important seats', this implies that I, or someone, must have taken him round and introduced him to people he thought were of higher status than his first companions. But he found it impossible to conceive that an elaborate wedding party should be as unstructured as this one was. There were no place cards, as he must have been aware; very well, there must be some hidden agenda. Hierarchy of position, he felt, there must be; if not open, it must be concealed, engineered in some way behind the scenes. The concept of the *important seat*, in his mind, was ineradicable. His introduction as 'the new brewery manager' probably derives from the habit within the family of referring to Guinness as 'the Brewery'. I can quite imagine that I may have introduced Saunders to some elderly lady cousin as 'the new Managing Director of the Brewery'. She would not have understood the term Chief Executive, which was his title. She could well then have introduced him on to someone else as 'Brewery manager'.

Saunders' reaction following my daughter's wedding is an illustration of how sensitive people manufacture slights; yet his sensitivity was not quite without reason. *Nightmare* has it that 'apart from the Moynes, the Guinness family largely excluded them from all but the most formal social functions'.[4] The exception made for my father and his family reflects the fact that Bryan liked him and maintained the sort of cordial relations that he had kept up with Beaver, Smiley and McNeile. The general impression Saunders had of social coolness in the family may reflect the feelings of Benjamin's wife, Miranda, who from the very beginning felt that there was something wrong with Saunders, and sometimes, in private, would say so. People have these feelings and they influence behaviour. If Benjamin himself had been a more socially active person, his wife's *malaise* might have had less effect. He did, if intermittently, do his best; according to *Nightmare*, Benjamin once wrote to him 'that the family considered me as an adopted Guinness'.[5]

Whether justifiably or not, Saunders did have this sense of being cold-shouldered by the Guinness family in whom at one time he thought he might find roots; we have seen that he once asked Bryan to look on him as a son. It may not be too imaginative to postulate that Sir Jack Lyons and his helpful friends made him begin to see his real roots as being in the Jewish community with which until then his only contact was his ancestry. Here were people with real money and real power, people who really counted in the social scene. When did one ever see a member of the Guinness family at one of the smart charity balls at the Dorchester or Grosvenor House? Even if they were there it would be at someone else's table, and they would be pretty backward at the tombola and the auction of the Ford Fiesta. Saunders' new friends would have their own tables, a sign of access to real money. They were the sort who could throw in millions to a bid battle and talk to others who could throw in more. The Guinnesses had a façade, but when you poked it your finger went through canvas. Sir Jack and his Jewish contacts had substance. After a holiday on Gerald Ronson's yacht, Saunders asked Michael Hadfield, a Guinness executive, 'Why can't we have a yacht like that? We are bigger than Heron.' Hadfield answered, 'Ronson owns Heron; you don't own Guinness.' Saunders was perhaps reflecting his disenchantment with the family when he said at a Board Meeting that directors should not expect to stay free at Champneys as a perquisite. (As far as I am aware he himself was the only director who ever stayed there; presumably he paid the bill.)

During the early part of 1985 there were two further minor acquisitions. Neighbourhood Stores, the UK operator of Seven-Eleven all-night shops, was purchased at what certainly seemed to me like a very high earnings multiple. This was a Bain suggestion. In the United States, Thomas Ward negotiated the acquisition of Richter, importers and distributors of gourmet foods; this was a better fit than might seem likely at first sight, because in the United States Guinness is counted as a gourmet, or at any rate a speciality, beer.

Then, in June 1985, came the bid for Bells Distilleries. Bain had identified this some time before as a suitable target to be taken over; in April, after months of discussion, Saunders agreed to go for it. The operation turned out to be a bitterly contested and expensive battle which queerly anticipated the later events around Distillers in that a surprising number of the same names crop up in the story, sometimes in different roles. Saunders drew the wrong lessons from it. He succeeded in the face of considerable difficulties. He regarded his success as an invitation to future ruthless advance; he should have seen his difficulties as a warning.

The first and least of these difficulties was with the Guinness family. Bells was by far the largest of the new acquisitions so far, and it would have to be for Guinness shares. This would increase the capital of the Company by about 60 per cent, thus reducing the family's proportion, already down to about 20 per cent at most, to say $12\frac{1}{2}$ per cent. However, events had moved on since Purssell's abortive rights issue. The Company was progressing spectacularly under Saunders. All of us were feeling more prosperous. If this wonder-worker needed to issue more shares to further his strategy, so be it. The family holding was already less than the 25 per cent which would have given it certain negative rights. There seemed no reason to suppose that any of us would lose our seats on the Board; it seemed clear, to me at least, that the presence of the family continued to be of use to Saunders from the point of view of image, giving him a veneer of the old cosiness which could easily be helpful. We could not foresee quite what use was to be made of this.

I do not think the reduction in our percentage was much mentioned in the family. What was mentioned was my father's moral objection to investing in spirits. Bryan was no longer on the Board himself but Finn and I were, so his views would be represented. Bryan thought distilled liquor harmful and never provided it in his house; he regarded the distilling industry as one which should be left alone. Beer and wine were all right in his eyes, whisky was not. This is a defensible point of view, although it can also be attacked and even mocked. At all events he held it. When the Bells proposition came up to the Board, Finn voiced the strong objection which we knew my father would have expressed. I suggested that Benjamin should try to talk my father round, and he agreed. Just what went on between them we shall never know, but their relationship was warm, and it would seem that Benjamin did not, in the end, have any great difficulty.

Bells had grown impressively over the previous ten years from being a smallish independent Perth-based distiller to owning a brand which outsold all others in the United Kingdom and, at its peak, had an astonishing 25 per cent of the domestic market. The company had made an important recent diversification by acquiring the Gleneagles Hotels group, but essentially, like Guinness, it was a company with a single very successful product. Profits had surged from just over £3 million in 1974 to £35.17 million in 1984. This advance can be attributed in the first place to the sleepiness of Distillers, that odd dinosaur at which we shall be looking again. Distillers' salesmanship was slack, its reaction to competition was slow and complacent, its gentlemanly management was wedded to a quiet life. In this way it left an opportunity in the Scotch whisky industry for a smart competitor. Of such, the smartest was Bells' chairman, Raymond Miquel.

Miquel was a phenomenon in his way. His father was a Channel Islander of French extraction who worked in Glasgow as a chef and married a Scot. (Some forebear must have come from the Mediterranean area, because Miquel is a Catalan name.) Raymond Miquel trained as an engineer, and joined Bells in 1956. He distinguished himself quickly, joined the Board in 1962, and by 1973 was Chairman and Managing Director. He was a dark, thin, intense man, energetic and desperately competitive. An exercise fanatic, he ran for miles every morning. On one occasion, during a hurdle race, he fell and broke his wrist. Despite what must have been acute agony, he picked himself up, continued, and ended the winner. He was very strict with his salesmen. Their shoes had to be clean, on pain of dismissal. At sales dances, they were allowed no more than one glass of whisky during the evening, and forbidden to dance with the same partner more than once.

There was some sense to this. Clean shoes do make a good impression on a salesman's customers. As to the dances, these were mainly given to entertain the customers, licensed victuallers and their wives. Miquel's regulation ensured that even the dimmest of these wives would get her dance with a salesman, and that her partner would be decently sober. Even so, these requirements betray the mentality of the sergeant-major rather than the officer, and Miquel was not particularly popular among the officer class in Scotland. Having risen from the ranks, he was not connected by birth to anyone in the Scottish Establishment, a concept which is more nebulous than is often supposed but nevertheless has a certain reality. This need not have excluded him from it; any Establishment will accept whose who have reached the right status, given a certain amount of charm and clubbability, and as Managing Director of a successful distillery Miquel would have found all doors open to him. But he was essentially a loner. He was also too obviously strenuous, even in a country like Scotland which traditionally rather respects strenuousness.

One toe on which Miquel had recently trodden rather hard was that of Peter Tyrie, Chief Executive of Gleneagles Hotels which, besides the famous golfing hostelry, also comprised three other important hotels: the North British and the Caledonian in Edinburgh and the Piccadilly (now the Meridien) in London. The hotels had been privatized by British Rail in 1983 and bought by a consortium of institutions which had recruited Peter Tyrie to run them. Bells won Gleneagles in February 1984 on a hostile takeover masterminded by Morgan Grenfell; the price was £27 million which in many people's opinion was far too low. Peter Tyrie was not pleased to lose his independence after less than a year. He consented to go on running the hotels with a seat on the Bells Board; Miquel, who admired his competence, was keen to keep him. Machiavelli could have foreseen the outcome.

There were already in 1985 signs that Bells might have reached a plateau, or even passed its peak. Its domestic market share had fallen from 25 per cent to a still respectable 21 per cent. It had perhaps reached the largest size where it could be efficiently controlled by someone who, though an exceptional manager himself, did not find it easy to delegate. There comes a point in a company's development at which too much personal attention to detail by the Chief Executive becomes an actual handicap; what is then required is the ability to pick others who can be trusted to do the work – and to trust them. Saunders had this ability; Miquel did not. The Guinness team would whisper this point rather effectively during the takeover battle. It was probably right; if Bells had remained independent under Miquel it is quite likely that the company would have stopped growing.

'Will they fight?' I asked Saunders when he presented to the Board his proposal for the takeover; the idea of buying a company as the result of a battle never appealed to me, for the rather obvious reason that the contest was liable to drive the price too high. 'Yes,' said Saunders, 'Miquel will certainly fight like a tiger.' He continued with a thumbnail sketch of Miquel, much as given above, and said that on a human level he respected him and felt rather sorry for what was about to happen to him. Saunders felt, though, that Guinness needed Bells as part of its strategy to escape the Cuckoo Factor and to join the big league among companies. It flashed through my mind that in relation to Miquel Saunders was being a bit like Beatrix Potter's Fierce Bad Rabbit: 'He doesn't say please; he takes it!' There was also a flavour of Lewis Carroll's Walrus who, as Alice points out, at least feels a bit sorry for the poor oysters.

Saunders wrong-footed Miquel at every turn. All commentators have noted this, but, as is their habit in these matters, they have exaggerated its importance. The greater skill of Saunders and his team would only be of real significance if Guinness paid less for Bells than it would have done if Miquel had performed more deftly; yet the same commentators also agree that Guinness paid the highest possible price compatible with reason, perhaps a bit more. Where the relative skill of the Guinness public relations did have some significance was in creating for Saunders a reputation in the business world for effectiveness as a bidder. More damagingly, it helped the development of a sense of hubris, both in Saunders himself and in his merchant bankers, Morgan Grenfell.

Morgan Grenfell was thought to be the merchant banking star of the City following some victories over Warburgs. Its stardom would be transient; largely owing to the Guinness affair, it was destined to flare and subside like a supernova. Morgan Grenfell's men Anthony Richmond-Watson and Philip Evans coordinated the team which Saunders had carefully chosen for the Bells bid. Solicitors were Freshfields (Alan Peck) and brokers were Cazenove (David Mayhew and Anthony Forbes), with Wood Mackenzie also helping. Behind the scenes was another top broker: Sir Jack Lyons' contact, Anthony Parnes. Parnes, loosely connected as a 'half-commission man' with Alexanders Laing and Cruikshank, was a familiar figure in the Stock Exchange. He seems to have been respected more than he was liked, but everyone knew him. He was dubbed 'The Animal'. His role in the Bells bid was to monitor the stock market without his connection to Guinness being generally known.

Besides this London team, Ernest Saunders had recruited helpers in Edinburgh, because there could be doubts in Scotland about a major Scotch whisky producer being taken over by a non-Scottish company. These were indeed forthcoming; Saunders, in his first Scottish Press conference after announcing the bid, ran into hostile questions on the subject. This Scottish factor, as we shall see, played a part in sinking Saunders; but this was because he mishandled it, by no means because he disregarded it. At this stage he made two intelligent choices for his Scottish team. One was a top lawyer in Edinburgh's Charlotte Square, Charles Fraser of W. and J. Burness. Fraser was a prominent member of the great and the good of Edinburgh; he held the ceremonial office of purse bearer to the Church of Scotland. Nobody was more respected, or more familiar with the Scottish business community. The other was the Edinburgh merchant bank Noble Grossart, which was also at the centre of the Scottish Establishment.

There was a serious leak before the bid, despite intense efforts by all concerned to keep it dark. According to Dominic Hobson in his book about Morgan Grenfell, *The Pride of Lucifer*, a man called Brian Evans overheard a conversation in a club and, following this, invested £128,000 in Bells shares a few days before the bid was announced. He may have cleared £80,000 profit. To everyone's embarrassment he turned out to be the brother of the Morgan Grenfell executive Philip Evans, who was working on the deal. Philip Evans was grilled both by his firm and by the Stock Exchange surveillance unit, and the brothers were exonerated.

The leak forced Saunders to announce the bid a few days earlier than had been envisaged, on 14 June 1985. The terms were nine Guinness shares for every Bells share, and valued Bells at £347.2 million on the basis of the Guinness share price at that time. The news caught Raymond Miquel entirely by surprise; he was visiting Chicago at the time to talk with customers there. At first he was oddly complacent; he was so convinced of the absurdity of any bid by Guinness for his company that he did not even cancel his appointments in the United States but calmly visited New York and returned in his own good time, on the 19th. When he did get back his reaction was one of frank outrage. He consulted no experts to put a favourable spin on his case. In

London he gave Press conferences claiming that a Guinness take-over would be a catastrophe. It could lead to redundancies, and would be bad for the whisky industry. He himself would find it impossible to work for Guinness, and his top managers would leave. He cast doubt on Guinness's recent record, pointing out that most of the recent profit rise had come from cost-cutting rather than from increased sales. He laid it on the line: 'There is no price which is acceptable from Guinness for the control of Arthur Bell.' This is not the sort of language that any institutional manager likes to hear. Getting too high a price for one of his fund's holdings means securing a windfall boost to his investment record.

Miquel did however have a grievance with which it is very possible to sympathize, and he at once complained about it. This concerned the role of Morgan Grenfell, which had been merchant banker to Bells until about six months before. According to Dominic Hobson,[6] Miquel had heard a rumour that the bank might be preparing a bid for his company on behalf of Guinness and asked the Chairman, Christopher Reeves, if this was true. Reeves denied it. The fact was, though, that although Guinness did not start seriously preparing the bid before March 1985, it was certainly being discussed as a hypothesis before the end of the previous year. Christopher Reeves was presumably not aware of this; if he was, Miquel's question would certainly have embarrassed him, especially as Bells paid Morgan Grenfell a fee of £20,000 around that time for research on British Caledonian Airways, which the company had considered taking over, and on Gleneagles Hotels which it had taken over. However, merchant banks were becoming less unconditionally attached to their clients, less loyal. To use the jargon, they were moving from being client-oriented to being transaction-oriented, which being translated means that they no longer conformed to the ethics of the old-style American gangster who considered that a decent man was one who stayed bought.

The man who had picked up the rumour of the bid in late 1984 and warned Miquel was Lord Spens, an executive with the merchant bank Ansbachers. Spens had handled the Bells account for Morgan Grenfell when he had worked there up to 1982 and remained friendly with Miquel. Spens then became engaged by Bells for their defence against Guinness. His first step was to ask Bells' lawyers, Denton Hall and Burgin, to obtain a court injunction to stop Morgan Grenfell acting for Guinness. The decision was taken, rightly or wrongly, not to go to law but to have recourse to the Takeover Panel. The Panel's Executive reprimanded Morgan Grenfell, but this had not the least practical effect because the ticking off was not backed up by any requirement that Morgan Grenfell should stop acting for Guinness. Spens thereupon asked for a hearing by the full Panel. Morgan Grenfell's Chairman, Christopher Reeves, went along in person, for if the firm had been compelled to withdraw from the bid it would have cost it millions in fees, as well as further millions for unwinding sub-underwriting agreements with several institutions. He made this point, and it must have weighed with the Panel, because they found for Morgan Grenfell. Sir Jasper Hollom, who chaired the meeting, even rebuked Spens on the grounds that the complaint had been frivolous; this was hardly complimentary to the Panel's own executive which, however ineffectively, had ruled Morgan Grenfell to be in the wrong. Spens later commented to Peter Pugh: 'You have got to remember that the Takeover Panel was set up by merchant bankers for the good of merchant bankers. When they heard that Bells had only spent £20,000 with Morgan Grenfell in the last two years and that Guinness had already spent £6 million that was the end of the case.'[7] Cynicism is of course the prerogative of the loser, but the fact remains that the impression left by the Panel was an unfortunate one; it seemed to be simply on the side of the big battalions, as Voltaire remarked of God.

Lord Spens' rejected submission to the Panel is worth quoting here. 'Legal considerations apart, a climate in the market in which a long-standing and trusted financial adviser can, without any sanction, just abandon his client and actually apply his efforts in opposition to his client, is one which the Panel and all its supporting institutions should strenuously try to combat. It will not go unnoticed that the potential rewards to the leader of a successful attack on Bells are very great and, if this is seen to be the only motivating factor of leading merchant banks, the others will follow, and trust in the City's institutions will go out of the window.' This prediction was as accurate, and at the time as unheeded, as those of Cassandra. The Panel's decision sent very much the wrong message to the financial community in general, and to Morgan Grenfell in particular. Had it gone the other way, it could have given the City the stitch in time that saves nine. As it was, it weakened the framework of accepted practice in the City, with fatal results in the Distillers bid.

In the meantime, nobody in the City seemed to mind much. The Panel again supported Guinness when Morgan Grenfell complained to it about certain attacks by Miquel on the Company that resulted from his uncontrolled rage rather than from any cool examination of the facts; Miquel was reprimanded. Nothing came, either, of the furious complaints in Parliament launched by Bill Walker, Conservative MP for Perth – Bells was in his constituency.

Bells called in Warburgs to help, and though they had come late on to the scene they did their best. They did at least force Guinness to raise its bid. On the public relations front, there were noises in Scotland about this great Scottish company being taken over 'from the South': Bill Walker and his colleague Nicholas Fairbairn were complaining away for all the world like Wagner's Rhinemaidens bewailing the theft of their gold.

However, the Scots were not in any way unanimous. Two eminent Scottish businessmen in particular took opposite views on whether to recommend acceptance of the Guinness bid for

Bells. Sir Thomas Risk, Chairman of the Bank of Scotland, turned down a request from Saunders to tell the Trustees of the Bank's pension fund to accept the Guinness offer, presumably because he felt that Bells should stay Scottish. Sir Norman Macfarlane, a director of the Perth-based insurance company General Accident, which held 12 per cent of Bells, was more hardheaded; he and the rest of the General Accident Board took the view that price was to be the deciding factor. On that basis there could be no argument; the bid price of 258p was nearly double the price at which Bells had been standing before the bid. Had the bid failed, the price would have plummeted. Saunders had a meeting with Sir Norman, and was to tell James Saunders: 'Sir Norman was pleasant, he listened and asked questions, including some about supply arrangements for whisky bottle caps.'[8] (Whisky bottle caps are one of the products of Macfarlane's company, Clansman Group PLC.) There is no suggestion that Sir Norman angled for the Bells contract for caps at this meeting, nor any reason why as an expert in the field he should not mention them, but in view of subsequent events it may well be that Saunders' raising of the topic is malicious in intent. Bill Walker, MP, railed against General Accident: 'These people, who have made millions out of Bells' very fine performance down the years, have now sold Bells down the river.' Politicians do say these things, which is perhaps why their profession does not always enjoy the highest of reputations. The shareholders and policyholders of General Accident would have had cause for complaint if, through the action of their Board, the opportunity had been lost of realizing this investment at such a favourable price. By this token one can ask whether Sir Thomas Risk, in refusing the bid, was giving due priority to the interests of the Bank of Scotland's pensioners.

Bells produced its considered rejection of the bid on 12 July. For shareholders, the best news in this was a dividend increase of 50 per cent together with pre-tax profits well above the previous year's level. (But then how is it that prospective bid victims so often conjure up sudden dividend increases of this order? If they are justified, what does this say about their previous treatment of shareholders? If they are not, and shareholders stay loyal, what does this do to their investment?) Guinness was rubbished; its management was said to be heavily dependent on outside consultants, meaning Bain of course. Bells then asked the Secretary of State for Trade and Industry, Norman Tebbit, to refer the bid to the Monopolies and Mergers Commission. There was no obvious case for this, and Tebbit declined to oblige.

Guinness practised brinkmanship for a few weeks; rather than raise its bid, it threatened shareholders that it might walk away, leaving the price to fall back to where it was before the battle. This did not work. Bells, on 5 August, provided a revised profit forecast with an even higher dividend promise. Two days later Guinness replied by raising its bid by about 10 per cent to some £370 million – the Guinness share price had fallen a little since the start of the bid. The exact terms were four Guinness ordinary shares, then priced at 270p, plus £2.65 which could be taken in cash or in the form of a Convertible Unsecured Loan Stock, for every five ordinary shares in Bells, therefore just under one Guinness share for each Bells share.

Miquel rejected the new bid as contemptuously as ever, but Peter Tyrie of Gleneagles sabotaged any further effort to frustrate Guinness. Tyrie had no love for Miquel, and it clearly made little difference to him whether his company remained a subsidiary of Bells or came under Guinness. Tyrie issued his own recommendation to shareholders dissociating himself from the rest of the Bells Board and recommending acceptance of the new offer. He had in fact been working secretly for Guinness for at least a fortnight before he came out into the open, employing his own merchant banking advisers, Quayle Munro. This firm submitted an invoice to Guinness for £50,979.61 for, among other things, 'perusing of Bell's Board minutes of July 24' and reporting on them to Guinness's advisers, Noble Grossart.[9] The inference has to be that these minutes came from Tyrie.

The aftermath was unexpectedly friendly. Saunders really did value Miquel's expertise and invited him to continue to run Bells; he accepted. True, he left fairly soon, but he drove off into the sunset in the Aston Martin with personal number plates which Saunders allowed him to keep, together with a life membership of Gleneagles golf club. He has preserved a dignified silence since.

ELEVEN

Going for Distillers

The Distillers Co. Ltd, DCL or Distillers for short, was one of the largest companies in Britain. It was also one of the oddest. In a sense it was more like a trade association than a single company. It started in 1926 when most of the major Scotch whisky producers, together with the gin distillers Booths and Tanqueray Gordon, came together in a mass merger. Most of the components were private family businesses some of whose owners, then or later, might prefer to own a shareholding in a major public company, which could be sold on the market, rather than an unmarketable chunk of an unquoted concern. What was unusual was that this was a merger between equals, and remained so; no one took anyone else over, and the component companies retained their management autonomy, their own Boards and company headquarters. There was a parent Board, but its yoke was easy and its burden was light; it left the component businesses to run themselves, each with its own Sales Department and its own London headquarters. Subsidiarity ruled.

The strangest thing is that such a ramshackle arrangement could have lasted for sixty years. For most of that period it seemed to work, but this was essentially because the Scotch whisky industry was such a goldmine. Distillers' secret was that the prestigious brand names – Johnnie Walker, Dewars and the rest – enabled it to add enormous margins to its products. An additional factor in this may have been the high rate of tax; a margin that looked big in relation to the cost of production was not high in relation to the actual selling price. These margins ensured that the industry in general, and Distillers in particular, would make good money even when mismanaged.

Mismanaged Distillers certainly was. It never positioned its brands, that is, it never aimed a particular brand at a particular market segment but allowed them to compete wastefully against each other. Its distributors were uncontrolled. It benefited from the worldwide passion for Scotch whisky which developed in the 1950s and 1960s. Even the French took to it, claiming that it was better for the liver than calvados or brandy. Distillers took advantage of the demand by quietly charging more for exported whisky than for what was consumed at home. However, when Britain joined the EEC it soon became established that differential pricing within the Community was against regulations. So as to preserve the profits on its whisky exports, Distillers took its leading brand, Johnnie Walker, off the UK market in 1979, continuing to sell it abroad at the higher price. This was what gave Raymond Miquel his chance. Distillers' market share fell in the ten years from 1974 from 54 per cent to 20 per cent, most of the lost percentage going to Bells.

Distillers did, however, suffer one appalling disaster which was due as much to bad luck as to bad management. Like so many of Guinness's fiascos it was in the pharmaceutical field, though it dwarfed anything suffered by Guinness. Distillers had a chemical division which bought the rights of a tranquillizing drug, Thalidomide. Invented in Germany where it was called Contergan, the drug seemed excellent and without side effects, and was often administered to pregnant women. All seemed well until mothers began giving birth to babies without limbs, without eyes, with hands directly attached to shoulders. Hundreds of people's lives were ruined, and Distillers had to pay out millions in compensation. The public relations effect was worse than the purely financial cost because the company had stubbornly resisted having to pay out.

Profits and turnover, it is true, continued to rise; the figures looked quite reasonable, as did those of Guinness before 1979. But when account was taken of the enormous assets of Distillers in the form of property, equipment and undervalued whisky stocks, there was no doubt that it was seriously underperforming; profits could, many thought, have been at least doubled by competent management.

What kept Distillers for so long from takeover or shareholders' rebellion was its sheer size. But size alone could not preserve it indefinitely. An angler fish can gulp a morsel many times as big as itself, if necessary dislocating its jaw for the purpose, and digest it at leisure; thanks to various techniques developed in the United States, a company can do the same, assuming that the profit projections look right and are believed by the bankers with clout. By 1985, Michael Milken and the other 'junk bond' experts were sowing terror among conservative managements in the United States.

John Connell, Distillers' Chairman, was never complacent about Distillers' prospects. He was from one of the old management families, although his background, unusually, was in the gin rather than the whisky side. Since his appointment in 1983 he had tried to rationalize the company, in particular closing a few plants and facing the unpopularity of making people redundant; but his colleagues, gentlemanly and conservative Scots, did not allow this policy to go very far. Connell knew what should be done, but in the end he could no more preserve the old regime at Distillers than Turgot or Necker could avert the French Revolution.

By the 1980s Distillers' Scottish roots were more apparent than real; most of the directors had taken that high road into England which Dr Johnson had told James Boswell, teasingly, was the 'noblest prospect which a Scotchman ever sees'. They lived in the Home Counties; James Gulliver and his advisers, mischievously alluding to this, were to give Distillers the code word 'Ascot' when they were preparing their bid. Board Meetings were held and top management decisions made in London. All the same, the major distilleries were in Scotland. The company was very much perceived as a pillar of Scottish business, especially by the Scots and not least by the directors themselves.

Aware of Distillers' attractions to a possible predator, Connell had talks early in 1985 with Allied-Lyons, one of the new giant brewing conglomerates, with a view to a merger. Allied-Lyons itself was licking its wounds after nearly being swallowed up by the Australian group Elders-IXL. For whatever reason, Distillers' discussions with Allied-Lyons came to nothing.

When the bid for Distillers did come, it was from a rather unexpected source: Argyll PLC, now best known for its Safeway supermarkets, whose Chairman was James Gulliver. Gulliver was a formidably successful Scottish entrepreneur, his career easily outstripping that of Ernest Saunders, with whom events were to encourage people to compare him. Starting in management consultancy, he had moved into food retailing and done brilliantly, first as head of the Fine Fare supermarket chain of Gary Weston's company, Associated British Foods. He then operated on his own account with two other Scotsmen, Alistair Grant who had worked with him at Fine Fare and David Webster from the merchant bank William Brandt. The three of them bought control of a firm called Oriel Foods which was later sold to the American company RCA for £11 million. James Gulliver Associates, as their company was called, eventually bought back Oriel Foods for nearly £20 million, and then showed Gulliver's potential as corporate angler fish by buying the much larger company Allied Suppliers from Sir James Goldsmith for £104 million. The Argyll Group was formed in November 1983. Though its interests were mainly in retailing, Argyll did include a small drinks company called Amalgamated Distilled Products which produced whisky and rum.

In the eyes of the Distillers Board this did not begin to make Gulliver acceptable. Bill Spengler, one of the directors, expressed their feelings when he said, 'Gulliver deals in potatoes and cans of beans . . . we are selling Scotch.' These distinctions have progressively come to mean less and less in the modern business world. But then the Distillers directors were scarcely modern. Gulliver, however able and successful, was in their eyes nothing more than a jumped-up grocer. What would he do to their company, how would he cope with the mystique of Scotch whisky and the craftsmen who made it? If Distillers must lose its independence, let it at least be to a company with some of the same traditions; which of course was where Guinness would come in.

Gulliver and his colleagues formed their intention to bid for Distillers in 1984; at current market prices their quarry was three times the size of Argyll. They decided to wait a year, despite the possibility of another predator appearing; they realized that their company was likely to grow more during that time than would Distillers, and their City advisers, Samuel Montagu and Charterhouse, felt that this period was needed to consolidate Argyll's rapid growth during the past few years. When Guinness launched its bid for Bells, Argyll was rather reassured; Guinness had been among the companies it thought might be interested in Distillers, and this seemed to eliminate it. Gulliver told Kochan and Pym: 'My own view was that Saunders made a fatal error in . . . buying a brand which was already successful and paying a top price for it.' Miquel and his advisers, Warburgs, in fact approached Gulliver and asked him to come in as a 'White knight' to save Bells from Guinness, but Gulliver felt the price was too high.[1]

In any case, what interested him was Distillers; and he was already making his preparations. Events in the New York market, and indeed Gulliver's own experience nearer home, showed that a smaller company could certainly take over a larger one. All the same, it would clearly be very helpful if a powerful ally could be found to help with underwriting the securities to be issued. Just such an ally seemed to appear, providentially, on the scene.

Gulliver was approached by Ian MacGregor of Lazards, former Chairman of the Coal Board and of British Steel. Mac-Gregor suggested that Gulliver might have a look at Distillers, which seemed to be underperforming; Lazards might be able to help through its connection with GEC, the mammoth electrical engineering group, and its Chairman, Lord Weinstock. GEC owned 4 per cent of Distillers and, almost more to the point, had a billion pounds of cash. Weinstock felt that he might use some of his resources to help liven up Distillers. He had already put out feelers to the Distillers management about possible cooperation and had been rebuffed. He might now help finance a takeover by Argyll.

Weinstock and Gulliver met and a plan emerged in the early summer of 1985, under which Weinstock would commit its Distillers holding to an Argyll bid and also be responsible for a very large part of the underwriting. Gulliver was so convinced that this deal was in effect agreed that he refrained from picking up in the market more than 1 per cent of Distillers shares; a holding of 5 per cent or more would have to be publicly declared, and Gulliver regarded himself as being in concert with GEC. This was an illusion; Weinstock was in fact full of doubts. He told Kochan and Pym: 'When Gulliver wanted to do something, we thought in principle we ought to help him, but he translated this into a proposition to underwrite £350 million of Argyll stock on terms which were remarkably unattractive to us. This was turned down within ten minutes of my people putting the detailed proposition on my desk. All the same, we said we would help, and that he could tell other investors we were willing to join in.'[2]

There was a failure of communication here, for Gulliver spent July and August trying and failing to contact Weinstock with a view to clinching something like the deal he had turned down. It was perhaps Weinstock's continued willingness to give marginal help that was misleading to a congenital optimist.

In the last week in August there was a sudden spurt in Distillers shares from 313p to an all-time high of 360p; someone had clearly heard something. Lazards spoke to the Takeover Panel on Argyll's behalf; this move would appear to have been premature, and looks inept. For the Panel, understandably from its point of view, instructed Argyll to make a clarifying statement, which was issued on 2 September. But what, at this stage, could Argyll say? Having spent so much time chasing the GEC rainbow, it did not have the underwriting arrangements in place to make an immediate bid. In the end the wording was: 'Argyll does not intend to make an offer for Distillers at the present time.' The Panel made Argyll define 'the present time', and Lazards, on behalf of Argyll, agreed that this meant three to four months.

It must have been galling to Argyll and its advisers to learn, very quickly, that the necessary underwriting would be much easier to obtain than they had thought; GEC's help was not needed. As a result of this episode Argyll ceased to employ Lazards, who had indeed only come into the picture because of the abortive negotiations with GEC, and went back to Samuel Montagu.

This approach to the Panel, and the statement that then had to be issued, lost Distillers for Argyll. Had Gulliver simply launched a bid at that stage he would certainly have won it, probably at a price not much higher than 400p a share. In this way he lost what might have been the deal of the century, for Guinness was finally to acquire Distillers at well over half as much again, and the purchase was to prove highly lucrative even at that much higher level. The muddle with Lord Weinstock was also important; without that, Argyll could have spent the whole summer of 1985 putting his underwriting together.

The announcement galvanized the Distillers Board and they

began taking defensive measures. They took on Kleinwort Benson to mastermind the financial aspect, and within the company changes were made which simplified the decision-making process and increased motivation for middle management. It is extraordinary how danger will concentrate people's minds. Suddenly, too, there was a determined attempt to woo the Press and the City. Investment analysts were shown round the various distilleries and given presentations which they often found surprisingly impressive. City editors were asked to lunch. Sir Nigel Broakes, Chief Executive and creator of the Trafalgar House conglomerate, was recruited as a non-executive director. The long and complacent neglect of Scottish opinion was brought to an end, although the Scots were sometimes irritated by being addressed by people who were not quite at Board level. Public relations firms were hired. In short, Distillers under the lash of danger took some of the same strides into the modern business world that Guinness had taken on the arrival of Saunders.

In Distillers' case it was much too late, and much too obvious that it was all done under pressure. Some observers were impressed, it is true, but most were not. Even Distillers' excellent interim figures failed to impress when they were published in late November. They showed profits up by 40 per cent and an interim dividend up by 22 per cent, but the newspapers shrugged these figures off, emphasizing a change in accounting practice which made exact comparison difficult.

Distillers considered various defence schemes during its three-month period of grace, including the stratagem known as the 'poison pill' under which a potential victim takes over another company to make it unattractive to the bidder. At one time Distillers even considered bidding for Argyll itself. It was probably wise not to go in for a poison pill; with a bid signalled, the motive for such a move would be too clear to everyone, and it would probably not have been allowed to succeed. Another possibility was a 'white knight': a friendly merger or takeover with a powerful partner to frustrate Argyll. Seagrams, the American distiller, was mentioned, but without result.

It was in this role that Guinness was seen by the Distillers Board. Serious contact seems to have started with Charles Fraser, who it will be recalled was a key Scottish legal adviser to Guinness in the Bells takeover. Bay Green of Kleinworts went to Scotland to sound out opinion there. He met Fraser, who told him that Scottish opinion had turned against Distillers; it was felt that a takeover by Argyll would do the whisky industry good. Fraser, who did not himself like the idea of the takeover, had gathered that this was the view at a meeting of the influential Scottish Council for Development and Industry at Gleneagles Hotel. Ernest Saunders had been there, making Scottish friends, and Fraser talked to him about Distillers. Guinness might join a consortium to bid for Distillers, Fraser thought. Saunders' feeling at the time was rather that he might get hold of some brands.[3] It seemed too soon after the Bells acquisition for any full bid to be made by Guinness.

Or was it? Saunders' advisers were certainly beginning to think that it was not, and he himself was receptive, if at times doubtful. Already in October 1985 he had told Olivier Roux that if Argyll did come up with a bid for Distillers, Guinness would have to consider a counter-bid. His discussions with Fraser at Gleneagles must have encouraged him. Roux tried to dissuade him; his view was that after buying Bells Saunders ought not to consider another bid for at least a year. Roux was to be consistently sceptical of the wisdom of going after Distillers at all. Yet even he was evidently intrigued by Distillers. Kochan and Pym tell us that at a lunch with Hoare Govett, Distillers' stockbrokers, in late October 1985, Roux took a keen interest in the Company's problems and let it be known that Guinness would like to help against Argyll.[4]

This does not mean that he was in favour of Guinness making a bid; he was not. All the same, he had not resisted when Saunders, a couple of weeks before, had instructed Bain to analyse the possibility. They were, of course, delighted to do so; following the Bells takeover Guinness was Bain's second biggest client in the world and by a very long way its biggest in Europe, responsible by itself for more than half the revenue of Bain's three European offices. But it was the Morgan Grenfell directors who most consistently pushed Saunders towards bidding for Distillers; James Saunders states this[5] and others confirm it. Shortly after his meeting at Gleneagles with Fraser, Saunders talked to Christopher Reeves and Graham Walsh, Morgan's head of corporate finance. It was a time of runaway boom; there was a strong bull market on world stock exchanges accompanied by a frenetic series of gigantic bids financed in ever more sophisticated ways. Reeves and Walsh felt that in these circumstances Guinness was still too small to be secure. They suggested that the world drinks business was going to be dominated by giant companies and Saunders saw their point: 'You either had to be up there with the biggest, or resign yourself to becoming a regional or specialist operator.'[6] This thinking was typical of the time. It would also, as it happened, suit Morgan Grenfell very well if Guinness were to employ the bank in a successful mega-bid at that particular juncture; Morgan Grenfell was to sell its shares to the public in the following year, and a multimillion pound fee, added to its earnings, would have a very favourable effect on the price the public could be asked to pay for their shares.

Saunders took some time to be convinced. If Guinness needed a big deal, why should it not go for his old company, Beechams; or perhaps Boots? In any case Guinness was involved in a number of smaller deals and there were other areas besides the drinks business that could be expanded. The health division was one; Guinness already owned Champneys health farm and was just taking over Cranks, the chain of health food restaurants. On the retailing side there was a suggestion of a joint venture with Underwoods, another Morgan Grenfell client. It was in connection with this proposal that Saunders first met Roger Seelig, a young high-flyer among Morgan's corporate finance directors. Saunders was at once impressed by his quick and original mind, and was influenced also by Reeves, who described Seelig as 'the most entrepreneurial man in the bank'.[7] Following his determination always to secure the very best people, that same determination that was at the basis of the odd-looking compromise that enabled him to hold on to Roux, Saunders grabbed Seelig as the man to run the Guinness account.

Whatever his doubts, and despite Roux's frank scepticism, Saunders seemed to be drawn inexorably towards making a bid for Distillers by a kind of gravitational pull. Morgan Grenfell wanted it, Charles Fraser wanted it, Distillers themselves were desperate for it. Benjamin Iveagh was enthusiastic. When Saunders tackled him about the project he must have been in one of his occasional moods of high euphoria: 'He was completely positive and said he would support any move I wanted to make. He said the family could have been the British Rockefellers or Rothschilds, with the Guinness Mahon bank as well, but they had lost their way. So anything that could put the Guinness family back in the big time he was in favour of.'[8]

Saunders told Morgan Grenfell that he would prefer the brands to the business. Only if there was a call for a white knight would he consider making a full bid. That condition was very easily met; John Connell was a desperate man. Guinness seemed incomparably better than Argyll; it was an old firm, in the right trade, with a reputation for expertise as well as benevolence and a family still in apparent control. Saunders was a newcomer, but the Guinnesses seemed to get on with him and his manner was that of a gentleman. The manner of the wolf, in Little Red Riding Hood, was that of a grandmother.

On 2 December, exactly three months after its statement prompted by the Panel and on the very first day that it was allowed to do so, Argyll bid for Distillers at 485p per share, valuing the Company at £1.9 billion. Later in the month Bain, together with Morgan Grenfell and Guinness's accountant Alan Bailey, completed their 'impact analysis' projecting the effect of acquiring Distillers on Guinness's earnings per share. This valued Distillers at £2.7 billion or 670p per share. The sceptical Roux had told the team to adopt the most conservative possible criteria in evaluating Distillers, rather hoping that the result might rule out a Guinness bid. Even on this basis, though, the case for a bid was made, and Roux had to admit it. From then on, David Mayhew of Cazenoves and Roger Seelig of Morgan Grenfell became convinced that this major deal was possible, and took the lead on behalf of Saunders. Roux himself, from now on, concentrated on minimizing the risk to Guinness. He agreed to it subject to three conditions: the bid was to be well below the figure of 670p a share, Distillers' directors must agree it unanimously, and the costs should be underwritten by Distillers if the bid failed. This last condition, known as the 'merger agreement', would generate a great deal of discussion. The Distillers Board accepted it because they were desperate not to fall to Argyll. For myself, it was what reconciled me to the bid for Distillers which otherwise seemed appallingly risky. I was to be irritated, rather than worried, when a City colleague cast a good deal of doubt on whether the merger agreement could be enforced; this was at a stage when it was much too late to do anything about it. In retrospect I think my colleague was right; as we shall see, the legality of the arrangement was at best doubtful. Roger Seelig tried to get the proposition dropped, but Roux insisted, probably because he knew the Guinness Board would not have agreed the bid without it. But if Argyll had won Distillers, would it in sober truth have been bound to honour, out of the resources of the company which it now owned, an undertaking which had been entered into purely to frustrate it?

The reasoning behind the indemnity was that Guinness was entering the contest essentially at the request of Distillers, as a white knight. To risk the tens of millions that would be incurred if Guinness's offer proved abortive, swallowing up a noticeable part of a year's profits, could not be justified to the Guinness Board. Thomas Ward, separately it seems from Roux, also understood the Guinness directors well enough to know that we would only accept it if there was an indemnity for the fees. Everybody concerned seemed to be quite satisfied that the arrangement was proper; directors not in the know were blissfully unaware of the legal arrangements which were to go on behind the scenes, or of the existence of an influential body of opinion, notably in the DTI, which believed it illegal.

Distillers' last dim hope that they might remain independent was based on the possibility that the Office of Fair Trading might refer Argyll's bid to the Monopolies and Mergers Commission. It is hard to see why such a reference should have ever been thought likely, though it had been asked for by the Scottish Conservative and Unionist Industrial Committee. Argyll's existing spirits production would not make enough difference to Distillers' share of the market to create anything near a monopoly, and it was improbable that a Government dedicated to the free market should see anything detrimental to public interest in Distillers being controlled by a food retailer. Following the recommendation from the Office of Fair Trading (OFT) Leon Brittan, the Secretary of State for Trade and Industry, laid down on 9 January 1986 that the bid need not be referred. There were still doubts in the OFT, perhaps reflecting the Scottish Conservatives' view; according to Roux,[9] Saunders met an official of the OFT a few days later and received the impression that some of its members would like an alternative to Argyll as a bidder.

Even so, Argyll's bid was cleared, which meant that the Distillers Board had only one hope of escaping acquisition by Gulliver, and that was a merger with Guinness. Naturally they would rather have stayed independent, but a merger with a gentlemanly company which talked the same language ought to have left them playing a continuing part in management, perhaps even the preponderant one. Saunders would run things, of course; he had revitalized profits at Guinness, no doubt he would do the same with their businesses. Their Chairman, John Connell, hoped to chair the merged company with Saunders as Chief Executive.

In the Guinness camp it all looked rather different. Even at that stage a fairly full price was being paid for Distillers. If this was to be justified, the profits would need to be pushed up smartly and soon. Saunders, helped by Bain, would need the same sort of free hand that he had enjoyed at Guinness. There is no evidence that he, or any of his team, ever envisaged any other pattern. This need not necessarily mean that Saunders was determined from the outset to clear out all the Distillers directors; but it does indicate that, if they stayed, they would have to do as they were told. Yet Guinness still needed its takeover to look like a merger, essentially because of the indemnity on fees; the more apparent difference there was between Guinness's prospective relationship with Distillers and that of Argyll, the more likely it was that the indemnity arrangement would stick.

However, Charles Fraser, backed by Distillers' advisers Klein-worts, told Saunders that Connell would not be acceptable in Scotland as Chairman of the merged company.[10] They felt that the new Chairman should be brought in from outside and that he should be a Scotsman. The name of Sir Thomas Risk was suggested. A solicitor by training, and a former Chairman of the Standard Life Assurance Society, Risk was Governor of the Bank of Scotland, which had just become Distillers' main bank. It replaced the Royal Bank of Scotland, which Connell had sacked for having joined Gulliver's bid team. Risk met Saunders several times on 17 and 18 January. At first he turned down the offer. In the end, after discussing the matter with a colleague at the Bank and following considerable pressure from Saunders and Roger Seelig, he agreed to accept the Chairmanship. There is a difference here about the implied terms of the appointment. *Nightmare* has Saunders saying 'that what we now wanted was a Scottish Lord Iveagh'.[11] Perhaps Saunders did say this, but by Roger Seelig's account[12] Risk made it very clear that there was no prospect of his being anything of the sort. He produced a list of requirements which included placing the Company headquarters in Edinburgh and active care for the interests of Scotland, in the matter of redundancies in particular. The impression Seelig got was that Risk might easily want the interests of Scottish employment put before those of shareholders, when they conflicted. Risk also stipulated that most of the Company's banking business was to go to his Bank of Scotland. Much doubt was to be thrown later on the idea that he would ever have made this a requirement – the Bank of England was to describe it as 'unthinkable' – but that was at a later stage when Saunders was seeking reasons to explain why he no longer wanted Risk to be Chairman. The insinuation was that Risk had raised the question of the banking business as a new condition, which would indeed have been unworthy of a senior banker. To have mentioned it at his first encounter with Saunders, before agreeing to the Chairmanship, was not unreasonable. Risk was an active Governor, and it was natural that he should want to make sure that this new and possibly time-consuming appointment should bring some benefit to the bank.

The stipulation about the banking business was actually the easiest of Risk's conditions. Saunders must have known quite well that if Distillers was ever to earn enough to justify the price that Guinness was going to have to pay, there would have to be rationalization of management and of the works which would be likely to involve redundancies in Scotland on an appreciable scale. The idea of the Scottish headquarters for the Group was also not helpful. It seems extraordinary that Saunders did not see at this stage that these requirements would make it impossible to work with Risk. Rather than accept them, Saunders should either have looked for another Chairman or dropped the bid altogether.

Edward Cecil Guinness, First Earl of Iveagh and the first Chairman of the Company.
Photograph courtesy of the Honourable Rosaleen Mulji.

Ernest Guinness, Vice-Chairman.

Walter Guinness, first Lord Moyne,
Director of the Company and the
author's grandfather.

Rupert Guinness, Second Earl of Iveagh
and the second Chairman.

Bryan Guinness, Second Lord Moyne,
Vice-Chairman and the author's father.
All photographs courtesy of the
Honourable Rosaleen Mulji.

Enter the toucan:
an advertisement
from 1935.

If he can say as you can

Guinness is good for you

How grand to be a Toucan

Just think what Toucan do

The famous man with the girder advertisement from 1934. Both photographs reproduced
by kind permission of Guinness Brewing Worldwide Limited. All rights reserved.

Mass robbery: one of the best known of the menagerie series from 1939.
Reproduced by kind permission of Guinness Brewing Worldwide Limited.

Anthony Purssell, Ernest Saunders'
predecessor. Reproduced by kind
permission of Guinness Brewing
Worldwide Limited. All rights reserved.

Not the chairman: Sir Thomas Risk.
Trevor Humphries/Financial Times.

The adversary: James Gulliver,
Chairman of the Argyll group. Ashley
Ashwood/Financial Times.

Simon, Second Viscount Boyd,
Director. Photograph by Alec Lessin
courtesy of Viscount Boyd.

Benjamin, Third Earl of Iveagh, Chairman of the Company appearing at the trial, 12 March 1990. Financial Times photograph by Tony Andrews.

Thomas Ward and Ernest Saunders. Financial Times photograph.

THE LONDON EVENING
STANDARD

CITY PRICES

FRIDAY 9 JANUARY 1987 20P   INCORPORATING THE EVENING NEWS

'Poor man will have to accept it' says director Jonathan Guinness

SAUNDERS 'MUST STEP DOWN'

ERNEST SAUNDERS . . . resignation may fend off confrontation.

JONATHAN GUINNESS... "We could force his hand."

THE Guinness family wants Ernest Saunders to stand down as chairman of the famous drinks group.

They are happy for him to remain as chief executive while the DTI investigation into the company continues, but believe it is not in the company's interests that he should hold both jobs at this time.

Main board director Mr Jonathan Guinness tells me: "Saunders is a man under intense pressure and the pressure on him must be relieved.

Mr Guinness, who is with City bankers Leopold Joseph, comments: " It was perfectly sensible at the time (last summer) for him to take on the two roles.

But now Mr Guinness believes circumstances have changed. "The chairman's role at the moment is to fend off attacks from the media and organise the lawyers. In the

by David Hellier

meantime as chief executive he has a major business to run.

" The poor man will have to accept it."

Mr Guinness was talking ahead of a crucial meeting of the full board next Wednesday, when Saunders's position and other problems surrounding the company will be discussed.

Though other members of the family were not available for comment, it is understood the views expressed by Jonathan Guinness are shared by the other members.

These are believed to include Lord Iveagh, the former chairman of the company, and one of Mr Saunders's staunchest supporters in the past.

Assuming the family does not change its mind between now and the board meeting

next Wednesday it seems highly likely Mr Saunders will indeed have to relinquish the position of chairman.

It is also possible, some sources say, in the light of this significant shift in support that he will move to head off a confrontation by resigning the chairmanship before the meeting.

Sensible

Jonathan Guinness says the board, headed by Lord Iveagh, is taking the view that any sensible shareholder would hold at the present time.

Mr Guinness, who is also a director of City bankers Leopold Joseph, comments: " It was perfectly sensible at the time (last summer) for him to take on the two roles."

There is little doubt that the non-executive directors, appointed as watchdogs of the company, take the same view.

I believe they have been seeking to persuade Mr Saunders to step down as chairman all this week.

So far he seems opposed to the idea, but the Guinness family's views which I have outlined may change his mind.

"We could force his hand, but I do not think that will be necessary" said Mr Guinness. "He will see the force of this."

The Guinness family hopes a new chairman can be appointed who will be able to work with Saunders.

Mr Jonathan Guinness indicated that the family has already approached possible replacements.

The five independent "watchdog" directors, as they are known, were brought into the Guinness boardroom last August to placate City opinion after Mr Saunders had changed his mind about a plan to bring in an outside chairman, Scottish banker Sir Thomas Risk.

Gray — President Reagan is smiling after a successful operation — Yeh, well try asking him about the Nicaraguan operation

'What you can't tell police...'

by Dick Murray

THE FULL extent of Lambeth Council's lack of co-operation with local police is revealed today in confidential instructions given to town hall staff.

It tells staff that in dealing with council work they have no obligation to meet police and that police officers must, in the initial instance, always be refused permission to enter and search council premises. Staff are told that if police ask to enter council premises to carry out surveillance

duties "in no circumstances" should this be given—without first going through official channels in writing.

The instructions say: "If you are approached by the police for use of council premises for surveillance you must inform the named person /designated person in charge of department) immediately, who will then liaise with the director and chief (chairman) concerned and inform the Police Committee Support Unit.

"In no circumstances should council employees allow police to enter or use council premises.

Continued Page 2, Col 3

Southwark Crown Court, the scene of the trial. Photograph by J. B. Goldman.

Ford Open Prison. By kind permission of HM Prison Service.

On Saturday, 18 January *The Times* carried an article by Kenneth Fleet, a consistent Saunders supporter, saying that Guinness was about to bid for Distillers. Guilliver rang Saunders, at first succeeding only in reaching Thomas Ward. Ward denied the story, but promised to get Saunders to ring Gulliver. Saunders did ring, from his car telephone, and there are again two rather different accounts of what was said in *Nightmare* and *The Guinness Affair*. Both agree that the conversation was abruptly cut off. James has his father prevaricating: 'I told him that Guinness was not interested in making a *contested* bid for Distillers' (my italics).[13] This could mean that any Guinness bid would have to be agreed by the Distillers Board, in which case Saunders was telling no more than the truth. But in another sense, with Gulliver already on the scene, any bid for Distillers was inevitably contested anyway. Kochan and Pym, quoting Gulliver, have Saunders saying without equivocation: 'We are certainly not interested in bidding for Distillers.'[14] It was only two days before the bid was to be announced, so Saunders could not have admitted his intention to bid; it was odd that he rang back at all. But then why did Gulliver pursue him on the telephone? He must have known that, whatever the facts, he would get a denial. He did not believe the denial anyway. He sent observers to Morgan Grenfell's office in the City and Distillers' headquarters in St James's Square to see if there was any unusual activity on that Sunday, and in each case found that there was.

Nobody had told John Connell about the discussions with Risk until they were completed; Connell still thought he was going to be Chairman but was presented with the *fait accompli* by Saunders, who drove over to his house near Walton-on-Thames immediately after receiving Risk's acceptance late on the Saturday evening. Saunders informed Connell that his own advisers, as well as those of Guinness, regarded him as having no credibility. He might have complained that Saunders had been negotiating behind his back with his Company's advisers, and with Risk whom he knew personally anyway, without his being allowed any input. He would have been justified in protesting very sharply at this discourtesy; that he lay down under it indicates what a weak hand he was conscious of holding. Saunders pushed his luck, insisting that full agreement had to be reached by the following night, Sunday, or it was all off. Connell gave way again.

The following day the sixteen Distillers directors met at their St James's Square office at 3.30. They carried on into the night because Distillers' own lawyers insisted that the Board had to be unanimous. Some directors took a great deal of convincing, especially on Guinness's demand for a guarantee of its costs. One told Kochan and Pym: 'I knew of no point in which we had put anything to Saunders which he had accepted . . . we were actually bending the knee left, right and centre.'[15] His instinct was sounder than that of the majority who still thought that this was to be, in the words of another director quoted by Kochan and Pym, 'a benevolent meeting of two like-minded companies'.[16]

The Guinness Board were summoned to Portman Square on that Sunday evening to authorize the bid so that it could be announced the next day; they were obliged to hang around until they had word that Distillers had agreed it. I was not there, having an annual engagement in Spain. We had been told there might be a Board Meeting and I had sent my apologies. What was afoot? There had been Press speculation about Guinness bidding for Distillers; I felt and hoped that this was unlikely, just four months after winning Bells. On Monday morning my telephone rang; it was Alan Scrine, Company Secretary of Guinness. He told me the news.

'Oh, no!' I groaned.

TWELVE

The Battle in the Market

Guinness's terms, as they had to, outdid Argyll's by a long way, but were well below the 670p per share which Bain and the accountants had worked out as the amount Distillers was worth to Guinness. The terms were eight Guinness shares plus £7 in cash for every five Distillers, with a cash alternative of 585p per share. After the bid, Sir Thomas Risk was to be Chairman of the Company, John Connell Vice-Chairman, and Saunders Chief Executive. Besides them on the main Board would be four Guinness directors, including Benjamin Iveagh, and four from Distillers, namely David Connell (John's brother), Bill Spengler and Sir Nigel Broakes, together with Charles Fraser. The remaining Guinness and Distillers directors would sit on two subsidiary Boards, responsible for the two sides of the business. Company headquarters was to be located in Scotland.

The proposals about the Board did not delight me, for I was to be relegated to a directorship of the brewing subsidiary. Simon, Viscount Boyd, the Deputy Chairman, was still more put out. He had been assured that he would have a seat on the main Board, yet his name was not on the list as first published. With some difficulty he got hold of Saunders and was told that his omission had been a clerical error. Boyd was inclined not to believe this, in which, according to Alan Scrine, he was quite correct. All the same, when he made a fuss, Saunders rectified the omission and in *Nightmare* he still claims that it was a mistake. This is a small matter, no doubt, but worth noting. Boyd was becoming disenchanted in any case. He did not immediately resign from the Guinness Board, feeling that this would be wrong in the middle of a bid battle; but he did so on 9 May, three weeks after the final success of the bid. He and I had a talk; my feeling at the time was that he was being unadventurous. But his experience was not quite the same as mine. As Deputy Chairman he was in closer touch with the management than I was as an ordinary director, and the fact that he was kept in the dark about most things was rather more obvious to him. To me, what was important was the exciting future that Saunders seemed to promise for our Company; a future, which, let us not forget, did in fact materialize. Saunders' successor, Anthony Tennant, was to reap, admittedly with great skill and panache, where he had sown. No balanced view can be taken of the whole story unless this is borne in mind.

However, during the Guinness bid for Distillers this was only a hope for the future. When Saunders tried to get journalists to concentrate on his vision of a great drinks company bestriding the world with its brands, he very often did not succeed. He still seems to resent this; during his first Scottish Press conference after the bid was announced he complains that 'it was as if they were all reading from the same script, one penned by Argyll'.[1] The questions, when they were not about employment in Scotland, concerned the prospect that the Office of Fair Trading (OFT) would advise the Department of Trade and Industry (DTI) to refer the bid to the Monopolies and Mergers Commission (MMC). It is odd that Saunders does not see how natural it was that the journalists should concentrate on this subject; a referral to the MMC was entirely predictable. The combined share of the Scotch market of Guinness and Distillers would be about 38 per cent, and the normal procedure was to refer any merger that would give a company more than 25 per cent of the British market in any product. What is more, since the MMC always took many months to rule on any matter submitted to them, a referral would very likely mean that Argyll's bid would go through. All this was fairly obvious; there need have been no 'script penned by Argyll'. Saunders' surprise that the newspapers should concentrate on the problems of the bid and ignore his vision for the Company shows some loss of touch with the habits of the media. As an expert in handling the press he would normally have realized that journalists are always more interested in the present than in a hypothetical future, and they are also, and rightly, suspicious of anyone too insistent on talking his own book. As against this, though, the Saunders vision was in fact to catch on with certain financial journalists; they too would later suffer a certain loss of face which was only partly deserved because, as said, the vision did materialize: after Saunders' ruin.

The agreement that Distillers should meet the bid costs of Guinness did not feature in the offer document, but it soon leaked out and caused much bad publicity. The Association of British Insurers expressed disapproval, as did other investors' representatives. It simply seemed unfair, assuming that Guinness, like Argyll, was just a common or garden bidder. Even if the Guinness bid was in some sense a friendly merger that would result in a better company than would emerge if Argyll won, many observers thought the playing field should be level; after all, the greater merit of the Guinness bid could only be proved after it succeeded.

Not long after the costs agreement became known, Samuel Montagu complained about it to the Takeover Panel on behalf of Argyll. The Panel's executive rejected the complaint. Samuel Montagu appealed to the full Panel, who also endorsed the deal; according to Kochan and Pym, this was a close decision.[2] It would seem, in any case, to have been another odd one. For one thing, the Panel seem to have regarded the amount of Guinness's costs, then estimated at about £20 million, as not material. It is true that as a proportion of the size of the bid – £2 billion – the estimated costs only amount to 1 per cent. But surely the size of the bid is not the relevant figure. What is important is the effect on Guinness's profits of having to meet the costs in the event of failing. If the fees incurred through an abortive bid would be likely to discourage a bidder, then the question as to whether those costs are guaranteed is clearly significant. In round figures, £20 million represents 23 per cent of Guinness's pre-tax profits for 1985, which is hardly trivial.

Then again, Argyll had what was considered a very possible case under Section 151 of the Companies Act 1985, which forbids a company from helping anyone else to buy its own shares. Argyll was confident enough of its case, even after its rejection by the Takeover Panel, to issue a writ against Distillers on 6 February. This writ was dropped, there being little point in pursuing it at that stage, but in issuing it Argyll gave a very clear signal that if it won the bid battle it would take legal action to frustrate the costs indemnity; also, that it had been advised that such action would have some hope of success. This reinforces doubt as to whether in the event of Argyll winning the day Guinness would have recovered its bid costs. The final figure for these was to be (according to different estimates) at least £100 million and perhaps £120 million. The figure would have been much lower in the event of failure, but even if it had totalled, say, £60 million, Saunders and his team would have had a lot of explaining to do to shareholders.

It turned out much later that the legality of the merger agreement was more doubtful than any of us was led to believe at the time. The legal question turned on whether Distillers would be prohibited from paying Guinness's costs by Section 151 of the Companies Act, which bans a company from helping to buy its own shares except in certain circumstances. One exception is when the financial assistance is given as part of a larger purpose, and in good faith in the interests of the company concerned. Anthony Salz, of Freshfields, was of the opinion that the merger agreement did come within the larger purpose exemption, and he took counsel's advice from Anthony Morrit, QC, who said that it probably did. As a layman, one can see that this is plausible; after all, the merger agreement was designed to promote a reorganization which the Distillers Board were genuinely of the opinion would be beneficial. All the same, there was enough worry in the Distillers camp that perhaps the exemption did not apply for the Distillers Board to ask for, and get, the promise of an indemnity from Guinness in the region of £25 million. Naturally none of us outside directors was told anything about this. In my case, at least, I should have exploded; not merely because of the amount involved, but because to engage in a transaction which is sufficiently doubtful for an arrangement of this kind to be thought necessary is hardly responsible. Since it was only the merger agreement that induced me to tolerate the Distillers bid at all, that would have been the end of my support for Saunders.

There was worse. Among those who believed that the merger agreement was illegal was Philip Bovey, a solicitor who had just been appointed Deputy Director of the Department of Trade and Industry. He had told the Takeover Panel of his views, and later seen Anthony Salz of Freshfields to whom, without completely committing himself, he gave the impression that his inclination was to the Argyll view of the matter.[3] This should have been taken much more seriously than it was, because it showed that the DTI were against the merger agreement and would, accordingly, be inclined to make difficulties. Their hostility to Saunders dates from then. But since Guinness's bid costs, following an increased offer price in February 1987, had escalated to around £47 million, Saunders and his team probably thought they had no option but to go on. They were playing for high stakes with the Company's money.

Besides issuing its writ on 6 February, Argyll increased its offer for Distillers, making it £2.3 billion which was just £100 million ahead of Guinness's figure. At the same time the Argyll team attacked Guinness's share price; according to Olivier Roux,[4] a jobber in the market was telephoned after hours, presumably with a large selling order for Guinness, with the result that the shares were marked down from 285p to 276p. This seems to have been the first blow in the market battle which was to involve Guinness in a share support operation of such enormous proportions. It did not catch Guinness unprepared. According to Roux, Saunders had already in December, before the bid, discussed market tactics with Roger Seelig of Morgan Grenfell and Anthony Salz of Freshfields.[5] On this occasion, though, the Guinness side seem to have been caught napping. Roux telephoned Cazenoves who organized support.

Five days later, on 11 February, the OFT recommended to the DTI that Guinness's bid should be referred to the MMC. On the criterion of British market share alone this was inevitable; and market share, at the time, was flavour of the month for the OFT in these matters. Some time before, in July 1984, Norman Tebbit as DTI Secretary of State had made a statement which amounted to ruling that a threat to competition was the only consideration to be borne in mind by the MMC when considering a possible merger. This was in line with the free market or *laissez-faire* theory of economics in which Mrs Thatcher's Government on the whole believed. Guinness's prospects of avoiding a referral depended on the way in which this was interpreted. If competition within the UK market was meant, the case was clear; by the standards laid down, the proposed Guinness–Distillers combination was a threat and should be referred. Any argument to the contrary would be a blatant case of special pleading. On the other hand, whisky was a product not just for the UK market but for the world market. Most went abroad, and common sense suggests that it would be foolish to insist on the industry in Britain remaining fragmented and slackly run simply so as to maintain competition within this one smallish country. Such blind adherence to free-market theory would indeed make the Government a slave to dogma, as the opposition always accused. Whatever applied in the British market, if Scotch whisky was to compete in the world market it needed a really strong combine with the right expertise. The plausible argument was advanced that neither Distillers by itself, nor Distillers in combination with a chain of supermarkets, was likely to do as well as a group in which the brands and resources of Distillers were managed by Saunders. He had proved by his recent record that he possessed the expertise to make good use of brand names and their mystique all over the world. The case was not only put privately to the decision-makers, but also announced to the public in the form of a Press advertising campaign. Saunders signed one such advertisement: 'Once in every decade or so there comes a chance to create something really significant on an international scale. Something which is bigger, by virtue of its name and what it is, than all its parts put together . . . Something which is a cornerstone of Great Britain Ltd in the international market place. Something which not only leads the way to long-term prosperity but which also creates wealth and jobs . . .' With this positive approach were allied other advertisements designed to make the flesh creep; in one there was a table of international whisky brands showing that the Japanese Suntory was world market leader: 'A chilling statistic for those of us who remember the British motor-cycle'. Guinness's own success, under Saunders, was highlighted in another advertisement; clearly this was the management needed to safeguard this vital British export industry.

This argument might have been expected to be the more telling in that neither everyone in the Government nor, by any means, all civil servants, had been intellectually won over to *laissez-faire*; Sir Gordon Borrie himself, the head of the OFT, has now been made a peer and sits on the Labour benches in the House of Lords. Saunders was to tell James: 'We answered all the OFT's questions, and we were getting favourable indications that they were sympathetic to the international approach.'[6] In these circumstances the decision to recommend a referral came as a blow.

For the moment it was still only a recommendation. The Guinness Board met on 13 February and authorized Saunders to increase the bid to a maximum of 670p, this being, it will be remembered, the figure that Bain worked out on the conservative basis insisted on by Roux as the highest at which a Guinness bid for Distillers would add to Guinness's earnings per share. The Board agreed to this but expressed caution; particularly in view of the obstacles that were appearing, we did not give 'victory' in the bid an absolute priority. If I intervened at this meeting – I am not sure whether I did or not – it was certainly in this sense.

The decision as to whether to refer the bid to the MMC was now up to the Secretary of State for Trade and Industry, who at the time happened to be Paul Channon. He had been recently appointed in succession to Leon Brittan who had resigned following the tangled affair of Westland Aviation. Channon's appointment, when announced, had depressed Saunders: 'Channon was related to the Guinness family and would want to demonstrate his impartiality by stabbing us in the front as well as in the back.'[7] This worry was unjustified; what Channon did, as was entirely proper, was to rule himself out of deciding and hand the matter over to his junior minister, Geoffrey Pattie. Pattie, on 14 February, followed the OFT's recommendation and referred the bid; to have overruled the OFT woud have been an exceptional act which would have required a strong and obvious case to be made out for it. Neither Channon nor, indeed, Brittan could have done very differently without sticking out their necks further than it is customary for ministers to do; that they might have acted with regret is beside the point.

Yet Guinness, it is clear, had not expected a referral. Saunders and his supporters thought their assiduous lobbying had succeeded. Even before the announcement of the bid, Thomas Ward had assured Charles Fraser that there was no need to worry about the OFT.[8] Roger Seelig told the *Financial Times*: 'We clearly would not have embarked on this course without taking full benefit of the informal guidance procedures of the OFT.'[9] The implication here is that some fairly strong indication, even perhaps an informal assurance, had been given at that stage. In fact it would have been risky to the point of irresponsibility to proceed with a bid that was certain to be fiercely contested without having received something of the sort.

Actually Saunders' representations did have their effect. What happened next indicates that the OFT's recommendation to refer was distinctly reluctant. There may even have been a tinge of guilt that Guinness had been led on by the 'informal procedures'. Charles Fraser told Saunders what to do. He was a director of United Biscuits, which was the subject of a bid by Imperial Group. This had been referred, and replaced with a reverse bid by United Biscuits for Imperial. To prevent another referral, United Biscuits had put Golden Wonder and its brand of crisps up for sale. The essential requirement was that any new bid should not create the same dominance of the market as the old one; which meant in practice that Guinness/Distillers should undertake to dispose of one or more of its whisky brands. The same idea of selling off some brands was suggested to Thomas Ward by Roger Seelig, who also knew about the United Biscuits moves because Morgan Grenfell acted for that company. Fraser recommended two specialist counsel, Jeremy Lever and John Swift, to advise.

With Swift and Bill Young of Bain, Saunders went to see Sir Godfray Le Quesne, a judge who was Chairman of the MMC, to ask that the first bid be allowed to lapse; this was necessary if a second bid could be validly made. This first interview on 17 February was followed by more on the 18th and 19th, to which, besides Swift, Saunders brought Seelig and Ward. *Nightmare* only mentions the first interview and has it going well; Le Quesne and Swift knew and liked each other, so Saunders could more or less leave it to them to sort matters out. Kochan and Pym give a rather different account. 'The two sides were hardly equally matched. On the one side was the judge acting by himself and without other members of his commission. On the other was the Saunders entourage of John Swift, Ward, and Seelig, applying 'unrelenting pressure', wearing down the '62-year-old judge' ('poor old chap' is the subtext here) with 'persuasion and table-banging, smiling and threats' and with no breaks for coffee, lunch or dinner.[10] This seems far-fetched; Le Quesne, after all, was in charge and would have decided when to take breaks. Had Saunders and the others behaved in the offensive way described, he could have sent them all packing; they were the ones who were soliciting a favour. For much of the colour in their description Kochan and Pym rely on Sir Alex Fletcher, a former minister and adviser at the time to Argyll; an unusual choice of informant in that he was not at any of the meetings himself. Roger Seelig, who was, has told the author that the Guinness team were 'deferential, though perhaps rather pushy in exploring the boundaries'.[11]

Late in the afternoon of 19 February the Saunders team came away with what they wanted. The argument that had won Le Quesne over was that if he disallowed the new bid it would hand Distillers over to Argyll, depriving Distillers' shareholders of the choice between different managements and of the prospect of getting yet more for their shares.

That same evening there was a meeting in the Guinness offices at Portman Square. Roux, with the Guinness financial team, had put together the conditions of a new bid including the disposal of certain brands. Saunders, Roux, Ward and the others were joined by four directors of Morgan Grenfell, including Reeves and Seelig, and David Mayhew from Cazenove. Saunders was reluctant to go ahead then and there with the new bid; he wanted time to think about it. The Morgan Grenfell contingent told him this was not on. If the new bid was not made the very next morning, it was likely that the Guinness share price would fall, perhaps by as much as 10 per cent. This would make the bid that much more expensive in terms of Guinness shares and would probably make it impossible to underwrite. Both Reeves and Seelig were very emphatic on this. Saunders, in *Nightmare*, tells a rather different story; his line is that he was not just hesitant, but definitely wanted to drop the bid. 'I had had enough. I had kept my doubts to myself before, but this time I expressed them to the group . . . I saw ahead the nightmare of more OFT lobbying to get this new bid through, with the possibility that the press and the Scots lobby might get us referred again.'[12] By his account the Morgan Grenfell team, backed by Ward, argued furiously in favour of going on. Roger Seelig, according to Saunders at his trial, was 'impassioned and powerful'.[13] Seelig denies this on the grounds that it would have been improper at that stage for Morgan Grenfell to push an unwilling Saunders into making a bid. It is true that, as Saunders puts it, 'the bank could no doubt see the millions of pounds in fees disappearing',[14] and this was particularly important for the Morgan Grenfell directors personally as it would affect the price at which shares in their company could be issued later in the year, as was planned. Certainly the Morgan Grenfell people would have been disappointed if the bid had not gone ahead, and this may have contributed to the heat with which Reeves and his colleagues argued against Saunders' request for time to think about it. However, they would have taken a serious risk in pressing Saunders, before witnesses, to go on with the bid if he had shown positive reluctance as opposed to hesitancy. Then again, if Saunders had wanted to withdraw rather than merely delay, Roux would scarcely have remained silent. He was against the bid at all stages, and if Saunders had really turned against it, Roux would have spoken out in his support. As it was he remained, in Saunders' expression, inscrutable.

This view is corroborated by the fact that a few days later, on 25 February, Roux was to tell John Theroux of Bains that he was uneasy about the way the bid was developing and to ask to be removed from Guinness. Theroux told him to stay there and work hard.[15]

To go back to the meeting on the 19th, Saunders says he rang Benjamin Iveagh to tell him that Guinness had permission to make another bid but that he did not want to do so. He expected Iveagh to back him in this view, but instead found that Benjamin asked him to think again. He then says he rang Simon Boyd who 'was even stronger than Iveagh, talking about duty and would I think about it again?' Simon has no recollection of being telephoned and adds: 'Indeed it would have been very uncharacteristic if he had asked my opinion about anything so important. What I do clearly remember . . . was that the referral represented a heaven-sent opportunity to get out of something which I had a gut feeling was proving much more difficult and complicated than we had expected.'[16] Saunders says he then rang Benjamin again and said that if the new bid did go ahead he would need Thomas Ward in London to help him, and that Ward 'would want us to make it worth his while financially'. Iveagh said the costs were underwritten, 'so what did it matter?' It is impossible to check up on either of Saunders' conversations with Benjamin, because the latter is dead; but the exchange about Ward's remuneration, if accurate, goes rather little of the way towards justifying any claim that Saunders had Board authorization to give Ward a fee of £5.2 million for his efforts.

Seelig does remember Saunders going out of the room to telephone; it is likely that he rang Benjamin to say Morgan Grenfell was insisting that the bid be launched next morning. It has to be said, too, that although one must doubt the literal accuracy of Saunders' account, it can be allowed to have a certain subliminal truth; the fact that he wanted time to consider before launching the new bid shows that he did have doubts, and the fact that the Morgan Grenfell team gave in such forceful terms their advice that it was 'now or never' shows that they were desperate for the bid to go ahead.

The following day, 20 February, Guinness came out with its new bid. The value was £2.35 billion, about £50 million more than the last Argyll offer, and the Company committed itself to sell enough whisky brands to get the prospective share of the UK market down to 25 per cent. The Annual General Meeting of Guinness took place on 27 February; it was very positive. Saunders asked shareholders to write to their MPs, to the OFT, and to Mrs Thatcher as Prime Minister to urge that the new bid be cleared. But on 3 March, when the formal document for the new bid was issued, Saunders gave a Press conference at Portman Square, which was 'the most awful meeting I had had to cope with. You would think that I was facing the Argyll press corps . . . I was treated to a barrage of hostile and critical questions.'[17] It is hard to see just why the atmosphere should have been so bad at that exact moment, except that the impression was growing that Saunders was being allowed to get away with too much. Saunders took it as an insult rather than a warning.

It was not certain that the promise to get the prospective market share for whisky in the United Kingdom down to 25 per cent would suffice to gain clearance of the new bid from the OFT: Borrie refused to give any indication on this matter before seeing the proposals in detail. It just had to be assumed that the sale would suffice for this purpose. The simplest way of disposing of enough market share would have been simply to sell off Bells, but Saunders would not do this. He recognized that Miquel had left Bells in exceptionally good order, with a good brand, an excellent industrial operation and a well-drilled sales force. Ward, much of whose function at this time concerned negotiations with the Distillers Board, persuaded David Connell to agree the sale of four brands from Distillers – Claymore, Haig Gold Label, Buchanan Blend and John Barr. One, Real Mackenzie, was to come from Bells.

There was some trouble about Real Mackenzie because its sale contravened an undertaking given during the Bells takeover. Lord

Spens, still indignant on behalf of his client Miquel, wrote to the *Financial Times* about Guinness 'flagrantly' abandoning its promises 'in the pursuit of naked ambition'.[18] In the light of what was known at the time, Lord Spens's protest seemed over the top. It was unlikely that anyone would actually suffer through the disposal of Real Mackenzie, and the time to have made this protest would have been when, and if, the buyer of the brand was shown to be inflicting redundancies or other evils. Then why did Lord Spens sound off like this? Like the journalists who were offensive to Saunders at the Portman Square Press conference, he had a feeling that there was something not quite right, something 'bent', in the attitude of the Guinness team. It is true that at that exact stage, even with total knowledge, there could have been only minor criticism of their actual behaviour in the Distillers bid. The serious breaches of convention and ethics still lay ahead. But a bent attitude leads, under stress, to bent behaviour; and Spens' letter now looks prescient.

The Argyll team reacted to Saunders' success with the MMC by going to law yet again. They asked the High Court for a judicial review to challenge Le Quesne's ruling; when this was turned down they went to the Court of Appeal. Here too they failed, but Sir John Donaldson, the Master of the Rolls, giving his judgement on 10 March, criticized Le Quesne for taking on his own the decision to allow the first bid to lapse. He ought, said Donaldson, to have called in his colleagues on the Commission of which he was Chairman. Donaldson's reason for nevertheless allowing the decision to stand was that 'deals had already been made that depended on the decision'. This implies that Le Quesne's dereliction cannot in his view have been really serious, for otherwise Donaldson would hardly have failed to give it preference over commercial considerations. He perhaps had in mind, though he does not seem to have made, the rather obvious point that since the first bid following referral was in practice dead, it would hardly be constructive not to allow it to be buried.

Who was to buy the five whisky brands that would be sold? Saunders suggested that they might be 'parked' with Morgan Grenfell who could then sell them off at leisure, but it soon became clear that the OFT would not allow this; it would have looked altogether too artificial. Saunders then approached Lonrho which owned a whisky distiller, Whyte & Mackay. Lonrho's Chief Executive, Tiny Rowland, was always game for a juicy deal. Agreement was soon reached. Not surprisingly, given the pressure of time on Guinness and Distillers, the price was extremely low: £3.5 million. How much this bargain basement sale added to the final cost of the Distillers bid is impossible to calculate exactly, but the amount must be appreciable; the short-fall to both Guinness and Distillers of the sum received, compared with the real value of the brands, whatever this was, constituted in effect another bid cost. Again the stakes edged upwards.

It is hard to see why an unnamed observer quoted by Kochan and Pym should have described this sale as a 'sleazy little deal';[19] it was done openly, its special purpose was public. The low price was determined, as prices of deals are apt to be determined, by the relative positions of the participants: in this case by the fact that the seller was in a tearing hurry. Those looking for sleaze in this affair can find plenty elsewhere; there is no point in attributing it where it is not applicable. As the battle hotted up, each side accused the other while indulging in its own low blows. Someone discovered, and told the *Observer*, that James Gulliver's *Who's Who* entry incorrectly stated that he had been educated at Harvard; he had only taken a three-week course in marketing there. (Scott Fitzgerald's Great Gatsby is similarly known as an 'Oxford Man', but then it is he himself who reveals that he spent only a few weeks at Oxford.) It was a nine-minute wonder. Gulliver launched a series of advertisements designed to knock Guinness; one of them showed a dustbin full of Guinness's main brands. This upset Saunders; 'You toucha my brands, I smasha your face' was his motto. He was determined to sue Argyll for the insult. Freshfields, Guinness's usual legal advisers, proved too lukewarm for him on this matter; he bypassed them and instructed Sir David Napley, of Kingsley Napley, to sue both in Britain and the United States. Napley issued writs such as one sometimes gets when fighting a parliamentary election, which have little real significance. I received one once when I was a candidate and ran round to my agent with it. 'Don't bother,' he said, 'this happens all the time at elections. You won't hear any more after it's over.' Sure enough, I did not; and in the matter of Argyll's advertisements Freshfields were right to be sceptical. Guinness's cases against the advertisements were quietly dropped.

On 21 March Sir Gordon Borrie gave the required assurance that he would not recommend the new bid for reference to the MMC. The day before, Saunders was told that this would happen. He consulted with Morgan Grenfell and the other advisers as to whether, if Argyll increased its offer, as it was almost certain to do, Guinness should match or outbid it. Saunders and Ward both wanted to increase the bid, but Seelig, for Morgan Grenfell, advised against doing this. He said that at the level the contest had now reached, an increased price for Distillers in terms of Guinness shares would simply make the price of Guinness shares fall commensurately, leaving the bid no more attractive to Distillers' shareholders, while Guinness's shareholders would be left with a lower proportion of the combined Company, and would therefore suffer. This was fairly obvious; I remember my intense relief at a Board Meeting on 10 April when I spoke against raising the bid at the last minute, and Saunders said it had been decided not to do so. Argyll did indeed increase its bid, valuing Distillers at £2.5 billion, but Guinness did not respond, preferring, as now seems clear, to rely on the buying power of its supporters to keep its bid ahead.

Thus in the last days of March 1986 the contest moved to the stock market. Distillers' shareholders could choose between

Guinness offering shares, at a price around 325p, worth about 705p per Distillers share, with a cash alternative of 630p, and Argylll, whose share offer was worth just under 700p but with a cash alternative higher than Guinness's, at 670p. Since both cash alternatives were below the value of the share offers, it may be thought that the difference in favour of Argyll was only of academic importance; this was not altogether the case, however, as would soon be apparent.

It is certain that both sides engaged in market support operations, but there is an imbalance in the information available. On the Guinness side it has been established that the Company paid large fees that were kept confidential, not least from its auditors, which have mostly been repaid. Both the fact that the fees were secret, and the fact that the recipients repaid them when they became known, indicate that there was thought to be something wrong with them. On the Argyll side, though, much less is known. It is certain that the market was supported, but allegations of impropriety have been only vague, and none has been investigated. Support of a market is not of itself improper; it was certainly evident to me at the time that support was taking place on both sides. The extent to which this created a false market is mitigated by the fact that it was well known, and well aired, in the Press: the *Birmingham Post* said on 7 April that 'both sides will make sure there is somebody in the market propping up their shares all the way', and the *Scotsman*, on 14 April, 'The share prices of both bidders are now no more the result of pure market forces than the price Mrs Thatcher got for British Telecom or the outcome of your average wrestling match on TV.' Or, one may add, the outcome of the boxing match in the Damon Runyon story where each contestant has bet on the other and each, accordingly, unleashes low blows so as to be disqualified.

On Guinness's side it seems that the market support was arranged in reaction to events, not planned beforehand. As the battle progressed, more and more share purchases were required to keep shares in Guinness at a level where its bid was competitive with Argyll's. The price had risen to a point where the prudent investor would have been inclined to take his money and run, given all the uncertainties. Some private shareholders will have been kept in by a reluctance to incur capital gains tax; this factor cannot be measured, but it is likely that without it the market support operations would have needed to be several million pounds greater.

Among the largest buyers of Guinness shares were Schenley Industries and Bank Leu. Schenley was an American whisky distributor which dealt in some of Distillers' products, and whose President was Meshulam Riklis. Schenley invested about £60 million in Guinness shares during the bid; and later, in November 1986, was given the distribution contract for Dewar's whisky. At the end of the bid Schenley had more than 5 per cent of Guinness, which under the Companies Act it ought to have declared, but did not. Schenley was already mentioned as a likely market supporter of Guinness in *The Times* of 21 March 1986, though this was probably no more than a shrewd guess based on the known fact that it distributed Dewar's whisky in the United States. *The Times* coupled its name with other companies that as far as is known were not involved at all. These were Nestlé as Saunders' former employers, Lonrho as beneficiaries of the forced sale of the whisky brands, and the French drinks group Pernod.

Nobody at this stage mentioned Bank Leu. This Swiss private bank had as its Chairman Arthur Fuerer, a friend of Saunders whom he had brought on to the Guinness Board. Bank Leu bought £130 million worth of stock altogether, some during the battle, some afterwards to keep the price up. It was guaranteed against loss on a very large scale. Nor, at this stage, did they mention a third important supporter, the American arbitrageur Ivan Boesky, at that time regarded as something of a magician in New York.

Other supporters were organized by Sir Jack Lyons, the consultant to Bain who was a personal friend of Mrs Thatcher, and Anthony Parnes, the stockbroker who as seen in chapter 10 was attached as a 'half-commission man' to the firm Alexanders Laing and Cruikshank. The official broker to the bid was Cazenove, but Parnes was employed on a confidential basis both to report what the market was saying and also to help recruit buyers. He had good contacts in the Jewish community, to which he himself belonged. Lyons and Parnes introduced two important supporters. One was Gerald Ronson and his Heron Group, which was one of the largest privately owned concerns in Britain; he and his companies bought about £25 million worth of Guinness shares against a fee and an indemnity against loss. The other was Ephraim Margulies, Chairman of the commodity company Berisfords which owns British Sugar Corporation. He and his group supported the bid to the tune of about £15 million. In addition, Roger Seelig introduced a Swiss resident, Mrs Seulberger-Simon, who through Cazenove bought about £17 million worth of Guinness shares. She too received a fee and an indemnity.

Much of the support seems to have been arranged at a moment's notice under the stress of day-to-day market activities; one of the stockbrokers, perhaps normally Parnes, would report that a couple of million Guinness shares needed to be absorbed, and then one of the influential 'friends' of the Company – Parnes himself, Sir Jack Lyons, or someone else – would arrange for an investor such as Gerald Ronson to come up with the money: if necessary on the basis that if they eventually lost on the deal they would be indemnified.

The Bank of Vienna, then known as the Zentralsparkasse und Kommerzialbank Wien, or Z-Bank, bought just under £2 millions' worth. In the context of the other amounts we have mentioned this was too small to matter; had anyone sat back and considered the implications, however, they would have realized that it was vital to keep the number of separate deals as low as possible because each one was liable to cause its own problems, and the more there were, the more likely it was that problems would surface. That the Z-Bank should have been roped in for such a comparatively minor amount is an indication that the support operation was conducted reactively, rather than as the result of a strategy.

On 18 April 1986 Guinness secured just over 50 per cent of Distillers and declared its bid unconditional. The market deal that seems to have turned the trick was Bank Leu's purchase of 10 million Distillers shares from Warburg Investment Management on 17 April. In connection with this last-minute deal it became apparent that Argyll's higher cash alternative had a certain importance, even though both cash alternatives were below the offers in shares. Under the takeover rules, the bidders or their supporters were not permitted to offer more than their respective cash alternatives. When the block came on offer, Samuel Montagu, on Argyll's behalf, at once offered the 660p they were permitted to bid. Guinness or its supporters were limited to 630p. However, Cazenove offered 700p per share and secured the block. Because of Cazenove's known connection with Guinness, Montagu complained to the Takeover Panel, which was unable to ascertain who the buyer was; it accordingly accepted that there was no connection with Guinness, and rejected the complaint. Much later, the name of Bank Leu emerged, and later still it was learnt that the purchase was in effect on behalf of Guinness. Comment is superfluous.

Immediately after securing control of Distillers, the Company made arrangements to buy in about 9 per cent of the merged Company in the form of the holding of Distillers shares accumulated by Morgan Grenfell. The shares would be cancelled, and would therefore no longer overhang the market. This was a perfectly legal move, provided it was made public and had the formal consent of shareholders, which was obtained. The operation, costing £350 million, was arranged quickly: it was announced on

22 April. It seemed likely to stabilize the market in the shares, and did so for a time. I also presumed that it would absorb all the loose shares that, as was perfectly obvious, the bid had generated.

For that, however, it was wholly inadequate. The proportion of the combined Company held by supporters who would wish to sell was not 9 per cent but certainly more than 20 per cent. This made Saunders' position distinctly rickety. For it to become secure, it was essential that the Guinness share price should remain at a level where those who had bought against an indemnity could sell without having to call on it. Whether Saunders saw quite how crucial this was is doubtful. Certainly he made efforts to generate favourable publicity and keep the price up, and in this he was for a time successful in terms of brokers' recommendations. However, what he did during the next few months wrecked the effort. He had made many enemies; it was crucial that he should make no more. Yet he proceeded to do just that.

THIRTEEN

Making Enemies

After succeeding in the bid, Saunders behaved in a notably high-handed way. This attracted bitter criticism, which had nothing to do with the market support operation, because those details were still unknown. The argument between him and his detractors was one in which both sides, in their terms, were right. The Saunders line was that he had paid a top price for Distillers and it was crucial that the forecast profits for the combine should be realized immediately. This worry was perfectly genuine; Roux's original maximum figure of 670p per Distillers share had been left well behind in the heat of battle. There had to be a rapid change in the way Distillers was operated; after all, it was precisely the existing inefficiency of the operation which had made the takeover possible and necessary. The critics countered that Saunders had secured control of Distillers subject to conditions which he agreed to. If he disregarded these conditions, he broke his word. Saunders' task, therefore, if it was to be carried out properly, was more complex than he would admit; he had to make Distillers profitable, but also to honour his commitments.

Or at least the essential ones; for he could certainly have got away with some modifications. There was one alteration in particular which he made with my encouragement. He had promised to change the name of the company and was tinkering with neutral-sounding ones like United Brands. I said, 'Ernest, please think again about the Company's name. Guinness happens to be the name of one of our major brands. Every mention of the Company, at present, advertises that brand. Don't throw this away; and don't think, either, that I am making this point out of sentimentality.' He said he agreed with my reasoning; he had probably already decided to retain the name anyway, for this was very much in line with his thinking. Nobody seriously objected; what's in a name?

But Saunders was not going to content himself with selective or cautious deviations from what he had promised. One after the other, he repudiated all those arrangements set out in the offer document which limited his absolute power to do what he liked. Anger mounted at this, especially but not only among the Scots, and the matter became known as the Risk Affair because comment centred on the rejection of Sir Thomas Risk as Chairman. There was also much indignation north of the border when it became known that the headquarters was not after all to be in Scotland. Much of this feeling was based on the view that offer documents should be regarded as inviolable; the word 'sanctity' was used. In retrospect it seems to me that Saunders' critics did not make the best of their case. It was fairly easy to maintain, after Guinness had won Distillers, that it was the duty of the directors to run the Company in the interest of share-holders as they saw it at the time; that where they perceived this interest to conflict with undertakings in a bid document, they had not just the right but the duty to disregard the undertakings. Saunders obtained a legal opinion to this effect from Freshfields, and indeed as a general proposition it must be the case that the present interest of shareholders can override past undertakings. Circumstances do change.

The sanctity of undertakings made in offer documents, then, is a matter of morality rather than law. This is not to belittle it; morality is older than the law, and in particular the principle that one ought to keep one's word, even when not bound to do so by having signed a contract, is an important foundation of civilized behaviour. In the specific case of takeover documents, Hamish McRae put the matter neatly in the *Guardian*: 'If you say in an offer document that you plan to do certain things with a company should you take it over, then . . . you are surely obliged to carry these out . . . the practical issue is that if you do not accept this principle the offer document in a takeover bid would become wholly worthless. Shareholders would be forced to make up their minds . . . on the basis of information to which they could attach no credibility whatsoever . . .'[1] In practice, though, this general principle can come into conflict with other considerations. Sir Nicholas Goodison, Chairman of the Stock Exchange, was to put it like this: 'There are occasions, however rare, when a board finds it necessary to depart from the precise terms of intentions stated in listing particulars.'[2] The insistence by Saunders' critics on sanctity as a general principle came over as rather pedantic; in the case of Sir Thomas Risk, many felt that if he and Saunders did not get on he had better not be appointed. As to the dropping of the proposal to situate the Company headquarters in Scotland, this was not reversed after Saunders' fall, even though his successor, Sir Norman Macfarlane, was very consciously a Scot.

Where the offer document ought to have been respected was in the matter of the Distillers directors. It was they, much more than Risk, who had a grievance when Saunders decided to disregard it. Risk simply received an offer which was then withdrawn; he had reason to feel sore, but he suffered no injury. The Distillers directors did suffer injury. They were blatantly double-crossed. Their support for Guinness against Argyll, extending to a guarantee of costs without which Guinness could not have moved, was given in consideration for an assurance that they would retain a leading role in the combined Company. By behaving exactly as Gulliver would have done had he won the battle, Saunders dishonoured this bargain. The reason that Saunders' critics in the media did not highlight this is that the

Distillers directors were discredited. On the whole the media do not give much space to losers, especially gentlemanly ones. In particular, too, they were discredited in Scotland, where Saunders' bitterest opponents were to be found; we remember that it was Charles Fraser, who of all Saunders' advisers was probably most in touch with Scottish opinion, who told him that John Connell was not acceptable as Chairman of the combined Company and who first put Risk's name forward. Even so, since it was the Distillers directors who were genuinely aggrieved by Saunders' actions, to disregard their plight was to give an advantage to Saunders in formal argument.

The advantage was misleading, for most people knew perfectly well that he had done wrong. John Chiene of Wood Mackenzie came out with it; begging Saunders at the last minute to think again, he said, 'You may well get away with it this time. But make one mistake after that and the City will be on you like a ton of bricks. You'll be eating up all the goodwill.'[3] Much the same point was made in the Lex column in the *Financial Times* after Saunders' new proposals were made public: 'It will be a long time before anyone loses such accumulated City goodwill in the space of a day as Mr Saunders has achieved by a shameless divergence from the terms of the "merger" with Distillers.'

Saunders showed himself curiously obtuse in this matter; he never really saw what the fuss was about and there is little sign that he sees it even now. This is partly because disapproval of him was never unanimous; he had influential defenders right to the end, not only in the financial Press but in the business community. His cavalier attitude may also owe something to the influence of Thomas Ward, who as an American corporate lawyer was accustomed to a business atmosphere where if you have the legal right to do something, and you think it is to your advantage, you just do it. In law, the Distillers directors were powerless; they had already given the game away in January. As to the sanctity of the offer document, Freshfields' opinion was clearcut: Guinness could disregard it.

But this was a purely legal opinion; it had nothing to do with whether what Saunders proposed to do was morally acceptable or, more to the point, whether it was advisable. For most people have moral standards on which there is a measure of agreement; to be seen breaching them is to excite disapproval which can translate into a very real threat. Saunders' non-legal advisers were categoric. Wood Mackenzie resigned as Guinness's stockbrokers. Even more significant, though, was the attitude of Morgan Grenfell. Saunders must have known that this firm, which had masterminded the bid and repeatedly gone as close as possible to the limits of what was permissible, would not press him so hard on this point unless there was substantial reason. It is frankly amazing that he did not take their attitude as the ultimate red light. Charles Fraser, who had done so much to smooth Saunders' way in Scotland, was horrified. Again and again these advisers begged Saunders to rethink before it was too late. He paid no attention.

His own case, as expressed in *Nightmare*, is that he could do nothing else. Guinness executives had to be put in charge of the Distillers businesses immediately; Vic Steel, who had been running Bells, was given the drinks, and Shaun Dowling took esponsibility for all other Distillers interests. Bain were introduced to look at costs in detail, as they had at Guinness. Kochan and Pym produce the striking image of 'the Bain people . . . swarming all over the bloated body of the company'.[4] Naturally this was resented, as it had been at Guinness. Saunders says in *Nightmare* that at one conference 'a number of Distillers managers came up with the most extraordinary, aggressive and arrogant remarks to me about how I would never get the changes through, and I didn't know what I was up against'.[5] One is reminded of Saunders' account of his reception when he went round to J. Walter Thompson to shake up the Guinness advertising. Did the managers in fact dare to talk to the new boss in this way? If they did, it shows that they were accustomed to being run on a loose rein. The way it looked when one was on the receiving end is shown by what one Distillers man told Kochan and Pym: 'He was so awful; instead of saying we're all members of a new team and basically going forward together, he said, "You're now members of the Guinness company and I will be sending out instructions to you on how you will conduct yourselves." '[6]

Saunders talks of being anxious about the results because the first profits announcement would have to be made in November. This was particularly the case since Distillers, to make their figures look better, had according to him been 'loading' sales to the United States, persuading the distributors to take more than usual and more than was being consumed. Clearly this would have to be followed by a period when deliveries, and accordingly profits, were below the average. The urgency of dealing with all these matters, and in particular of getting costs down, meant that they had to be given priority. 'I thought we could deal with the Board, the administration and the location of the offices later,' Saunders says,[7] implying that at that stage he was still intending to implement the offer document.

This is not altogether convincing. No one at Distillers resisted either the Bain invasion or the management shake-up. The directors were certainly ready for change. Immediately after his victory, Saunders told John Connell that he was to lose his executive position, even though it had been specifically stated in the offer document that he was to retain it. He could stay as non-executive head of Distillers. Saunders says that John Connell 'didn't like it, but he accepted the situation'. Interestingly, Saunders adds that he told Sir Thomas Risk about this, who 'did not demur'.[8] This destroys most of Saunders' case for dropping Risk, because it shows that he accepted Saunders' view that Distillers needed to acquire immediately what he calls an 'action-oriented command structure' under himself as executive Chairman of the Distillers subsidiary and with Steel and Dowling in charge under him.

The reason why Saunders could perfectly well have dealt with John Connell and the others in a way that they could have accepted is that they were demoralized. They knew the old ways had to change; some at least of them could have been useful. John Connell himself made a constructive announcement, immediately after the bid had succeeded: 'The creation of a British-owned drinks company of this truly international scale is a momentous event. In harness with Guinness we can now look forward to a future which is brighter with promise for our brands, for our business and for Scotland.' If Saunders had taken a little trouble with the Distillers directors he could certainly have got them on side – or most of them, in which case he could have dropped any who were recalcitrant. My brother Finn's remark that family directors of Guinness may not do much good, but certainly do no harm (quoted in Chapter 5) could also have been true of the old Distillers directors. Some of them might even have been capable of fitting in with Saunders' 'action-oriented command structure'. Even if the attempt to accommodate some of Distillers' people resulted in some temporary loss of efficiency, this would have been acceptable in order to avoid the public relations disaster that was in fact to ensue. The simple fact seems to be that Saunders was intoxicated with success. He had come too far too fast, believed his own publicity, and would tolerate nobody on the Board who was any less under his thumb than the existing Guinness directors.

His treatment of Sir Thomas Risk was both clumsy and arrogant. Risk had kept in some sort of touch with the progress of the bid battle by occasionally visiting Guinness's offices in Portman Square; he rarely got to see Saunders himself but usually managed to have a talk with Ward.[9] Such contact was always at his initiative; he might have expected Saunders to have informed him of what was going on, while realizing of course that this was a very busy time. What did surprise him was that after the bid Saunders continued to remain silent. Risk took a short holiday, but as soon as he returned he began trying to speak to Saunders. 'I started getting heavy breathing from Risk,' is the way Saunders expresses this in *Nightmare*;[10] but surely it was to be expected that the man who was to be head of the merged business should at that stage have wanted to find out what was in the Chief Executive's mind. The Guinness Board met on 9 May; among other matters addressed, Simon Boyd's resignation was accepted and Saunders was appointed Deputy Chairman in his place. There was no move to implement the new arrangements as detailed in the bid documents. It was not until nearly a month after the bid that Risk made contact with Saunders who was about to leave for the United States with Ward and with Vic Steel, the new head of Guinness's distilling arm. The purpose of the trip was to talk to subsidiary businesses and distributors, and also to investors. These included Ivan Boesky, of whom more shortly. Risk came chasing after him; *Nightmare* claims this was at Saunders' suggestion,[11] but Kochan and Pym imply that it was at Risk's own initiative.[12] This is more probable, for Pugh adds the detail that Risk paid his own expenses for the journey; if Saunders had dragged Risk across the Atlantic he would surely have offered to pay. Originally the meeting was to be in New York, but this was changed to Washington. Steel dined with Risk on Saturday, 17 May; Risk said little to him, but according to Saunders in *Nightmare*, Steel warned him that 'my meeting with Risk would be difficult, as he was irritated at having had to come to the US at all'.[13] The following day, Sunday, 18 May, Saunders and Ward saw Risk in his hotel room and continued their talk over lunch.

Accounts differ as to what was said. It is agreed that Saunders emphasized the management problems at Distillers and the fact that he needed a free hand to deal with them. According to *Nightmare*, Risk took the offensive: 'When are we going to move the head office to Scotland and change the Company name?' Asked how he saw his role, he said, 'In company law there is just a chairman, and the chairman is the boss.' He brushed aside Saunders' account of the management problems and made it clear that he would want a considerable part in running the Company, organizing the non-executive directors, determining the agenda for Board Meetings, telling executives what to do. His manner was 'icy and at times sneering'. Saunders ended by saying, 'Your views on the chairman's relations with the management . . . are so different from my understanding and intent when we got into this that I will have to discuss it with Lord Iveagh before we go any further.'[14]

This account cannot be relied on. It is too clearly in Saunders' interest to make out that Risk would have been an impossible Chairman. Apart from this, it is inconceivable that an eminent banker with plenty of other responsibilities should have proposed to tie himself down in this way to a detailed second-guessing of the executives in a large and complex concern. It is also hard to see why, on this account, Risk should have shown such hostility so soon; irritation at crossing the Atlantic hardly explains it. Peter Pugh, to be sure, cites indications that before the Washington lunch Saunders had already made up his mind that Risk was likely to be a nuisance.[15] The day after the bid closed, Saunders said to John Connell, 'I'm not sure Risk is going to be Chairman.' A couple of weeks later, but before the Washington lunch, Ward asked Distillers director Sir Nigel Broackes when Saunders could be Chairman. These remarks, or similar ones, may have got back to Risk; if he was cool and rather wary at the Washington meetings, this could explain it.

In any case, Kochan and Pym's account[16] is very different from that in *Nightmare*, and much more plausible; it essentially agrees with that of Pugh. They maintain that Saunders came straight out with the statement that the problems in Distillers required an executive Chairman to tackle them and that he would have to take the post, to which Risk replied that Saunders was 'daft'. Besides insisting that Saunders could not just walk away from his commitments, Risk made the reasonable point that the difficult decisions that needed to be made, particularly in Scotland, made a non-executive chairman more rather than less important.

The salient point which emerges from all accounts is that the meeting was not a friendly one. This was Saunders' true failure. After this Washington lunch, even if things had been patched up between the two men, their relationship as Chairman and Chief Executive could never have been easy and would most likely have been impossible. Trust would never have been total. Ward did his best; *Nightmare* has him 'cautiously trying to hold the middle ground',[17] while Kochan and Pym, never fans of Ward, say that he, 'in his usual deceptive manner, gave the impression of agreeing with Risk'.[18] Ward's diplomatic approach at least prevented relations being broken at once, and it does seem that Risk was left with the impression that Saunders could still be brought to see sense.

What is strange is that Saunders failed to see that relations with Risk, even if impossible in the long run, had to be kept cordial at this stage. There was the aftermath of the market support operation to take care of; whatever credence we place on Saunders' claim not to have known the impropriety of what was done in the market, he certainly knew that much clearing up was needed. At that precise moment he ought to have been using all his negotiating skill, all his charm, to keep in with Risk. This would have greatly mitigated, and might even have prevented, the weakness in the Guinness share price that was to cause so many of the guarantees given during the bid to be called. Even if Saunders never intended from the start to honour his bid promises, this was not the time to let the mask slip. To take for a moment and for the sake of argument the standpoint of a total cynic, he could have given Risk a timetable, promised implementation in six months, and then gone back on it at that stage. In view of what was to happen, Saunders would probably in fact have been quite glad not to go back on it. But then at that stage Risk would no doubt have been noticeably less keen to take up his appointment. A timetable, from Risk's point of view, would have represented an advance, for there was nothing in the bid document to say when the changes were to take place.

Did Saunders at any stage intend to appoint Risk or retain some of the Distillers directors? This question will never be answered because nothing can be proved, either way, about anyone's past intentions. His line is that he did, but that Risk turned out to be a legalistic and obstructive pedant and the Distillers directors worse than useless. Others believe that the promises were never intended to be kept. My own view, for what it is worth, is that in making the commitments Saunders was not deceitful but reckless; that is, he intended to keep to them if convenient, but never took them very seriously. He was told that he would have to make certain undertakings in order to get together this new, incomparably powerful vehicle for his ambitions; very well, he would make these undertakings, then when he was in control he would see. Some nitpickers might object a bit if he went back on his promises, but others could sort this out while he got on with ruling his new empire. His expensive public relations consultants, his even more expensive City advisers: what were they there for if not to take care of these matters? If you employ a valet, you don't pick up your own clothes. When I was a witness at Saunders' trial, his defence counsel, Richard Ferguson QC, put it to me that I might regard the fuss over the Risk Affair as being somewhat overdone. This suggestion rather surprised me, and I replied that on the contrary I regarded the matter very seriously indeed. Ferguson certainly caught this attitude from his client.

It is often supposed that Saunders was worried that Risk, as a banker, might ask awkward questions about some of the market support operations. This theory smacks of hindsight. If these problems really loomed large in his consciousness immediately after winning the bid, Saunders' logical reaction would have been not, at any cost, to rock the boat. This was certainly to be the attitude of his City advisers, notably Morgan Grenfell who were acutely aware of the problems. Here again, Saunders' attitude appears to have been that these problems were for others to sort out; but it was rather odd that he paid no attention to those others when they begged and pleaded with him to think again about Risk.

Risk kept his counsel when he returned to Britain, for he still thought Saunders might be persuaded to fulfil his undertakings. He did mention his worries to Charles Fraser and Nigel Broackes, who were to be his colleagues on the new Holding Board. Lord Rockley, Chairman of Kleinwort Bensons who were Distillers' merchant banking advisers, was also brought in. It appears[19] that both the DTI and the Bank of England were given indications at this stage that Saunders might be going back on the bid documents. The Guinness Board met on 12 June; Benjamin Iveagh, well briefed of course by Saunders, gave an exposition of the management's point of view from which it emerged that the pattern envisaged in the offer document might not be adhered to; the important consideration was that the management could operate unhindered. There was to be a study on how the Board should be constituted so as to facilitate the working of the Company.

I am afraid I was rather pleased at this, because it seemed likely that the existing Guinness Board, including myself, would be kept on. It was reasonable to suppose that if Saunders wanted a Board that did not obstruct him, then he would see his existing Board as filling the bill admirably. Nearly all of us were Saunders enthusiasts: especially those who spoke for large shareholdings. We would give him as little trouble as any conceivable group of people. Possibly we ought to have asked ourselves just how

Saunders was in danger of being obstructed by the proposed directors, why he was so insistent on an absolutely free hand. We ought to have wondered whether he was becoming power-obsessed or, worse, whether he wanted to get away with impropriety. Certainly we – and I in particular as director of a merchant bank – ought to have been worried at the possible breach of undertakings, particularly to the Distillers directors. My own attitude, more felt than thought, was that I had never wanted Guinness to bid for Distillers anyway, that the Guinness shareholders had certainly paid right up to the limit, although fortunately Saunders had seen sense at the end and not increased the offer yet again. Now, though, here was this enormous and powerful company run by someone who had proved himself a business genius. If I had anything to do with it, he should not be held back by people I was induced to think of – never having met any of them – as bureaucratic nonentities. My mood was further improved by a sight of the good interim results for Guinness – not of course yet including Distillers – to be declared on 16 June. I felt altogether that

> *God's in his Heaven,*
> *All's right with the world.*

This was not the view in the City. Saunders had a succession of eminent visitors from there, trying to induce him to do what he had undertaken. Among them was Christopher Reeves, Chairman of Morgan Grenfell. Of all people, Reeves ought to have been taken seriously by Saunders, considering the vital role his firm had played in the takeover. Saunders also saw David Walker of the Bank of England; he too was clear that things should be patched up with Risk. Saunders had dinner with Risk on 26 June; the conversation was 'perfectly polite',[20] but also perfectly inconclusive, except that Risk said he wished to see Benjamin Iveagh for a Chairman-to-Chairman meeting, and

Saunders promised to arrange this. On 2 July, Roger Seelig suggested a compromise; given that Saunders could not get on with Risk, perhaps another non-executive Chairman might be found, of whom Risk, as well as Saunders, would of course have to approve. But who in the world, at that stage, could be approved by both Saunders and Risk? That Seelig should come up with an expedient with such a very slim chance shows a certain desperation; again, this ought to have given Saunders pause.

It did not. The next Guinness Board Meeting was on 8 July, and on that occasion Saunders told us frankly that Risk had proved impossible. He mentioned the possibility of a compromise candidate, but to appoint someone unnamed seemed less than satisfactory. So who was to be Chairman? None other than Ernest Saunders. Benjamin Iveagh would be kicked upstairs to the honorary office of President. Otherwise things would remain as they were; the new Board was a dead letter, there was no mention of anyone from Distillers coming on.

Saunders' assumption of the Chairmanship of the Company was one of the worst moves he made. Iveagh, at that stage, still had a good deal of credibility, and he was completely under Saunders' control. It was foolish to throw this asset away. Later there was to come a time when Saunders would have dearly liked to restore him, but by then he was a spent force, no longer acceptable to the authorities. At the time the move looked to me like an extra, unnecessary, slap in the face for Saunders' critics, liable to provoke them even more. Benjamin's own reaction to the move was strange. Simon Boyd remembers discussing it with him and reminding him of a principle enunciated by their grandfather, Rupert Iveagh: 'Others run the Brewery, we say who will run it.' Benjamin replied: 'I will continue to run the Brewery.'

The new arrangements were not announced at once. On 10 July, two days after the Board Meeting, Risk went round to Portman Square for the meeting he had requested with Iveagh. He found Saunders and Ward there, and asked them both to leave the room. They did so, and Iveagh told Risk straight out that it had been decided not to appoint him as Chairman. Saunders and Ward returned, and Risk left. Through no fault of his own, he had been placed in an invidious position. Despite all the allegations and insinuations from the Saunders camp, and there were to be a good many of these, it will have become clear to the reader that he had been given no chance to prove himself either acceptable or unacceptable. He had been used and discarded; Saunders might have said of him, as Frederick the Great did of Voltaire, 'When one has sucked the orange one throws away the skin.' Risk would no doubt have liked to walk away – he had been fairly reluctant to take the Chairmanship in the first place – but matters had gone too far for this to be feasible. As it was, he let it be known that he was willing to stand down if another acceptable Chairman could be found: Seelig's compromise. But it was already too late for this; Saunders was not to be deflected.

Nor, though, would he be forgiven; and nemesis was on its way. To go back to Saunders' visit to the United States when he and Ward had eaten their rather frosty lunch with Risk: that meal had been preceded by breakfast with Ivan Boesky, the famous – soon to be the notorious – 'arbitrageur'. At that time Boesky's name was one to conjure with, even if some people were a little sniffy about his aphorism 'Greed is good'. He had made a huge fortune on Wall Street and was immensely powerful, definitely a man to have on your side in a takeover battle. There was at the time no hint that he ever did anything improper; the impression given was that he made his money by the ruthless use of his placing power, by making things happen and then reaping the profit.

Saunders and Ward met him for breakfast, and in *Nightmare* Saunders gives the impression that the reason for the meeting was simply that he was a 'high flyer' who might be able to help with acquisitions in the United States. 'It is in this context that one needs to look at Ward's recommendation with regard to our

$100 million investment with one of Boesky's investment funds that summer . . . he could put us in touch with key people . . .'[21] This is more or less the same as the account Saunders gave the Guinness Board about his relations with Boesky when he told us of this investment.

What he did not tell us, for the good reason that he did not know it, is that a few days before he partook of coffee and rolls with Saunders, Boesky had already been fingered as an insider trader by Dennis Levine of Drexel Burnham Lambert. Shortly after Levine exposed him, Boesky had come to a confidential deal with US Attorney Rudolph Giuliani, as a consequence of which he went around wired for sound so that his contacts, too, could be caught. It seems likely that Boesky's personal bugs were already in place during that breakfast, and one may assume that the listening detectives were laughing up their sleeves at the Guinness people – the phrase 'Limey suckers' may have crossed their minds – who were respectfully arranging to invest $100 million with this man they were about to expose. Certainly it was Boesky's revelations to the US authorities that triggered the DTI's appointment of inspectors to inquire into Guinness, and Saunders' prosecution for fraud. Boesky had supported Guinness during the bid for Distillers, and now that it had won, he was among the sellers of large quantities of Guinness shares who were having to be accommodated by new market operations, public and private. Exactly what the extent of Boesky's support had been is still not known. Certainly he was a large seller of Guinness shares after the bid, but when and through whom he had bought them and how many he had held is a mystery. One unconfirmed theory is that he was originally supporting Argyll and that some of his assistance to Guinness consisted simply of changing sides and unwinding his pro-Argyll positions.

Guinness's investment of $100 million in Boesky's limited partnership can only be rationally explained if it is understood as a payoff for this help. For one thing, it would make Guinness by far the largest holder in the fund with 30 per cent of the equity; none of the others put in more than $28 million. Again, an industrial firm will almost always be able to find better use for its resources than to put them into a mutual fund. Such an investment might be a suitable home for surplus cash, although many would be inclined to say that cash that was surplus to this extent would be better returned to shareholders. Guinness, in any case, had no surplus cash; it had already increased its borrowing ratio quite sufficiently by buying back its own shares, as we shall see.

A few days after the breakfast meeting the cash for the investment was paid over, before Saunders even consulted his Chief Executive's Committee (himself, Roux and Steel); this Committee endorsed it on 28 May.

The investment was not even mentioned at the Board Meeting of 12 June, but it came up on 8 July. It rather spoilt for me what was otherwise a fairly congenial meeting; it was then that the Board decided to make Saunders Chairman and keep everything else as it was. The Boesky investment, though, seemed inexplicable. For the first time since Saunders' arrival, I felt the sort of unease with which I had become familiar under the old regime. It was like hearing about films again, or caravan sites. I asked for an explanation of it. Ward said it was a way into the American market, that Boesky had an excellent record and would produce a good return. Saunders then intervened, saying that there was not time to discuss it at the meeting but he would see that I received the underlying documents. For further explanation I should talk to Roux.

The documents were not reassuring. They showed in particular that Ivan Boesky, the 'general partner', with a comparatively small investment, would be entitled to 40 per cent of the profits after debenture interest and liable to only 10 per cent of any losses. After failing several times to get hold of Roux, I rang Ernest Saunders. He told me to talk to Ward rather than Roux. When I got on to him, Ward admitted that the documents did not look good. But, he said, Boesky had been very helpful with the Distillers bid; and he was also a good ally to have if Guinness was to be an international group. Not only that, but his record indicated that we should get a 20 per cent return on our investment. All right, the investment was perhaps unorthodox; but it should be regarded as a strategic one. To my shame, I left it at that. After all, the investment had been made, and it might turn out as Ward said.

So the Boesky investment remained for the next few months as a ticking time bomb. In the meantime, though, the Risk Affair reached its crisis.

FOURTEEN

Saunders Takes the Halter

On 11 July 1986, the day after Iveagh had given Risk his marching orders, Saunders gave a party at Knoll House, his graceful seventeenth-century residence at Penn in Buckinghamshire. The idea was to invite the directors and managers of Guinness and Distillers to celebrate the 'merger'. It was a grand affair with a marquee on the lawn, but it appears that not everyone enjoyed it. The fact is that any such party, in order to be an unalloyed success, would have had to be given at least two months earlier. Too much had happened, too much more was clearly about to happen, for all those present to be relaxed. Risk had already been told by Benjamin that he was not wanted, though this was still secret. The Distillers directors were being shown the cold shoulder, and John Connell was still displeased at losing his executive role. In *Nightmare* we are told that when Carole Saunders introduced herself to John Connell's wife, saying, 'I'm Carole Saunders, I'm so pleased to see you,' the reply was a cool 'I'm *Mrs* Connell.'[1] John Chiene and Scott Dobbie of Wood Mackenzie almost failed to turn up at all, because a few days before they had failed to make Saunders think again about Risk. Chiene's final plea has already been noted. At a meeting with Ward just before they went in to Saunders, Ward had insinuated that Risk was demanding more business for his Bank of Scotland. The pair from Wood Mackenzie reacted badly to this because they felt that Risk, as an eminent banker, would simply not have done it. Nor did he; yet the insinuation was not completely baseless. Risk in fact made this request in January[2] when first offered the Chairmanship. This was scarcely improper; Risk was not eager to accept the Chairmanship at all, so it is hardly surprising that he should have made some such suggestion. At that stage Saunders, desperate to have him on board, made no objection. For Risk to have demanded more business for the Bank of Scotland as a new condition in July would have been very different, in fact unworthy of a senior banker. The suggestion that he did this was offensive as well as disingenuous.

I was not invited to the party at Knoll, and only heard about it after the event. I was not invited, either, to a function Saunders had given at the Méridien Hotel in Piccadilly during the Distillers bid; nor was Simon Boyd, at that time Deputy Chairman. Simon was rather embarrassed because someone asked him why he had not been there at a time when he did not even know that the party had taken place. This contributed to his later decision to resign from the Board. The fact is that Saunders' attitude to us family directors, as to many other people, fluctuated in line with his view at a given moment of our usefulness. The Company Secretary, Alan Scrine, noticed this as regards Saunders' treatment of him, and others say the same. The way Saunders used and discarded Risk was a more dramatic example. Simon Boyd describes[3] how just before the Bells bid Saunders was 'all over' him. This, Simon thinks, was because he knew various senior City figures socially. But he was reticent about using these friendships to make business contacts for Saunders, and Saunders himself found during the Bells bid that he could succeed just as well using his own more junior contacts. As for me, I was the straw at which Saunders would grasp just before his dismissal, when it was too late for anyone to help.

The first public intimation that Risk was to be dropped and Saunders intended to make himself Chairman came in the *Sunday Times* business section two days after the party at Knoll in a piece by Ivan Fallon, the City Editor. Fallon was an admirer of

Saunders who according to *Nightmare* used to call him every Thursday for a possible story.[4] This time he was rewarded with a scoop; Saunders told him what he was going to do and why, and secured just the article he wanted. In form it was a leak; there was no official announcement from the Company. Still, when a senior journalist writes in the confident terms used by Fallon on this occasion, the leak is generally taken as being true. Fallon wrote that Saunders 'has performed one of the great wonders of the modern commercial world'. If he was to make the most of the brands and assets of Distillers and make the necessary cost savings, he needed a free hand – 'and there is just the possibility that he won't get it. The key man was [sic] to be the august Sir Thomas Risk, Governor of the Bank of Scotland and Distillers' principal banker.' Note that Risk's proposed appointment is here assumed to be a thing of the past. 'On paper and in the heat of battle, that sounded fine. Events since have changed the perspective, however. Lord Iveagh's willingness to step aside should permit Saunders to assume the role of executive chairman.'[5]

Fallon's piece stirred up a hornets' nest. Alf Young of the *Scotsman* at once got hold of Charles Fraser who confirmed some of the background to the story and then expressed, on the record, his total disapproval of the moves should they take place; since they had not been announced or even formally decided he could quite properly do this. Alf Young's story appeared on Monday the 14th, quoting Fraser. *The Times*, whose City Editor, Kenneth Fleet, was like Fallon a consistent Saunders supporter, carried the other point of view on the same day. This included the allegation that Risk had demanded more business for the Bank of Scotland.

That same Monday morning Guinness officially announced the changes, and the fat was properly in the fire. The Guinness share price slumped; Ward called Fraser and threatened him with a law suit because of what he had said to the *Scotsman*. This, according to Kochan and Pym, scared Fraser, though it is hard to see why.[6] Certainly Fraser was an eminent man whose words carried weight, but Guinness's share price would certainly have suffered even if Fraser had remained wholly tight-lipped, as his defence counsel in any law suit could have pointed out.

It was not only the stock market which reacted on that Monday. The Bank of England, too, was concerned with the dishonouring of the undertakings in the offer document. Robin Leigh Pemberton, the Governor, summoned Saunders, Ward and Benjamin Iveagh to a meeting in the afternoon with himself and his deputy, George Blunden. According to *Nightmare*, Saunders told Leigh Pemberton that it had become impossible to work with Risk. 'We had to deliver the profits to the shareholders, and to do so required flexibility in terms of timing and implementation, but Risk had refused to see the point, and we had taken legal advice about where our fiduciary duties lay.' At the end of the meeting Saunders felt that Leigh-Pemberton 'basically accepted the situation', though Blunden remained unhappy. Blunden was the Bank of England official concerned with City self-regulation, and his continuing doubtfulness is certainly a truer indication of the 'Bank's view' than the emollience of his chief, who would have been concerned for the amenities during the interview.[7]

There was naturally much criticism in the newspapers the following day, Tuesday, 15 July, but it was not unanimous. Lex in the *Financial Times* said Saunders had used his promises on Board composition to get the Scottish institutions on his side, and had then gone back on them with explanations 'so vague as to be insulting'. Hamish McRae in the *Guardian* was also critical, saying the effects would linger for a decade. On the other hand, Kenneth Fleet of *The Times*, as usual, supported Saunders, rather imprecisely blaming the Scots for making a fuss and adding: 'Distillers needs strong management and a massive dose of constructive interference. It was not likely to get it with a "balanced" board. From the point of view of the City, and the Bank of England, the situation created by the latest Guinness moves is serious but hardly critical.' On the same day Wood Mackenzie resigned as stockbrokers to Guinness. Charles Fraser severed all connections with the Company, ceasing to act as its Edinburgh lawyer and resigning his post as Chairman of Morgan Grenfell Scotland, since Morgan Grenfell were remaining as Guinness's merchant bankers. The decision to stick with Guinness must have been a finely balanced decision for that firm, for they had been trying very hard to persuade Saunders to accept Risk. Christopher Reeves told him that Risk had written him a letter 'which had been a model of how a non-executive chairman should act'. Saunders paid no attention, and still sees this and other approaches as the result of lobbying by 'Risk and his allies'.[8]

Also on that Tuesday, Morgan Grenfell came up with a logical solution to the Risk Affair which would probably have patched things up quite acceptably, but for the improprieties of the market support operation during the bid, which were still unknown. Their reasoning was that if anyone could be thought to have been aggrieved by Saunders' changes in the Board arrangements as compared with the offer document, it was the recipients of those documents, namely, the Distillers and Guinness shareholders. The right thing to do, therefore, would be to hold an Extraordinary General Meeting of the Company and put the issue to them. If they agreed after the event to what had been done, this would validate it and stop all argument. Saunders agreed, and if the irregularities of the market support operation had remained hidden, he might have been able to consolidate his empire. Given time and much emollient publicity, he might then have become a respected leader of British business. His critics would have continued to grumble, but their access to the serious news media would have diminished until their complaints became forgotten. From time to time one meets someone with a lurid story about the past of some admired and successful tycoon. Sometimes it may be true; who knows? The newspapers probably already know it, but shrug it off.

Saunders might have taken longer than usual to reach this degree of impregnability, because the authorities were very, very angry; all the angrier in that they had stretched several points to suit Guinness during the bid and incurred criticism for so doing. To have given permission to mount the new bid after referral to the Monopolies and Mergers Commission was, after all, a big favour. Powerful people, especially though not only in Scotland, wanted to 'get Saunders'; and when enough powerful people want to get someone, they often succeed. What doomed Saunders was that the Guinness share price remained below the level at which the bid's supporters would have forgone their illegal payments; the Risk Affair ensured that this would be the case. Sooner or later it would all inevitably come out.

For the moment, though, much of the disapproval spent itself in futile gestures. Malcolm Rifkind, the Scottish Secretary, summoned Saunders to a meeting and for an hour or so subjected him to a 'tongue-lashing' (Kochan and Pym),[9] 'personal abuse' (*Nightmare*)[10] or a 'pompous wigging' (Ivan Fallon in the *Sunday Times*),[11] a good deal of which was to do with the probability that Saunders would not locate the Company headquarters in Scotland. As Saunders says, this was no doubt for the benefit of the Scottish Press. There was, as both men knew quite well, nothing concrete that Rifkind could do to Saunders, who eventually was able to walk out in disgust. Taken in isolation, the episode reflects more discredit on Rifkind than on Saunders. It is an example of the Government's recurrent itch to be seen 'doing something'. Nevertheless, seen as a symptom of attitudes among the influential, it should have shown Saunders that in the end his position was likely to be untenable.

Although Morgan Grenfell remained with him, Saunders saw that the problem had now moved beyond them because the controversy had become political. Therefore, an adviser with political contacts was needed. Sir John Nott, Chairman of Lazard Brothers, agreed that his firm should be special advisers to

Benjamin Iveagh and mastermind the Extraordinary General Meeting. Nott had been Defence Secretary during the Falklands War; he was a political heavyweight.

The Ministry which could be a serious threat to Guinness was not Rifkind's Scottish Office but the Department of Trade and Industry. Sure enough, Michael Howard, then the Minister under Paul Channon, told Guinness that if the Distillers' offer document was not implemented he would order a DTI inquiry such as was in the event to be instituted four months later. This started a convoluted set of negotiations between Guinness and the DTI in which Guinness's team was led by Nott, helped by Thomas Ward and by Anthony Salz of Freshfields. The key meeting was on 28 July 1986 at the DTI, when Saunders, Ward, Nott and Salz met Howard, with Philip Bovey and two other DTI officials. Howard Hughes of Price Waterhouse and Robert Alexander, QC, were there as well. At first the Minister threatened an inquiry, but he was talked round. The new scheme was to appoint to the Board a number of new non-executive Directors who would constitute a committee with power to appoint and remove the Chairman. Some of the new appointees had to be Scottish. Saunders accepted the move, if rather wryly, christening the non-executive committee the 'Sack the Chairman Committee'. The Guinness Board endorsed it on 31 July.

There is criticism to make of the authorities at many stages of the affair, but at this point they did well. The arrangement was unusual, in fact unique, but it would prove its worth in the crisis to come. If it had not been for the facts that were to emerge about the market support arrangements, the new compromise would have consolidated Saunders' position. He was placed under control, without being obstructed. Nobody was imposed on him. It was even left to him to choose the non-executive directors, the only stipulations being that they should include some Scots and they had to be acceptable to the DTI and the Bank of England.

Saunders says in *Nightmare* that he had plenty of offers. This would seem to have been the case. Only on the assumption that Saunders had many applicants to choose from can one explain the fact that all those who joined the Board were not only respectable but genuinely eminent. There was not a deadbeat or a passenger among them; all were chief executives of important and successful companies. Saunders, in *Nightmare*, goes all coy: 'It was quite thrilling to interview these famous people.'[2]

Four names were announced on 13 August 1986. They were Sir Norman Macfarlane, Chairman of the Clansman Group: Sir David Plastow, Chief Executive of Vickers: Anthony Greener, Managing Director of Dunhill Holdings: and Ian MacLaurin, Chairman of Tesco. Ian Chapman, Chief Executive of Collins, was added to their number following the Board Meeting on 2 December: with Macfarlane, he made up the number of Scots to two out of the five. But by the time of Chapman's appointment, much had happened.

The circular announcing the Extraordinary General Meeting and the motions to be discussed was sent to shareholders on 22 August. The day before, Ward told Bill Spengler, the Distillers director, that he was not wanted; he resigned at once, leaving David Connell as the only Distillers man on the Guinness Board. Spengler was particularly badly treated. He had always been a keen advocate of the merger with Guinness; he had been half promised an executive position and definitely promised a seat on the new Board. Before the merger he had commissioned a report on Distillers from the management consultants PA Strategy, which Saunders admits was well done, and gave him a good basis for action.[13] Spengler had also been used as hatchet man to get rid of some of his old colleagues and subordinates. It is not a pretty story.

The Extraordinary General Meeting was held at the Mount Royal Hotel, just round the corner from Guinness's offices in Portman Square, on Thursday, 11 September. The big, sombre hall was packed – from the platform it looked like standing room only – and the meeting ended in a triumph for Saunders. To be sure, he had more than enough proxy votes to ensure victory on the motions; but it was important to him to win the public debate. This was not only for the sake of image, but also because a large number of fund managers were there who could have changed their minds, and withdrawn their proxies.

Everything went right for Saunders on this occasion. Benjamin Iveagh was in better form than I have ever known him; perhaps he was fired by the knowledge that this was the last shareholders' meeting he would ever have to chair, for as we saw earlier, the task had always been a misery for him. Yet if he was capable of such a confident performance, why had he ever found it so difficult? Perhaps he simply happened to be in a better mood and better health than usual. He also had a very genuine regard for Saunders; he was not acting, but transparently sincere, when he told the meeting of his personal resentment of the attacks that had been made on his Chief Executive.

The case against Saunders was seriously mishandled from the floor by the first speaker, Graeme Knox of Scottish Amicable. His task was not easy, of course, after Benjamin's fluent defence of the proposals. Yet he had substantial points to make, and would have done better had his style been less hectoring and legalistic. Perhaps his heart was not altogether in it, because he told Kochan and Pym afterwards that during the bid for Distillers 'one of the things I really didn't like about the Guinness proposals was their board structure – the two-tier board farce was clearly never going to work'.[14] This was a good reason to oppose Guinness during the bid, and Knox was quite logically an Argyll supporter at that time; but once Guinness had won, it was unconstructive for him to oppose an attempt to change proposals he felt were farcical. This highlights a weakness in the reasoning of several Saunders opponents during the summer of 1986, and it is a point made in various forms by *Nightmare*; they put legal correctness before the practicalities of management. But even if insistence on keeping to the terms of the offer document for Distillers was nothing but legalism, it is a fact of life that many people will be legalistic. The practical way to look at legalism is as a problem which management needs to address, on a par with the tendency of people to get slack, or overrun their budgets. It is no good simply ignoring it. Saunders complains that he was forced to squander management time in dealing with the 'Risk Affair'.[15] Might he not in fact have saved time if he had tried to work with Risk and the others? Were the proposals in fact unworkable. We shall never know.

Knox's flop at the meeting was so complete that nobody spoke in his support. After his speech the meeting developed into the sort of good-humoured farce that often characterized question time under the old regime at Guinness. 'This is what Guinness meetings have always been like,' I remember telling one of the newcomers. The speaker after Knox was another Scot, but one who volubly and repetitively congratulated Saunders on beating the 'Scottish Mafia'. Like many who speak up at shareholders' meetings, he was a man with a grudge; in his case it was against the Bank of Scotland. Robert Maxwell was there, a paunchy, good-humoured giant of a man in red braces, a good example of the type known in French as a *faux bonhomme*, a false good fellow. He jumped up every now and then with an intervention, always supporting Saunders. An old-established Guinness shareholder, Declan O'Hegarty, a familiar figure at Guinness meetings for years, asked what the cost of the bid was. The answer given was a round £100 million; the true figure is certainly higher.

After the Extraordinary General Meeting the Board met, for the first time joined by the four new non-executives. Not surprisingly, the meeting went well; the new directors were entirely supportive, and the atmosphere was pleasant.

During the rest of the autumn, everything at Guinness seemed calm. The new management team was put into place: Vic

Steel to run the spirits interests – Distillers and Bells – Brian Baldock to be in charge of Guinness Brewing Worldwide – the beer company – and Shaun Dowling to be responsible for the non-alcoholic side. This was now considerable, for it included the hotels acquired with Bells – as well as the retail businesses, now including the French luxury food company Hédiard. Roux was still there, despite his intermittent desire to drop Guinness and get back to Bain from which, officially, he was still seconded. Saunders was also developing new Scottish links; it will be recalled that Distillers had dropped the Royal Bank of Scotland the year before because they had taken underwriting for Argyll. Now Saunders gave some business back to that bank, which was more than happy to have it. Yet during this period of outward calm, Saunders was worried about a possible investigation by the DTI, which had been threatened during the summer; he apparently told Alan Scrine to shred any 'inimical' documents, an order the Company Secretary was careful to ignore.[16] Saunders has always denied giving any such instruction.

A Morgan Grenfell director, Geoffrey Collier, got into trouble that November on a matter that had nothing to do with Guinness, yet has its significance for our story because the reaction foreshadowed the way the Guinness affair was to develop. Suddenly, it seemed out of the blue, he admitted having indulged in insider trading; he had bought a large holding in an automotive parts company called AE and made a large profit, on the basis of information about a bid for the company. He admitted the offence, resigned from Morgan Grenfell and cooperated fully with the police. It was a straightforward case, and he was eventually found guilty, fined £25,000 and given a suspended prison sentence. Morgan Grenfell suffered no immediate disadvantage from this episode; Reeves handled it shrewdly, so much so that the Press actually commended Morgan Grenfell for acting promptly against Collier. But the political atmosphere started heating up; one of those situations developed where each side in

Parliament tries to outbid the other in righteous indignation. Bryan Gould, Labour's Trade and Industry spokesman, wrote to Paul Channon as Secretary of State for Trade and Industry, suggesting that 'a couple of good prosecutions in the City would work wonders'.[17] Channon, not to be outdone, assured Parliament that he took an equally serious view of these matters. One of his officials went further, telling the *Sunday Times*: 'People want blood. Public opinion must be satisfied. We are under some pressure to prosecute.'[18] Channon appointed inspectors and immediately gave them powers for which the necessary legislation was still going through Parliament: to compel witnesses to attend hearings and give evidence under oath, to seize documents, to prosecute anyone who refused to cooperate. In Collier's case all this was unnecessary because he had already confessed; but evidently Channon felt that he had to be seen to be doing something. This kind of reaction by the authorities to presumed public emotion, in the Guinness case, was to cause confusion that still continues.

Collier and his family were subjected to a severe, if short-lived, press persecution. When he said to his wife that the newspapers might be interested, she had told him he was not important enough. The poor lady was to learn otherwise. Journalists besieged the Colliers' house, telephoned them incessantly, tramped through their garden, intrusively photographed their children. More ominous, from the point of view of the authorities, was that even with the full cooperation of Collier in this comparatively simple case it took them a full fortnight to get their evidence together. What is more, they had to agree to what amounted to a plea-bargain. According to the *Observer*,[19] Collier had intended to accuse a DTI official of perjuring himself at his bail hearing; Collier had then dropped this charge in return for the prosecution agreeing to be less aggressive. This may be what caused his prison sentence to be suspended. The fact that he walked free infuriated Labour politicians and the Press, but it looks as if this was due less to leniency than to incompetence.

Two other events that November did relate to Guinness. The first made no immediate stir; Schenley, Meshulam Riklis's trading company which had helped in the market support operation and was the distributor of Dewar's whisky in the United States, was given the valuable rights to the Dewar's trademark for nothing. The other event caused uproar. On 14 November 1986 Ivan Boesky was publicly disgraced and prosecuted for insider trading. He was given the benefit of a plea bargain because of all the helpful evidence he provided to the authorities since being wired for sound in May. The deal he struck was extraordinary by most standards. He was to pay a fine of $100 million – a record, but peanuts compared with the fortune he had made. He was also sentenced to three years in an open prison. The oddest feature was that during the final months he had been allowed to continue insider trading, cutting his liabilities by $1.32 billion and selling $440 million of securities; that is, the Securities and Exchange Commission permitted him to go on doing exactly what he was being prosecuted for. The SEC's Chairman, John Shad, explained later that this was done to avoid a collapse in the market; he also said, rather more improbably, that Boesky had not personally benefited from the trading.[20]

The news about Boesky worried me, and particularly the thought of what the new non-executive directors might say or do if, as seemed certain, our investment was in danger. Had they been informed of the investment, ought I to inform them? It is always easiest to do nothing, so I kept my head down. Our money should not be entirely lost; after all, there would be underlying securities. There was to be a Board meeting on 2 December at which I should have raised the matter if no one else had done so.

By then there were more things to think about, for on 1 December the DTI sent in inspectors to conduct an inquiry. The procedure for this was laid down only a short time before in

Sections 431 to 436 of the Companies Act, 1985. Two officials from the DTI arrived at the Portman Square headquarters, and others at Company offices around the country, and produced copies of a letter of authority to investigate the Company's affairs. The managers, clerks and secretaries were utterly bewildered; Saunders claimed, and still claims, to have been bewildered too. He informed Benjamin Iveagh, called in Anthony Salz of Freshfields, and appointed an additional public relations consultant, David Wynn Morgan of Hill and Knowlton, who moved into Portman Square.

That evening Guinness held a reception at the National Gallery to mark the Company's loan of a painting to the gallery. Everyone knew that the inspectors had gone into Guinness, and the occasion was held under a heavy and palpable cloud. Roger Seelig noticed a lot of whispering; Lord Rothschild, who would normally have made a speech of thanks about the picture, did not do so. Journalists were clustered round the exit and pestered Saunders in vain for a comment. It happened also to be the evening when Sir David Plastow gave a dinner for all the non-executive directors, old and new, at the Vickers offices high up over Millbank. I remember this as a friendly occasion, less overshadowed by the news of the inquiry than one might have expected. Saunders says that he had briefed Ward, who being a non-executive director was to be there, to tell the new non-executives about the Boesky investment, but I do not remember him doing this.

At the Board Meeting the following day, 2 December 1986, the Boesky investment certainly did come up, and caused such consternation as to imply that if Ward did mention it the night before it was under his breath. Ward and Roux defended it as best they could, which was not very well. I was not surprised when Sir Norman Macfarlane attacked hard. Ward did not help his case by saying, among other things, that the investment was a way to hold dollars, which would probably rise. This was an insult to the

intelligence of the new non-executives, who as serious businessmen knew quite well that the way to hold a currency is to get
a bank deposit in that currency, not to invest in a mutual fund.

I was in a dilemma. On this matter Macfarlane was clearly
right, because the investment, already in normal terms inexplicable, had become potentially disastrous following the exposure of
Boesky. It would have to be made public, sooner rather than later,
and might at worst have to be written off entirely. What would
the Press say? And the shareholders? Again I remembered my
feelings about the films and caravan sites, and felt sick at heart.
Yet I could not weigh in behind Macfarlane. I still believed in
Saunders and felt that if his position was jeopardized the
Company would suffer. He was under enough pressure, I felt,
with this inquiry which I was convinced was misconceived and
suspected was vindictive, originating from the influential
enemies he had made in the summer. It seemed unfair, too, of the
new non-executives to accuse Saunders of concealing the Boesky
investment from them. It was after all mentioned in the minutes
of the meeting of 8 July. I think I made this point, either at the
meeting or later to Macfarlane. It was a little disingenuous of me
to do this, because no one really expects a new director to check
all the back minutes carefully. This was a rather special case,
though; the new non-executives, having been put there to keep
an eye on Saunders, might easily have checked more than usual.
The fact that they did not do so tends to discredit Saunders'
insinuation, in court and in interview, that Macfarlane and
Plastow were out to get him from the very beginning. Had this
been the case, they would surely have gone through all available
documents, including minutes, with a fine toothcomb. Their
shocked surprise at the Boesky investment was not an act, but
quite genuine. They had joined the Guinness Board expecting a
congenial extra directorship with the duty of monitoring and
perhaps moderating a tough management; suddenly they found
themselves pitched into controversy that they had certainly not

looked for. It is true that Macfarlane in particular was to do very well out of it personally, but this is not because he devised a plot with this in mind; rather that he stepped, successfully, into a yawning breach.

The Board at its 2 December meeting discussed when and how to make the Boesky investment public. Ward's advice, which rather to my surprise was accepted, was to say nothing for as long as possible; he felt that with discretion all the money might be recovered. The hope of keeping it quiet for any length of time was, of course, forlorn. On 18 December a rumour surfaced in the *Independent* that the Guinness family had taken an interest in a Boesky fund. It was obviously not fair to the family that this falsehood should be floating around; unless promptly contradicted it would have given rise to offensive speculation in the newspapers. The Company came clean immediately; Saunders and Ward were still reluctant to do this and Sir Norman Macfarlane protested that the Press release was 'disastrous'. However, all the advisers had insisted that it had to be done. It was followed, not surprisingly, by some acid Press comment. The appointment of the DTI inspectors, by itself, did not convince the mass of journalists that there was anything really wrong at Guinness. It was when the Boesky connection became known that the Press became seriously hostile.

Saunders fought hard against the bad impression, and with some temporary effect. Kochan and Pym tell of a lunch at the *Financial Times* at which he spoke to assembled journalists for an hour and three-quarters. He spoke of the 'Risk Affair', and claimed that he was the victim of a Scottish Mafia. Apparently the journalists, not the easiest audience, were impressed; he still seemed to be in complete control.[21]

Olivier Roux was at that lunch, but he was becoming seriously estranged from Saunders, as would shortly become very apparent. On 19 December he left his office at Portman Square, never to return. From then on the fabric began to unravel.

FIFTEEN

The Fabric Unravels

At the same time as the DTI inspectors went in to the Guinness offices on 1 December, others went in to the firms that had, or might have had, information relative to the Distillers bid. In particular, they visited Morgan Grenfell. That firm, heartened perhaps by their recent success in containing the trouble over Geoffrey Collier, began by brazening it out. Christopher Reeves told the *Guardian*: 'People must come to their senses. It's not an investigation into Morgan Grenfell. It's an investigation into Guinness.'[1] This time, though, the trouble could not be contained. The atmosphere turned poisonous. Press interest was intense and hostile, given an extra bite because the previous image of Guinness had been so clean and cuddly. The cynics who man newspapers inwardly detest anyone or anything that has such an image, and nothing can equal their glee if they find it flawed. Their current baiting of the Royal Family is powered by this feeling. Not that this was a matter 'all got up by the Press'. On the contrary; in the early stages, feeling expressed privately in the business community was franker than in the Press which was hobbled by respect for the defamation laws. On the whole, to be sure, the stigma remained personal to Saunders. Edward Guinness, who was currently Chairman of the Brewers' Society, was in turn approached at a Christmas function by his predecessor Derek Palmar, and by the Society's director, Desmond Langham. Both told him separately that the scandal was doing harm to the whole brewing industry, though both also assured him of their continued personal regard for him, and indeed for Guinness as a company. Palmar's vehemence on the subject of Saunders was so intense that Edward felt he needed to pass it on to its object. Saunders did not take it as badly as might have been expected. 'I have always regarded you as the conscience of the Company,' he said. Whether the scandal was really harming the brewing industry is open to doubt; sales of stout rose and remained healthy during the time when the newspapers were constantly full of the scandal.

As soon as the inspectors had gone in it became apparent to Saunders that it would be impossible to work from an office that was constantly staked out by suspicious pressmen. Leaving his personal assistant, Margaret McGrath, to hold the fort at Portman Square, Ernest Saunders moved with his wife into a suite in the Inn on the Park to manage the crisis. There he held a series of meetings with different groups of directors, which although not official Board Meetings were minuted by the Company Secretary, Alan Scrine. After years of being, or at any rate feeling, frozen out in his office at the Park Royal Brewery, Scrine had been brought back to the centre. The meetings mostly took place at 7.30 in the evening, and were attended by those directors whom Saunders had been able to get hold of and who were able to come.

An important early question to be settled was that of legal representation in dealing with the DTI inquiry. Saunders told those present on 18 December that Freshfields, the main Company solicitors who had acted during the bid, also acted for Boesky and could accordingly be faced with a conflict of interest. They also, though Saunders did not mention this fact until a later meeting, acted for Morgan Grenfell and Roger Seelig. This does indicate that in the likely event of Guinness, and its main City adviser, each wishing to put a different slant on events so as to minimize its own responsibility, Freshfields might have been in a difficult position. But Saunders' choice of a solicitor to act instead of them surprised some people, and certainly proved controversial. He put forward Sir David Napley of Kingsley Napley.

Napley was a familiar figure to the public; all too familiar. A former President of the Law Society, he had made headlines more often than any other solicitor in the country except Lord Goodman, but in a very different way from that prince of high-level negotiators. *Private Eye* called Goodman the blessed Arnold; nobody, even in fun, ever called Napley the Blessed. He was a fighter, known for his high fees and his success in difficult cases. Saturnine, dry and precise, he radiated a sombre reassurance well calculated to comfort clients who were in bad trouble. He avoided cheerfulness, as an undertaker does, but was rather good company in private. I knew this, having once debated against him and accepted a lift back to London in his stately old Rolls-Royce. He had helped in the successful defence of the former Liberal leader Jeremy Thorpe on a charge of conspiracy to murder. Other clients had been Sarah Tisdall, who leaked Foreign Office secrets to the *Guardian*; Harvey Proctor, MP, and Commander Trestrail of the Queen's bodyguard, both caught up in homosexual scandals; and the family of Roberto Calvi, the Italian banker whose corpse was found hanging on Blackfriars Bridge. Saunders' family had consulted him in the past, and as we have seen he had prepared writs for Guinness in connection with the advertisements put out by Argyll during the Distillers bid to which Saunders had taken exception.

Sir Norman Macfarlane greatly disliked the proposal to take on Napley. He is not minuted as having objected to the appointment when Saunders proposed it on 18 December; but privately he regarded it as sinister. 'You only go to Napley as the very last resort,' was the way he put it to me later. There was general agreement, though, that Freshfields would have to be replaced; all the directors present on 18 December, including Macfarlane and Plastow, agreed that it was undesirable for them to continue as sole advisers to the Company, in view of the possible conflict of interest. However, they thought in terms of 'another firm of *corporate* lawyers to represent the Company'. (My italics: Napley was not primarily a corporate lawyer, so this is a coded way of opposing his appointment.) In the end Saunders agreed that he would resurrect Guinness's connection with Travers Smith Braithwaite, solicitors to the firm and the family since the 1860s whom he had eased out. He would approach John Humphries, the firm's senior partner; however, the reappointment of Travers Smith would be in addition to Napley, not instead of him.

On 19 December Napley met Iveagh and Ward; Saunders came in with Humphries. Napley said quite frankly to Humphries, 'We need your name; if I act alone people will think there is something wrong.' Ward was carrying some papers and remarked he was just off to Heathrow. 'Those aren't papers for the DTI, are they?' asked Humphries, lightly; Ward brushed this aside with an air of irritation. Alan Keat, another Travers Smith partner, came in 'to prevent me overcommitting myself'; Humphries' colleagues sometimes thought him impulsive. Ward said Freshfields thought there was not yet a conflict of interest; nevertheless Ward thought that such a conflict 'might well arise'. Ward felt that another firm of solicitors was needed in addition, and suggested that Napley might work with both Travers Smith Braithwaite and Freshfields.[2]

Napley was critical of Freshfields. He disagreed with their approach on the subject of conflicts of interests and with their suggestion that the Company, Saunders, the other directors and others involved should seek separate legal representation. 'It was desirable in matters such as this for all the parties to speak with one voice.' Desirable perhaps: but surely, in the situation now being reached, impossible? Napley's purpose here was clearly to protect Saunders, because if Saunders and the Company were firmly linked it would be less easy for anyone within the Company to say anything against his interests. The minutes quote

Napley as saying that 'it was very unlikely any conflicts of interest would arise between the Company, its directors and its officers'. As would soon become very clear, this was a notable piece of wishful thinking.

The following day, Saturday, 20 December, Saunders, Iveagh and Napley met with the three executive directors, Steel, Baldock and Dowling. They were all in favour of the change from Freshfields, as indicated by the minutes: 'Mr Steel, Mr Baldock and Mr Dowling referred to incidents within their areas of responsibility where Freshfields had taken action which seemed unsatisfactory.' But Baldock voiced the usual concern about Napley: 'if . . . the media became aware . . . that the Company had retained Kingsley Napley it was likely that the inference would be drawn that the Company was in some trouble and had . . . retained Sir David Napley because of his reputation in criminal legal matters.' Saunders told the meeting that Ward supported the move from Freshfields to Kingsley Napley but that Roux equally strongly opposed the idea. Napley said he regarded it as a gross error of judgement to tell the Press of the Boesky investment before telling the inspectors about it; he blamed Freshfields for this. Those directors present all supported the appointment of Kingsley Napley, jointly with Travers Smith or another City firm, to deal with the inspectors.

But then Sir Norman Macfarlane joined the meeting and began noticeably to assert himself as spokesman for the new non-executives, or the 'sack the chairman committee'. In the summer when Saunders had given them this name he had been joking; now the joke was no longer a joke. Macfarlane now said the replacement of Freshfields by Kingsley Napley should not be effected 'precipitately', and the other non-executive directors should be consulted first. Could it not wait until 23 December, when another meeting was scheduled? Saunders explained that the inspectors were getting impatient for some of the information required, mentioned Freshfields' possible conflicts of interest, and alleged that there had been a lack of communication from Freshfields. As to the Press announcement about Boesky, this had been drafted by Freshfields and Lazards and issued urgently at their specific request. Macfarlane said the Press release was extremely poorly worded and should not have been issued until the non-executive directors had commented on it. He feared that Freshfields might announce that they had been dismissed, which would damage the Company's image. Napley said he had offered to Freshfields to work jointly with them, but they had refused.

Shaun Dowling supported the decision to change solicitors, both because Freshfields acted also for a Boesky company and because, having advised Guinness during the Distillers bid, they should not be consulted by the Company in matters about which they might themselves be investigated. In the end Macfarlane seems to have been more or less satisfied; David Wynne-Morgan, the public relations man, came in and said the change of solicitors could be presented positively. Macfarlane said it would be 'very advantageous' if the change could be attributed to Freshfields' conflict of interest.

Two days before Christmas, on 23 December, there was another of these meetings, the only one at which I was present. All the executives and all the new non-executives were there, and Napley was in attendance for us to meet. Saunders told us that 'it was difficult to discover what subject the inspectors were really interested in', but it seemed to concern allegations about inducement to purchase shares. Otherwise much the same ground was covered as at the other meetings; I am ashamed to say that I defended the Boesky investment on this occasion, saying that Ward had satisfied my doubts. It would have been better to keep quiet, especially as I was not sincere; but my concern at the time was that at all costs Saunders' position should not be undermined. Whatever his mistakes, he seemed to me to be essential to the Company. Ian Maclaurin echoed Macfarlane's earlier insistence that the Board should be consulted on 'such sensitive and important matters as a change of legal representatives'. Yet by and large everyone was prepared to accept Saunders' leadership and await some sort of pronouncement, if not a report, from the inspectors. We are of course still waiting for the report.

Saunders' downfall, though, was now close. On 28 December the Press disclosed a dispute which arose between Morgan Grenfell and Ansbachers, another firm of merchant bankers, about the beneficial ownership of a block of 2.15 million Guinness shares in the name of Downs Nominees, a subsidiary of Ansbachers. The shares had been bought by an Ansbacher customer, Dr Ashraf Marwan, during the Distillers bid; afterwards he wanted to sell them. It did not suit Morgan Grenfell or Guinness that the shares should be put on the market. They were desperate at the time to keep the price as high as possible; high enough, in particular, so that those who had been enlisted in the share support operation would not need to call on their guarantees. In order to persuade Ansbachers to hang on to the 2.15 million shares, Morgan Grenfell arranged for Guinness to deposit £7,614,682.10 with Ansbachers, free of interest. This was the exact cost of the shares to Ansbachers, including all expenses. The so-called deposit would be repaid when the shares could be sold in the market at or above the relevant price of about £3.55. If this amounted to a purchase of the shares by Guinness, it was against the law, for a company may only buy its own shares with the leave of its shareholders. The strange thing is that at the same time, as we have seen, a perfectly above-board transaction was taking place through Greatbrand under which the Company was indeed buying large quantities of its own shares; the fact that this holding, not in the context a large one, was not simply added to the transaction through Greatbrand seems to exemplify the haphazard way in which the support operation was conducted. The deposit with Ansbachers was supposed to come to an end and be 'rolled over' on 19 May, though this did not happen. The Risk Affair removed all hope of Guinness reaching a level where

355p could be obtained in the market for a holding of that size; even the middle market price only reached 350p on one day in September. So the deposit was still outstanding in December.

In the meantime nobody admitted to owning the shares, and this led to an embarrassment when a dividend was paid on them. The cheque, of about £48,000, was paid to Down Nominees, the Ansbacher subsidiary in the name of which the shares were registered. However, following the payment of the £7,614,682 to Ansbachers, that bank regarded the shares as sold and as being the responsibility of Morgan Grenfell. Accordingly, Ansbachers sent Morgan Grenfell the dividend cheque. On 1 December, the arrival of the DTI inspectors at Morgan Grenfell gave rise to an urgent desire to get rid of the dividend, so the sum was returned to Ansbachers with a note saying it had been sent in error. At the same time Ansbachers' Chief Executive, Richard Fenhalls, had ordered an internal inquiry about the odd-looking interest-free 'deposit', and had not liked what he saw. The sum equalled the exact cost of repurchasing the shares, plus an indemnity to the client. Fenhalls went to the Bank of England who instructed him to tell the DTI. Dominic Hobson thinks it was from there that the story leaked to the *Sunday Telegraph*.[3] The Press had some fun with the story; the *Financial Times* referred to the 'genuine bouncing Guinness dividend cheque which nobody wants on the premises when inspectors from the DTI call'.[4]

This triggered Roger Seelig's resignation from Morgan Grenfell on 30 December. At first the firm put on a bold face. Its spokesman was positively arrogant to the *Sunday Times*: 'All we are saying is that we do not own the shares and never paid for the shares. We are not saying that Guinness, or anybody else, owns or paid for them. But what I can say is that Roger is surrounded by a clutch of lawyers and so are we.'[5] Morgan Grenfell's legal advisers, Slaughter and May, advised Seelig to leave immediately so as to limit the damage to the firm, in the hope that the others would be able to keep their jobs.[6] This did not work for long.

In the meantime came the event which really did for Saunders. Olivier Roux had been getting increasingly worried; now he decided that for his own personal protection he had to shop his colleague. After consultations with his solicitors and with Bain, Roux wrote an eight-page letter on 4 January 1987 to Sir David Napley with a copy to Sir Norman Macfarlane. This was to become famous as the 'Roux letter'. Later he came to an agreement with the Serious Fraud Office that he would be guaranteed immunity from prosecution in return for revealing all he knew.

The Roux letter listed eleven institutions or individuals who had been approached during the bid and asked to support Guinness. Many had been given an indemnity, that is, compensated for making a loss on their investment, as well as a payment for having made it. Roux admitted that he himself had helped in arranging this; in most cases he also implicated Saunders either as approving what was done or as actually ordering it. Others, notably Seelig and Ward, also came into the account. What was so damaging about the letter was that it gave clear and simple explanations of much that had been mysterious. This was true of the Ansbachers' 'deposit'. It was true also of the Boesky investment. Ward, said Roux, had proposed to him and Saunders that a suitable way of compensating Boesky for his support during the bid would be for Guinness to invest £100 million (*sic*: the figure was really $100 million) in Boesky's fund and that Saunders had agreed.

The largest transactions were with the Swiss bank, Bank Leu, whose Chairman was Arthur Fuerer. It had extended to Guinness two unsecured lines of credit at the favourable rate of 1 per cent over Libor, one of £50 million and one of £70 million. The £50 million credit had been used to buy Guinness shares; the £70 million had been used to buy 3 per cent of Distillers' share capital. (This 3 per cent was, we remember, purchased as the bid was closing, and was probably the transaction that swung the battle Guinness's way.) Roux said in his letter that he was 'shattered' when he discovered these transactions and protested strongly to Saunders; some such scheme had been discussed but he had ruled it out. However, when Saunders asked him to help in sorting out the position, he had arranged a further line of credit of £75 million to absorb a total of 24 million Guinness shares: 12 million from Ivan Boesky, 8 million from Heron Corporation, and 4 million from Ephraim Margulies. The intention was then to sell all the shares held by the Swiss nominee companies by secondary offerings, for which purpose the Guinness share price would have to rise to about 350p a share. Steps were taken to engineer these secondary offerings; Saunders went to the United States, continental Europe and Japan to prepare for them by getting Guinness quoted in those markets. The sales effort achieved considerable success; the combined Company did look a good investment proposition. By mid-July natural demand had absorbed some £65 million worth of these holdings. But the effect on the Guinness share price of the Risk Affair was such that no more could be sold at the necessary price.

Saunders was not himself sent a copy of the Roux letter – he takes exception to this in *Nightmare* – but Napley of course sent one round by messenger as soon as he received it on the morning of Monday, 5 January 1987. When it arrived, Saunders was meeting Brian Baldock and others to review the Press coverage on the Company, which was turning nasty, and to consider taking libel action where desirable. They agreed that a letter should be sent to staff, and Saunders decided to hold a meeting the following day, Tuesday, 6 January, to brief all directors who might be available with his reaction to this bad publicity; it would be held at Sir David Napley's office at 3 p.m.

Saunders had planned this meeting as an operation to patch up a leaking dyke; with the Roux letter the dyke itself collapsed. The meeting was a dramatic one. Benjamin Iveagh was not there, nor was Ward or Roux, but all the executives and the new non-executives were present. Napley handed us copies of the Roux letter; Sir Norman Macfarlane had been sent a copy direct by Roux, and had informed the other new non-executives. The rest of us had to read it rather quickly. This put us at a disadvantage; I certainly did not want to be bounced into agreeing to take any action on the basis of a long document which I had not had time to consider. Macfarlane asked Saunders if Roux's allegations were true; Saunders said it was the first he had heard of any of it. Napley said he had seen Roux on 30 December, and Roux had made certain statements on the basis of which Napley had prepared a document for him to sign; but Roux had sent word through his solicitors that he had decided not to sign. On Roux's letter, Napley pointed out that it constituted an admission of illegal behaviour by Roux himself. He had advised Saunders to tell Bain that Roux was no longer to come to Guinness's offices, and Saunders had done this and locked Roux's office.

Macfarlane, it turned out, had been in close touch with Roux, who was by arrangement waiting in the building. Macfarlane said he thought that Roux should be asked into the meeting; this was agreed, Macfarlane made a quick telephone call, and Roux came straight up. Macfarlane then asked Napley to leave the room. For a director who was not the Chairman to make this request of the man in whose offices we were meeting was a touch impertinent; however, the circumstances were rather exceptional, and Napley complied quietly. The reason why Macfarlane did not want Napley in the room became apparent when Roux made his statement, of which he had certainly given Macfarlane a foretaste. With Napley in the room, Roux would either have had a direct and embarrassing confrontation with Napley, or been severely restricted in what he said. He said that during and after the bid he had become more and more worried about certain transactions, but had not been able to bring himself to speak out. He now pointed out that he had opposed Napley's appointment, and said he believed that a cover-up was being prepared, to which he would not agree. He also knew that the auditors, Price Waterhouse, were concerned about certain matters. So he had consulted his own solicitors, who were also those of Bain, and written his letter.

Roux then left, and Macfarlane, backed by Plastow, said that Saunders ought to resign then and there. He refused, saying that this was a matter for the Board at a proper Board Meeting. This seemed right; it had now come down to Roux's word against that of Saunders, and I for one could not make up my mind immediately. At this stage no one expressed himself in favour of Saunders resigning except the new non-executives. The executive team, in particular, was to all appearances solidly behind Saunders. Vic Steel made the point that for Saunders to be sacked or suspended at this stage would be taken by the media and public as implying that he was guilty, whereas the facts were still unclear. After a bit Napley rejoined the meeting, and said that the Roux letter must be sent to the DTI inspectors. Macfarlane said he would himself take a copy to them, implying that he did not trust Napley to do this. It was, of course, unthinkable that a senior solicitor would fail to give the inspectors a document which he had promised in front of a dozen people to deliver; Macfarlane's insistence on delivering it himself was a calculated insult.

The meeting then discussed whether either Saunders or Roux or both ought to be suspended from their functions. It was finally decided that both should remain for the time being.

It seems with hindsight strange that any of us should for a moment have supposed that Saunders could survive the Roux letter. Even if he was ignorant of the details of the support operation, even if Roux was lying about his involvement, he could scarcely carry on. He was Chief Executive of the Company when these events took place, and had demonstrably been working almost full-time on the bid; such a degree of ignorance would indicate a level of incompetence which his career rendered unlikely. In any case, how could he have been ignorant to this extent? Roux was to carry conviction when he snapped at

Saunders' counsel during his trial: 'We were not running the Sock Shop.'[7]

Yet I kept my common sense at bay for several days. On Wednesday, 7 January, the day after the meeting at Napley's office, Macfarlane invited me to breakfast, with the idea of bringing me round to the view that Saunders ought to go. He was so scathing about Napley that I asked him whether he thought that appointing Napley was in itself a confession of guilt by Saunders. He back-pedalled a little, but explained: 'You only go to Napley as a last resort.' On Saunders he came out with: 'Can't you see the man is a crook?' My reply was on the lines that, crook or not, Saunders was running the business, and that the team of executive directors who were producing the current profits was solidly behind him. This, as Macfarlane knew but I did not, was no longer the case. Saunders had asked all the executives to write Macfarlane letters in his support. They did indeed write to Macfarlane, but Brian Baldock, for one, told Macfarlane that he was profoundly suspicious and disillusioned.[8] Baldock's letter was confidential, but since I was a director of the Company it would perhaps not have been totally improper at least to let me know the gist of it. Macfarlane evidently felt differently, and kept quiet about Baldock; so our breakfast ended in disagreement. All the same Macfarlane was probably not dissatisfied, for he will have become aware that my attitude was entirely dependent on the belief that the executives were still behind Saunders, and that it would change when I discovered that this was no longer the case.

He must have been irritated, though, by the letter I wrote to him immediately afterwards; unfortunately there is no date on it. I resurrect it because it brings to life again the way I saw things. 'Thank you for our breakfast and meeting which was certainly useful . . . Unfortunately it was belated, though. To be explicit, I take exception to the fact that four non-executive directors met without giving the rest the opportunity to attend. I don't claim that this meeting was either illegal or in the strict sense improper;

my standpoint is that it was mischievous . . .' and constituted a cabal.

My remarks may have discouraged the new non-executives from letting me in on their deliberations; this was a pity, because had they done so I could have come to see Macfarlane's point of view earlier than I did, and communicated it to others.

Later that morning Sir John Nott, Chairman of Lazards, visited Saunders and advised him to resign of his own accord. Macfarlane and Plastow then turned up; Saunders had Napley with him and also Scrine, the Company Secretary. No agreement was reached.

In the meantime, exposure was approaching from another source: Price Waterhouse, the Company's auditors. They and Guinness's own in-house accountants had been steadily becoming more worried about large invoices, running into millions, which seemed to have no satisfactory explanation. As early as May 1986, Keith Hamill, the Price Waterhouse partner directly responsible for the Guinness audit, overheard someone from Morgan Grenfell ask Alan Bailey, Guinness's chief accountant, whether he knew about up to £20 million of extra costs of the bid, and Bailey had seemed in the dark about these and 'uncomfortable'. Hamill continued 'nagging' Bailey about this and on 8 November demanded an explanation of four items: £25 million of acquisition costs unaccounted for, the £7,614,692.10 interest-free deposit with Ansbachers, the $100 million investment in the Boesky partnership and the £50 million deposit with Bank Leu.[9] Hamill made these statements at Saunders' trial. Bailey's own account was slightly different; without mentioning Hamill's queries, he said that he himself started to get concerned about some of the unexplained invoices in 'late August [of 1986] going into September because by then the total was about £15 million and I was concerned because of the total amount being kept confidential' – confidential from him, as he explained. He gives the impression that he alerted Price

Waterhouse rather than the other way round. This discrepancy is of limited importance; what is certain is that unexplained transactions of this size could hardly be kept concealed for ever either from the accountants employed within Guinness or from Price Waterhouse, especially as the year-end approached. On 25 November 1986, Howard Hughes, senior partner of Price Waterhouse, met Saunders and asked about the four items. Saunders said he would discuss them later. This did not happen, for on 1 December the inspectors were sent in. Hughes dined with Saunders and Iveagh in the Inn on the Park on 22 December. On that occasion Saunders told Hughes that if his senior executives had been 'over-zealous', this was because they wanted to get the bid out of the way. Any breaches of the City code on takeovers there might have been were accidental and technical. Hughes' reaction is not recorded.

However, as soon as they received the Roux letter on Monday, 6 January, Saunders and Napley showed it to Howard Hughes and his colleague John Salmon, and asked them to report on these matters. Hughes, according to *Nightmare*, 'said he would need to see the Board to review the implications of Roux's letter in terms of the Company's borrowing powers and the closing of the accounts'.[10] This indicates that he was already concerned about the Company's free reserves and whether it could pay the dividend it-had already announced, a matter which was to cause some stir. The following day, after the meeting in Napley's office, Sir Norman Macfarlane on behalf of the new non-executives also asked Price Waterhouse to report to the Board on the matters raised in the letter. The report was to be ready for consideration by the Board at the meeting scheduled for 14 January. This did not give the auditors much time, but they set to work quickly; in particular, paying a visit to Bank Leu in Zurich on 9 January. Their report is dated 12 January, and we received it on the 13th, the day before the meeting.

In the meantime events were moving fast. Saunders, realizing that the floodwaters were rising around him, decided as a last expedient to sacrifice the Chairmanship of the Company, remaining simply as Chief Executive, thus restoring the position as it had been before Benjamin Iveagh had retired. Iveagh himself, though, would no longer do; someone altogether more solid and credible was required. The new man would have also to satisfy Sir Norman Macfarlane and the other new non-executives, whose specific right it was to determine who was to be Chairman. In desperation Saunders approached me; specifically, he asked me to dine with him and Carole on Thursday, 8 January to discuss the matter. We ate in the brown dining room of the Inn on the Park, whose all too discreet lighting rendered the occasion physically, as well as metaphorically, rather a dark one. Saunders seemed full of fight, but the longer we discussed the possibility of finding a Chairman the more hopeless the prospect appeared. Who on earth, of sufficient stature, would consent to do it? A maverick would not be acceptable to the new non-executives or indeed to Saunders himself. I had no ideas and privately considered the prospect hopeless, but agreed to make inquiries. Suddenly, over the coffee, Saunders slumped in his chair, asleep or unconscious. Carole took charge smoothly, as if this had happened before. 'You'd better go, Jonathan,' she said, 'I can manage.' Impressed by her quiet confidence, I took my leave and went home, worried for Saunders but reassured that he had Carole to look after him.

Much later, at the time of Saunders' successful appeal to get his prison sentence reduced, doctors mentioned that he might be suffering from the premature onset of Alzheimer's Disease. This being a newsworthy complaint, the media picked it out of the appeal hearing, and many people who did not read beyond the headlines got the impression that a false diagnosis of the disease secured Saunders' early release. The record of the appeal makes it clear that this was not so; it was only mentioned as one of several possibilities, and there were other factors involved besides the medical one. However, in so far as the possibility of

Alzheimer's did occur to Saunders' doctors, it may well have been based on this tendency to fall suddenly asleep.

The following day, Thursday, the *Evening Standard* rang me to ask about Guinness; I tried to display confidence in Saunders' future. All the same, I had been struck by that moment of human vulnerability when he had suddenly fallen asleep; so without saying what had happened I emphasized that this was a man under stress, and said that for this reason he might give up the Chairmanship. The *Evening Standard* printed a report of the interview in its early edition of Friday, 9 January under the banner headline SAUNDERS MUST GO. I had underestimated the sheer newsworthiness of the idea that a Guinness family director might be publicly turning against Saunders for the first time, in the light of the obsession with Guinness in the news media. (The report made it clear that I was referring only to the possibility that Saunders might give up the office of Chairman, but anyone seeing the headline would naturally assume that I wanted him to resign as Chief Executive as well.) Saunders saw the story first, and rang me in a state of indignation; I told him that the newspaper had given my remarks a spin I had not intended. Saunders sent David Wynne-Morgan, the public relations man, round to see me at my office at Leopold Joseph in the City, and the two of us started to draft a correction. We were in the middle of this when Brian Baldock turned up and said he had to see me without Wynne-Morgan, whom I accordingly asked to wait outside. Baldock told me that I should not retract the *Evening Standard* story because he and the other executive directors were now convinced that Saunders had done wrong, was telling lies and would have to go. He was clearly harassed and upset, and also in a hurry, so I let him go without too many questions; it was evident, though, that he and the others now accepted the essential truth of the accusations in the Roux letter and did not believe that Saunders was ignorant of what had gone on. Saunders' last bastion was down.

At 5 p.m. those directors who could do so met at Lazards with Sir John Nott and his assistant Marcus Agius; there were five of us there, Edward Guinness, Vic Steel, Brian Baldock, Shaun Dowling and myself, enough to form a quorum. There was general agreement that Saunders would indeed have to go, or at least to stand aside while all the allegations in the Roux letter were properly investigated. Nott distributed a document from the solicitors Herbert Smith which made it clear that in the circumstances it was the duty of the directors to ensure that this happened, not least as an insurance for their own personal positions. 'If an executive director against whom serious allegations are made is allowed to retain his authority and further irregularities occur, how do directors answer the charge, "In the light of what you knew why did you not strip him temporarily of all his powers?"'

In their paper the solicitors made one point that needs underlining, because of the case made by Saunders' defenders, notably but not only in *Nightmare*, that it was unfair to get rid of him before he had a chance to defend himself and answer the charges. This was that directors cannot act like a court of law, which has the luxury – a luxury often, as we shall see in this case, used with a lavishness that amounts to serious injustice – of almost unlimited time to get at the truth. A Board must feel free to take immediate action in protection of the Company's assets, and indeed of its staff.

Nott, who we remember had urged Saunders to go some days previously, said that it would have to be the executives in a body who would get him to stand aside, because his case for staying rested on their support. So all four of them – Vic Steel, Brian Baldock, Shaun Dowling and Edward Guinness – left Lazards for Portman Square to confront Saunders. Steel shared a taxi with Edward. 'You are senior to us all, Edward,' said Steel, 'you had better be the spokesman.'

Was Edward in fact senior to them all? In terms of length of service he was, of course, but in terms of status he was not, because unlike the other three, he did not belong to Saunders' Executive Committee. Nevertheless Steel was right; Edward was the man to deliver the black spot. He had spent all his working life in the Company; he was also a member of the family. Edward was too modest, perhaps, for his own good; he tended to be seriously underestimated. He ran Harp Lager for a decade, a task which required diplomacy in handling the other powerful brewers in the consortium; he undertook Press relations just before Saunders' arrival, when nobody else was able or willing to do this. He was Chairman of the Brewers' Society, and performed well in the role which admirably suited his talents and his temperament. His normal retirement date would have been in the previous June, but Saunders had asked him to stay on until February to handle the tricky relationship with the Scots. We have already noted Saunders' remark to him: 'I regard you as the conscience of the Company.' When he repeated this compliment around the time of the Roux letter, Edward answered: 'A conscience cannot operate if it does not know what is going on.' Now, as often in the past, Edward was there when he was needed.

SIXTEEN

The Sacking of Saunders

We are still in the taxi with Edward Guinness and Vic Steel, on their way to Portman Square to confront Saunders. After agreeing to be the spokesman, Edward said, 'All right; but what do we do afterwards?' and went on to ask Vic Steel whether he would be willing to become Chief Executive. Steel was the obvious candidate for this post, because he headed the Company's largest division, its distilling interests. However, he said he did not want it. Edward spent the rest of the journey working out what he would say.

Everyone arrived at the Guinness offices not long after 6 p.m. Saunders was surprised to see Edward; he had called a meeting of the Executive Committee of which Edward was not a member. Edward told Saunders that he and the others had something to say to him and that they had better go to the Boardroom. When they were seated, Edward spoke quite briefly and to the point. Saunders had lost the confidence of the Executive Directors, he said. They were all agreed that he must step aside, at any rate while the DTI inspectors were conducting their investigation. Saunders asked if he would continue to receive his salary; they told him that as far as they were concerned he could, but that they had no power to commit the Board as a whole. Edward in particular is very clear on this point; Saunders, he says, was perfectly aware that the Board could not be bound by any suggestion the executive directors might make. Saunders proposed to consider the matter over the weekend and give his response on the Monday. Shaun Dowling was the first one to make it clear that this was impossible: 'It must be now,' he said, and the others all agreed. The media were circling like wolves; everyone was under pressure. It really was essential that the move be announced to the Press that night. Emotions were intense; these men were, after all, close associates who had worked as a team and had done so effectively. Steel, Baldock and Dowling had been chosen by Saunders, they were his men; as for Edward, he had been the first among the old management to see clearly that change was required and to push without equivocation for Saunders to be in charge rather than Purssell. To repudiate an inspiring leader – and Saunders was inspiring in his way – is never easy, whatever the reasons which make it necessary. Vic Steel was particularly upset, breaking down in tears, and Brian Baldock's eyes had been noticeably moist when he had visited me that afternoon. Saunders eventually accepted that the matter could not wait until the Monday, but asked for a few hours that evening so that he could see his lawyer, Sir David Napley, and also his wife. There was a short discussion – Saunders' idea of a new and independent Chairman was mentioned – and a Press statement was drafted to be issued when he had made up his mind. He was given until nine o'clock. 'Till nightfall,' interjected Shaun Dowling; the January night outside was already entirely black, and Dowling's remark struck, for Edward, the only light note in the proceedings.

Saunders rang Carole, and both went straight to Napley's office. Napley then telephoned the Guinness executive directors to confirm that Saunders would retain his salary and benefits; they again said that as far as they were concerned he could do so, but that Saunders could not stipulate it as a condition because such a decision would have to be taken by the full Board. Napley told them that Saunders agreed on this basis and that the Press statement could go out. Saunders turned up again at Portman

Square, accompanied by Carole and their daughter Joanna. Shaun Dowling handed him a copy of the Press statement and Executive Committee minute. They all repaired to the bar for a drink; the atmosphere became relaxed, even rather friendly. Now that the decision had been made, personal relations for that evening could return to the old footing. Carole told them, 'You know, he nearly left after the Monopolies Commission referral.'

Guinness PLC now had neither a Chairman nor a Chief Executive – additional proof of Saunders' unwisdom in making himself Chairman during the previous summer: he could equally well have been in a plane crash. It was imperative that someone be appointed at least as Chairman during that weekend, so as to be in place on the Monday. There was a great deal of movement and discussion during those two days. On Saturday, 10 January, Saunders' announcement was in the newspapers; it said he was standing aside. 'I feel personally that because of the uncertainty and disruption that has been caused to the business as a result of the Department of Trade and Industry inquiry, this action would be in the best interests of the company, its shareholders, its employees and my family.' That morning he flew to Geneva with Carole to see Arthur Fuerer, the Chairman of Bank Leu whom he had made a Guinness director; it is permissible to wonder whether this was just 'to say goodbye', as *Nightmare* puts it,[1] for Bank Leu had been the source of the gigantic loans mentioned in the Roux letter. From Geneva they flew to Dublin to see Benjamin Iveagh. *Nightmare* claims that Benjamin promised that he would see that the Company fulfilled the conditions which the executive directors had provisionally agreed.[2] This must be queried. Benjamin, who had sat on Boards since his twenties, is unlikely to have imagined that he had the power to ensure this. What he probably did was agree personally to support Saunders' terms and to try to get them ratified, as indeed the executive directors had done. Saunders and Carole flew back to London the following day, Sunday, 11 January, and entered Champneys health farm, which was owned by Guinness, for a brief rest cure.

That same Sunday there was a lunch party at the Wimbledon home of John Humphries, senior partner of Travers Smith Braithwaite, convened at short notice following a telephone call from Edward Guinness. The idea was to formulate an agreed policy in the emergency to put before the new non-executive directors who, it was accepted, were now in a dominant position. A key element of this policy would be the complete reinstatement of Travers Smith as the Company's solicitors. Edward and I were both at the lunch, as were Benjamin, who had flown over from Ireland, and also Shaun Dowling and Brian Baldock. Two other partners of Travers Smith were also present, Alan Keat and Roger Dixon. It was recognized that the new Chairman would have to be one of the new non-executives. But those present expressed a preference for Plastow over Macfarlane, and we agreed to try to achieve this. We felt that Plastow would be more balanced and emollient. There was no evidence for this view; all along Plastow had agreed with Macfarlane in every particular. Macfarlane had taken the lead throughout, however, and had therefore been the one to show his teeth. We did not consider Maclaurin, Chapman or Greener.

That Sunday evening the Guinness Board met at Vickers' offices, by courtesy of Sir David Plastow. It was quickly made clear that the new non-executives had sewn everything up. The solicitors would not be Travers Smith Braithwaite, but Herbert Smith, who had acted for Distillers. As to our suggestion that Plastow should be the new Chairman, this was politely turned down by Plastow himself; he would not have the time, he said, and in any case all the new non-executives had agreed that Norman Macfarlane should take the appointment. He turned out to be better at running the Company than any of us expected, or perhaps deserved: strong, shrewd and absolutely straight, yet capable also of a sensitive touch and by no means without charm.

He is, I think, a man of strong emotions; I saw signs of this on several occasions. To be emotional is by no means incompatible with being, as Macfarlane is, a man of formidable ability. The combination made him a dangerous enemy for Saunders, because he felt the extra rancour of someone who believes he has been deceived and exploited. Macfarlane started, let us not forget, as a Saunders supporter. Now that he saw him in stark terms as a crook, he not only showed no mercy, he pursued Saunders with what can only be called vindictiveness.

It was the Price Waterhouse report that decisively turned every member of the Guinness Board against Saunders and made us insist that he should not just step aside pending further investigation but be sacked forthwith. This may seem odd, in that most of the information the report contained was also in the Roux letter. But Roux had himself been intimately mixed up in the bid operations, and the view was tenable – just – that he was simply trying to unload on to Saunders the blame which was really his. This is indeed what Saunders himself has consistently claimed. Even at the time, though, there could be no suspicion of Price Waterhouse, and no question of retaining or rewarding a Chief Executive under whom the Company had done what was described by them.

The report is perhaps the more damaging in that its wording is so moderate. The introduction emphasizes 'the difficulty of drawing firm conclusions on the basis of this report'. Yet although many details are certainly missing, there was more than enough in it to enable us to form a view.

On that eventful Friday, 9 January, two representatives of Price Waterhouse had flown to Zurich to visit Bank Leu, and received copies of correspondence and other documents confirming what Olivier Roux had said in his letter about the two large deposits made by Guinness against Bank Leu's purchase of Guinness and Distillers shares. This visit followed a letter from Bank Leu to the new non-executives which 'confirmed that these transactions had taken place, although it differed to [*sic*] the Roux letter in the description of the form of the transactions'. During the visit, the Price Waterhouse men received copies of the documents relating to the transactions, on the basis of which they prepared certain questions. The Bank faxed these questions to its London solicitors, Allen and Overy, who advised that it need not answer most of them because it had supplied the basic information in the form of the documents. 'They considered that answers to the listed questions should be available from Guinness.'

Price Waterhouse, collating the information collected by them with that given in the Roux letter, give the following round-figure calculation of 'possible liabilities of Guinness to Bank Leu', that is, money lent to Guinness to buy its own shares, and Distillers shares at a time when following the success of the bid these in effect represented Guinness shares. Bryton and Pipetec were Swiss nominee companies; photocopies of the agreements with them are annexed to the Price Waterhouse report. Two are with Bryton, one countersigned by Thomas Ward and one by Olivier Roux; one is with Pipetec, countersigned by Roux.

	£ million
16 April: Agreement with Bryton per agreement	50
18 April: Agreement with Pipetec per agreement	75
	125
2 June: Bryton per the Roux letter	75
	200
Sales during June and July per the Roux letter	(65)
	135
Interest to date (estimate)	15
	150

Price Waterhouse then went on to consider payments 'which have been treated as costs relating to the acquisition of Distillers but for which the invoices 'did not give sufficient explanation'. They were:

	£'000
Marketing and Acquisition Consultants Ltd	5,200
J. Lyons Chamberlayne and Co. Ltd	300
Konsultat SA	3,000
Heron Managements Ltd	2,500
Pima Service Corporation	3,413
CIFCO	1,940
Erlanger and Co., Inc	1,495
Zentralsparkasse und Kommerzialbank Wien	254
Consultations et Investissements SA	3,350
Rudani Corp. NV	1,933
Morgan Grenfell	1,650
TOTAL	25,055

This list of unexplained payments would became very familiar to us in the months to come as the situation was clarified.

Marketing and Acquisition Consultants Ltd, a Jersey company, received its £5,200,000 as a fee to Thomas Ward for his services in the Distillers bid. It was arranged privately between Ward and Saunders without the Board knowing. Until 15 February 1993 all sorts of suspicions attached to it, as we shall see; but on that date a British court acquitted Ward of stealing it, thus establishing that it was properly paid.

The rest of the list represented fees, and indemnities for losses, for purchasers of Guinness shares during and after the bid. The exact amount of share support represented by the whole list is uncertain, but it was well over £50 million and may have reached £100 million.

J. Lyons Chamberlayne and Co. Ltd was a company belonging to Sir Jack Lyons and the £300,000 was for him.

Konsultat SA: This £3 million was also for Lyons. He repaid

Guinness in November 1987 an undisclosed sum in respect of these amounts.

Heron Managements Ltd: this sum, £2½ million + VAT, was the responsibility of Gerald Ronson; the company is part of his Heron Group. It was half of a £5 million success fee in respect of an agreement to buy, in the end, up to £25 million worth of Guinness shares.

Pima Service Corporation: the £3,413,000 represents the other half of the success fee for Ronson, with an additional indemnity of £800,000. Both sums were voluntarily repaid, very soon after Saunders was dismissed.

CIFCO (Compagnie Internationale de Finance et de Commerce) which received £1,940,000 billed as 'advisory service re Distillers PLC' can be taken with

Erlanger and Co. Inc. which got £1,495,000 billed as 'work in connection with the acquisition of Distillers'. Both of these were the responsibility of Ephraim Margulies. Anthony Parnes received £340,000 of the CIFCO payment; he was to tell the DTI inspectors that this was forced on him. CIFCO eventually repaid £1.2 million to Guinness, and Erlanger repaid the full amount it had received.

Zentralsparkasse und Kommerzialbank Wien received £254,000 in consideration for having bought just under £2,000,000 worth of shares shortly after the bid. They bought for their own account on the recommendation of Sir Jack Lyons, and repaid Guinness in February 1987.

Consultations et Investissements SA: this £3,350,000, invoiced as a 'corporate success fee', went to Anthony Parnes. It includes the £340,000 received through Margulies (see above) and was repaid.

Rudani Corporation NV: this £1,953,000, billed as 'fee for advising on the acquisition of Distillers', was for the account of Mrs Violet Seulberger-Simon, who bought through Cazenove about £17 million worth of Guinness shares on the advice of

Roger Seelig passed through the property developer Elliott Bernard.[3] The amount was repaid.

Morgan Grenfell: this £1,650,000 was separate from the main fee of more than £20,000,000, and was in respect of confidential market support operations. It was repaid to Guinness in full.

After giving this list, the Price Waterhouse report went on to deal with the investment in the Boesky partnership. It summarized the conditions of the investment, showing just how unattractive these were and implying that the Company would scarcely have made it except as a recompense for something else. Guinness had put in nearly a third of the money invested in the fund. Boesky himself would get 40 per cent of any profits the fund might make, and suffer only 10 per cent of any losses. The fund had already lost $72.3 million at the end of the year. 'A current statement of the financial affairs of the Limited Partnership should be requested immediately . . . Legal advice should be sought as to the precise effect on the Limited Partnership of Boesky's settlement with the [New York] Stock Exchange Commission.'

There was a section about the interest-free deposit with Ansbachers of £7,614,682.10. This made the point that the Board 'will need to establish . . . the commercial justification for placing funds in an interest free deposit account'.

The Price Waterhouse report made another very damaging point. The shenanigans around the Distillers bid had left the balance sheet of the combined Company in such a state that for technical, accounting reasons the auditors had to advise that 'the Board should urgently consider . . . what action should be taken in relation to the payment of the interim dividend declared on 10 December 1986'. This, being interpreted, meant that the Board was being told not to pay it until there had been some resolution of the 'uncertainties which prevail as a result of the matters discussed in this report'. The Board had to comply with this advice, to the acute embarrassment of every one of us. On the

Stock Exchange the shares were already quoted ex-dividend, that is, if they changed hands the dividend did not go to the buyer, but to the seller. This is normally taken as a guarantee that the dividend will be paid, so its indefinite postponement came as a shock, as well as an inconvenience to shareholders. The dividend was a second interim, designed to be paid at about the same time as previous final dividends had been paid; the year-end had been changed from 30 September to 31 December. It was eventually paid on 28 May, and a final dividend followed it on 10 June.

Even on the question of the dividend alone, there is a case for saying that a Chief Executive under whom the accounts could get into this state had shown himself unfit to run a public company. Had we not got rid of Saunders, the Stock Exchange might well have suspended the Company's quotation; the Labour front bench spokesman on City affairs, Robin Cook, had already called for this to be done. But the dividend was not the most important of the problems; it was a symptom, not a cause. The report told us very clearly that we had been kept completely in the dark about major transactions during the bid which on the face of it were in breach of company law and the rules of the City. To judge Saunders on this was, of course, a matter for the courts. But even if he was personally innocent, as he still maintains, these apparent improprieties happened when he was in charge.

The report was incontrovertible and utterly damning, and by the time of the full Board Meeting on Wednesday, 14 January we had taken it all in and concluded that it had to be accepted as representing objective fact, not just as a case which might be answered. Olivier Roux had resigned from the Board two days before, on the Monday. Saunders did not turn up at the meeting, although he was still a director. Arthur Fuerer did come, flying over from Switzerland; he was not allowed into the building but stayed outside in his car. Since he was, after all, still a director, it is rather doubtful whether this was proper; all the same, it avoided what would have been an embarrassing confrontation, since all the directors present were minded to ask for his resignation. The meeting decided that Saunders should be dismissed without any compensation from his position as Chief Executive, although by a quirk of company law he retained his position as a director until the next General Meeting. The Price Waterhouse report was considered to indicate such gross impropriety that the Company could only be saved by distancing itself completely from the Saunders regime. Nobody argued against this; Benjamin did not, nor did the executive directors. The Board also confirmed Macfarlane as the new Chairman.

The Press and television were waiting downstairs in force. They were told what had happened. Benjamin Iveagh was asked about Saunders and said of the man he had just helped to sack without compensation: 'Once a friend, always a friend.' What he meant by this must remain uncertain.

Immediately after the meeting, Macfarlane wrote to Saunders, telling him that the directors were unanimously of the view 'that all connections between the Company and yourself should be terminated'. The Board felt that developments since the previous Friday, when Saunders had agreed simply to stand aside pending the outcome of the DTI inquiry, had rendered this insufficient. 'Accordingly it has been decided that, with immediate effect, you will no longer be Chairman and Chief Executive of the Company . . . I am afraid that all your remuneration and other perquisites will cease forthwith', as would the appointment of Carole, who had been taken on as design consultant at £20,000 a year; this comparatively small impropriety, if impropriety it was, had shocked Macfarlane deeply, as he was to make clear to me in conversation. The letter also invited Saunders to resign as a director of the Company.

Was Ernest Saunders made a scapegoat, as his son maintains in *Nightmare*? The fact that this is very much a minority viewpoint, dismissed as absurd by the consensus of opinion, does not excuse us from examining it. James Saunders underlines

Macfarlane's remark in the letter quoted above that developments since the Friday had 'rendered the agreement to let Ernest stand aside on full pay with legal costs "no longer appropriate". In fact,' James comments, 'there had been no damning revelations *against Ernest*: the only developments that took place between Friday and Wednesday had been the resignation of Roux and the election of Macfarlane as acting chairman' (my italics).[4] In the narrow sense, it is true that there was no new accusation against Saunders personally. However, if this is meant to imply that nothing had happened between the Friday and the Wednesday except the resignation of Roux and the appointment as Chairman of Macfarlane, it is wrong. Something very important had happened – the appearance of the Price Waterhouse report. What that report did was decisively to raise the status of revelations already made, but made until then only by Roux who had himself been involved in much of the apparent irregularity and therefore could only be regarded as suspect. With Price Waterhouse backing the allegations, it would have been irresponsible to continue to wait for an inspectors' report that, in the event, has still not appeared nine years on; or indeed for the result of prosecutions which were not to take place until 1990.

In *Nightmare* James Saunders says: 'There was to be no corporate responsibility as far as Macfarlane was concerned.'[5] This was very true, and not only of Macfarlane but of all of us. We were determined to repudiate what had been done, promptly and totally. Accepting corporate responsibility for actions of which none of us had been aware would have been pointless masochism. But did the Guinness Board go further in its measures against Saunders than was strictly fair? It had a duty to run the Company; it had no duty to prejudge the result of a possible lawsuit. To sack Saunders without pay and in disgrace was right; quite apart from anything which he may have done against the law, there were plenty of ways in which his behaviour had made this the only course of action the Board could have taken. The Risk Affair had brought the Company into severe disrepute; the matter of the delayed dividend implied that at the very least the management was culpably out of touch with its auditors; the Boesky investment was wholly unsuitable in the first instance and had turned out disastrously. For his dismissal, the case seems irrefutable.

It is arguable, though, that the Company ought not to have refused to pick up Saunders' legal costs against any forthcoming prosecution. He was, by 1987, a longstanding servant of the Company. Right or wrong, what he had done had been on the Company's behalf. True, much that he ought to have reported to the Board had not been so reported and much of that looked, *prima facie*, indefensible. That is why at the time none of us stood up for his right to be given his legal costs. It is only now, years later, that I begin to think that in this respect our behaviour did not reflect the best traditions of a company like Guinness. There is, to be sure, a counter-argument here, which is that the Distillers bid enriched the Company as well as disgracing it. Agreeing to pay Saunders' legal costs would have been taken by many commentators as failing to distance ourselves from the scandal. Such commentators would have been wrong in logic and mean in intention, but the fact is that logic is in short supply in public life and meanness all too plentiful. The point would have been made, certainly in the Press and probably in Parliament too. Given the public mood then, this would probably have damaged the Company. Neither side of this argument occurred to me at the time, nor probably to any of us; we just wanted to be shot of Saunders and all his works.

In *Nightmare* we are accused of refusing Saunders access to documents and forbidding employees of Guinness to talk to him. As regards access to documents this is not true; he and his representatives were directed to go through Guinness's lawyers Herbert Smith for copies of documents, but Herbert Smith provided this facility when they were asked for it. Guinness employees were indeed forbidden to talk to Saunders, however, and this was possibly unfair.

We had nothing to do with cutting Saunders off from contact with Guinness employees: this was in fact imposed on Saunders as a bail condition by the Bow Street magistrates. Courts have these habits: they are accustomed to make this kind of condition where a person on remand may, for instance, threaten a witness with violence. This was unlikely to apply here. The prohibition is perhaps simply an expression of the general public disapproval of Saunders.

The news of Saunders' dismissal was none the less sensational for having been widely anticipated. The media were already full of the Guinness Affair, and the storm had spread from the City to the political world. This was not, as has been suggested, simply because a General Election was approaching; this may have helped concentrate politicians' minds on it, but the embarrassment and anger of Mrs Thatcher's Government went deeper than any immediate electoral worry. For Mrs Thatcher is not just a Conservative, but a Conservative of a particular type. She is a believer in an ideology; in her way, she is an idealist. The easy cynicism of the man of the world, so prevalent among practising politicians of all stripes and particularly among Conservatives, is foreign to her nature. Traditional Conservatism was at bottom sceptical of all ideology; pragmatic, worldly-wise, even a touch world-weary. Lord Gilmour, among the brightest of the pre-Thatcherite Conservatives, wrote in 1977: 'Probably the only thing that could prevent [a Conservative victory at the next General Election] would be for the Tories to go on an ideological "trip" and scare the voters.'[6] He was probably thinking partly of the *débâcle* suffered by Barry Goldwater in the United States Presidential Election of 1964. But as regards Britain in the late 1970s he was wrong. The revived nineteenth-century free-trading liberalism we now call Thatcherism was an ideology whose time had come, or come back. In the late 1970s it was James Callaghan's Labour Party that seemed morally stale, compensating for its lack of a majority with funny little deals and *ad hoc* manoeuvres, tacking constantly between the trade unions and the exasperated public. For once, the British public was ready to try a little ideology. The Conservatives won the 1979 election under Mrs Thatcher and increased their majority in 1983.

Mrs Thatcher was not at all world-weary; she believed in her market economy, both in the sense that it worked and in the sense that it was morally right. That it works, on the whole, has been demonstrated. But it must always be rather difficult to show that it has anything to do with morality, either way. The line is usually that any attempt to interfere with it, whether for moral reasons or for selfish ones, will make it less efficient. This makes believers in the market economy who have high standards of personal ethics, such as Mrs Thatcher, particularly sensitive to accusations that markets are rigged or corrupt. Conversely, their opponents who profess some form of socialism love to find reason to make such accusations. Hence the venom with which Government and Opposition competed to pursue the wretched Geoffrey Collier, as we saw in Chapter 14.

When the Guinness Affair erupted Mrs Thatcher reacted as if stung. Her view of the free market was predicated on honesty; genuine honesty, naïve as this may seem or even be. She was not pretending, but was truly upset by the gibes of the Labour Opposition about Guinness, led in this matter by John Smith who was Trade and Industry spokesman at the time. Mrs Thatcher felt that if City wrongdoing went unpunished it would give Labour the moral advantage and in the end endanger all she stood for.

She was certainly not going to accept that Morgan Grenfell, for one, should get away with the sole resignation of Roger Seelig. According to *Business*,[7] she told Nigel Lawson, her Chancellor of the Exchequer, 'I want Reeves and Walsh out today, not next week or next month but by lunchtime today.' The Bank of England summoned Morgan Grenfell's Chairman, Lord Catto, on Monday, 19 January, and told him that it would withdraw the firm's banking licence unless Reeves and Walsh both resigned at once. They did so the following day. The Bank of England then turned its attention to Ansbachers. Rodney Galpin, head of the supervisory department, summoned Richard Fenhalls, Ansbachers' Chief Executive, and told him that Lord Spens should resign immediately from Ansbachers' board. If this did not happen, 'the recognized status of the Company' would be 'put in question', in other words its banking licence might – read 'would' – be withdrawn. When Fenhalls reported this to Ansbachers' Board, he found that all his colleagues were most reluctant to comply, though of course they did so in the end. They also decided, however, that Spens' departure should be 'dignified and properly compensated', and he was later paid £79,000. Before then, the Bank of England had given Fenhalls to understand that Spens could go when his departure could do least damage to Ansbachers.[8] The abrupt change of mind by the Bank certainly implies that it was heavily leaned on, probably on 20 January; and it may be assumed that the impetus came from Mrs Thatcher herself.

We can only guess at her feelings about Sir Jack Lyons, who had given her lunch at Bain's office as recently as 7 January before resigning from that firm over the Guinness Affair at the end of the month. He was a personal friend, seeming exactly the type of businessman she admired.

In any case resignations were still not enough. Mrs Thatcher and her Government were determined that there should be criminal prosecutions. John Wakeham, Leader of the House of Commons, is quoted as saying, 'Get the handcuffs on quick.' The 'pressure to prosecute' that there had been over Collier was no more than a foretaste.

Cazenove was the target of fierce attacks in the media, directed in particular against David Mayhew, the partner who had dealt with Guinness. Whether this was accompanied by Government pressure is doubtful; Cazenove is not a bank, so the Bank of England did not have the direct hold on the firm that it did on Morgan Grenfell and Ansbachers. In any case Cazenove stood firm: Mayhew never resigned. He was eventually to be the object of a prosecution, but the case was dropped. On 29 January Cazenove made a public statement which conceded virtually nothing to the criticism. The firm said it had gone to its solicitors, Simmons and Simmons, who found that 'nothing in their inquiries had led them to believe that Cazenove was involved in, or aware of, any illegality'. When the Guinness share price had risen during the bid, Cazenove thought it was because the market expected Guinness to win. As to share dealings, 'a very significant number of transactions took place without our involvement'. There was no question, they said, of David Mayhew's future being in doubt.

But there is some evidence that at this stage Mrs Thatcher's attitude resembled that of the Queen of Hearts in *Alice*: 'The Queen's argument was that, if something wasn't done about it in less than no time, she'd have everybody executed, all round.' This was certainly in tune with the public mood of the day; Mrs Thatcher's attitude in this, as in so much, reflected a deep instinct for what many people were feeling.

SEVENTEEN

Clearing Up

The Guinness image now had to be restored. Not that the popularity of the brand had been impaired; on the contrary, sales of stout were noticeably buoyant during the period of the scandal. It was the Company, not the product, which was in disgrace. When people see the name of a product mentioned in their newspaper every day that product is kept in their consciousness, and in this restricted sense it is true to say that all publicity is good publicity. However, it was now urgent to clear up the mess, and to restore the reputation of the Company for straight dealing. For these purposes, much depended on Sir Norman Macfarlane, and on Shaun Dowling, who was in charge of the detailed work of clearing up. Dowling told me[1] that Macfarlane was an excellent front man, insisting that this was not meant to be patronizing; a crucial part of the task was precisely that of the front man, the man who would personify the cleansed image. He and the other new non-executive directors were well prepared; even before the receipt of the Roux letter they were sounding out possible replacements for Saunders should he have to go.

Specifically, they approached Anthony Tennant, Deputy Chief Executive of Grand Metropolitan and Chairman of its wines and spirits business, International Distillers and Vintners. The *Sunday Times* got wind of this approach and reported it on 4 January. The report also claims that Tennant had been runner-up to Saunders when Guinness first appointed him. This is unlikely. Had

Tennant been seriously interested at that stage, it is certain that Peter Guinness and the others would have considered no one else. He had started in advertising and marketing, then gone into brewing. In International Distillers and Vintners he had helped in the phenomenal and worldwide success of the pale whisky J & B Rare. The brand was said to have been popular with American business executives because its weak appearance enabled them, under the suspicious eyes of their wives, to get away with a drink a good deal stronger than it looked. Tennant was a well-known figure and the Guinness Board would certainly have seen him as not only professionally suitable but also likely to be congenial. His credentials would have completely eclipsed those of the unknown executive from Nestlé. Speaking personally, I felt I could hardly believe my luck when Tennant agreed to take the appointment.

Yet it was hardly surprising that he did so; it was after all a step up, from Deputy to Chief Executive, and the challenge must have been intriguing. He took over on 9 March. Until that happened, Sir Norman Macfarlane was in effect the Chief Executive, working with Saunders' team. Steel continued to run the distilling interests and Baldock to be in charge of the Breweries. The man of the hour was Shaun Dowling. His task was the more urgent in that Price Waterhouse needed to be satisfied that the dividend could be paid. It was a worrying time for all of us; we knew that Macfarlane still had to run his own business, and it seemed certain that he must be under considerable strain, as the man with the public responsibility. I remember worrying that he might not be able to cope. True, he had Shaun Dowling to back him up, and the sheer interest and drama of the situation would have been calculated to give anyone an adrenalin buzz; further, Macfarlane knew he would be well rewarded. Later, we voted him £100,000 a year. This was actually a rather moderate figure in the circumstances, but the Government was also to chip in with a life peerage.

So much depended on Macfarlane that I kept alert for any sign of strain. I noticed it once only. This was at a party in February at the Brewers' Hall in the City, given for the retirement of Edward Guinness as Chairman of the Brewers' Society. Like everybody present, I was on tenterhooks to see how Macfarlane would manage in his speech the difficult task of combining a gracious tribute to Edward with just the right amount of allusion to the scandal. He launched into the scandal from the start, how it was a shame and a disgrace to the Company, and I thought this right; it was best to get the bad bit over to begin with and only then to steer into the calmer waters of celebration and tribute. The trouble was that this switch never took place. Macfarlane went on and on about the scandal, with only the most perfunctory references to Edward. He's made his point, I said to myself; now he's just banging on. He should realize that whatever scraps remain of the solid old family image need to be used, and this is just the occasion to do so. He's on edge, nervous. Much more of this and he will be distancing himself from the Company when his job is to show solidarity. However, this occasion was only a ceremonial one, and if this is the only criticism I have of Macfarlane's behaviour at such a difficult period, it is in itself a tribute.

Yet the *faux pas*, if it was one, could be seen as a symptom of something more important and perhaps dangerous; namely, that Macfarlane's abhorrence of the way Guinness under Saunders had behaved seemed at times to transcend the rational, to be violent, visceral. Or was this reaction not entirely his own? Was his ruthlessness at least partly prompted by someone eminent hinting that ruthlessness would not be ill-regarded?

If so, this was no more than a contributory factor. Macfarlane's anger was not put on. Like that of Mrs Thatcher and of many journalists, it was absolutely genuine. British opinion is still divided between Roundhead and Cavalier, and the whole Roundhead tendency was outraged by the goings-on. There were as many people, of course, and still are, who fail to see what all the fuss was about. They are the Cavaliers, or some of them. Macfarlane, like Mrs Thatcher, is a quintessential Roundhead. The fact that he was in a position of power presented acute danger for Saunders, because it ensured that he would be pursued without mercy.

Macfarlane was firm with his fellow Scots. One eminent Scotsman wrote to him demanding that Guinness's headquarters should be moved to Scotland as promised in the bid document. Macfarlane used to send copies of such letters to all directors, and I remember writing to him on this occasion to say that had one not seen the signature one would have thought it came from a crank. Macfarlane did not weaken on the point; it was obvious that the *de facto* headquarters of the Company could only be in London, and to create a *de jure* headquarters elsewhere would be no more than a fudge.

At the same time as Anthony Tennant, the Board acquired, for the first time for years, a proper Finance Director. Olivier Roux's position as an employee of Bain running Guinness's finance officially as a non-executive director had been one of Saunders' most eccentric arrangements. The new man was Michael Julien, an accountant who had been a Group executive director of Midland Bank and helped to create the Eurotunnel consortium. His record shows rather more dash than is commonly associated with members of his profession; he left Guinness in 1988 to run Storehouse PLC, and later became Chairman of the holidays group Owners Abroad. He was a great talker, especially when compared with Anthony Tennant who would never use two words where one would do. Chief executives usually say more than finance directors, and indeed marketing men are usually more talkative than accountants. The Guinness Board Meetings were unusual in this respect.

Alternate Board Meetings were held in Scotland. The first one was in the Distillers offices in Edinburgh, but on one occasion we met in the City Hall in Glasgow, which is Norman Macfarlane's home town. Macfarlane is a man of civilized outside interests, especially in the graphic arts. He made this particular meeting memorable by organizing a visit to the Burrell Collection. This pleased me; it was clear that the Company was going to continue to favour the arts. A small point which I noticed at these first meetings was that when Saunders was mentioned he was at first still referred to by his Christian name, even by the Chairman. By about the third or fourth meeting, though, he was always Saunders.

Shaun Dowling always gave a report on the recovery of the improper payments, and the research into the share support scheme in general. These reports were considered so sensitive that they were never minuted; the minutes simply say that Dowling reported to the Board on the 'legal issues being dealt with'. The operation got off to a good start with the prompt action of Gerald Ronson, who spontaneously returned to Guinness about £5.8 million representing the payments to Heron Management Ltd and Pima Service Corporation. He accompanied his cheque with a letter drafted by his solicitor, Lord Mischcon, which was to be much quoted. 'I did not focus on the legal implications of what had occurred, nor did it cross my mind that City advisers and business people of such eminence should be asking us to join in doing something improper.' The phrase about not focusing on the legal implications was all too neat; it passed into the language, to join Lord Armstrong's 'economical with the truth'. There are times when a good phrase is a bad idea.

Soon after this the comparatively small amount of £254,000 paid to the Austrian bank Zentralsparkasse und Kommerzialbank Wien, or Bank of Vienna, was returned. This respectable, even stodgy savings bank had until then almost entirely confined itself to operations within Austria. The go-getting mood of the mid-1980s reached its Board, however, and induced it to plan an expansion into world markets. For this purpose it had established a London representative office with a view to promoting it to branch status when it generated sufficient business. The man in charge of the office happened to be a friend of mine, Dr Horst Tiefenthaler, and at the time I thought the Bank of Vienna could have made no better appointment. A systematic and indefatigable contact man, Tiefenthaler seemed the ideal person to pioneer the London market. He was what in the City is known as a lunch man, and as such he was one of the best.

Among the many contacts Tiefenthaler made in London, Sir Jack Lyons appeared to be one of the most useful. He had financial clout, long experience and eminent friends in politics as well as business, from Mrs Thatcher downwards. So when Lyons approached Tiefenthaler with a view to helping in the share support scheme after the bid, it seemed that this was a good quick way into the big time. Tiefenthaler at once contacted his chiefs in Vienna. They told him to go ahead provided there was a guarantee against loss, which in their country would not have been illegal. The amount bought was small compared with the other similar deals: less than £2 million worth of shares. Tiefenthaler told me at the time that his bank had invested in Guinness. This struck me as somewhat unexpected, and I said so. 'It's all right, it was on the recommendation of Jack Lyons and he will see that we don't lose,' said Tiefenthaler. This did not seem particularly sinister at the time and I asked no questions. I did, however, obliquely mention the matter to Saunders the next time we met. 'I learn that Sir Jack Lyons has been arranging for people to buy our shares,' I said. 'Yes,' said Saunders: 'he has been very helpful.' Soon after I saw the Austrian bank's name on the Price Waterhouse list I told Macfarlane what I knew. Shaun Dowling got in touch with Tiefenthaler who immediately secured the return of the £254,000. He and his bosses were already worried about the situation. Sir Jack Lyons had handed him some draft letters in December 1986 and asked him to get them retyped on Zentralsparkasse paper 'to avoid problems'. Tiefenthaler smelt a rat; he consulted his head office, and on their instructions refused to do what Lyons asked. The Zentralsparkasse was, therefore, already expecting trouble, and this no doubt explains its prompt repayment. With the return of what Ronson had received, this meant that over £6 million of the £25.5 million came back to Guinness within a month of Macfarlane's accession.

Sir Jack Lyons was also immediately cooperative and wrote to Macfarlane. He was responsible for two of the listed invoices and a small part of a third. J. Lyons Chamberlayne, one of his companies, had received £300,000, and the £3,000,000 for Konsultat SA of Switzerland was also for his account. The position was complicated by his statement that £750,000 of the latter sum had been used to buy from him a flat in Washington, DC: Thomas Ward was to deny this and say that on the contrary he himself had bought the flat. In November 1987 Lyons repaid Guinness an undisclosed sum, and later Guinness paid Ward the modest figure of $60,000 for the Washington flat. Lyons had also received a further £350,000 as part of the amount paid to Consultations et Investissements SA; the rest of which went to Anthony Parnes.

It might be useful at this point to consider the whole of the operation to support Guinness shares in the market, directly or indirectly at the expense of the Company, in connection with the Distillers takeover. It was not at all systematic, but represented a series of reactions, literally from day to day, to selling pressure in the market. This explains how comparatively small deals can have been concluded that caused a disproportionate amount of trouble: Zentralsparkasse, Ansbachers. At the start, Morgan Grenfell and everyone else clearly underestimated the amount of support that would be required. It was, of course, impossible to tell how much would be forced on Guinness and its helpers by the market operations of Argyll and its team. These undoubtedly took place, though there is no reason to suppose they were in any way improper. This area will always remain obscure. For one thing, a large proportion of the fees in the Guinness scheme was conditional on success, so if there was anything similar on the other side, the fees would simply not have been incurred. Again, the searchlight of the DTI inquiry was focused exclusively on Guinness and not at all on Argyll, rather as the Nuremberg war crimes trial excluded in advance any consideration of possible transgressions that might have been committed on the Allied side in the Second World War. A more general inquiry, covering the whole of the bid battle, might have been of more enduring value. As it is, it looks as if the purpose of the inquiry was not so much exploratory as inquisitorial; designed, that is, to provide evidence to be used in prosecutions that had already been decided in advance rather than to establish the facts without preconceptions. One not very hard story did surface about Argyll's support operations in the *Observer* newspaper of 16 July 1989. Michael Gillard alleged that Merrill Lynch, the large Wall Street firm, had organized support for the Argyll price and short sales of Guinness. No figures were given, nor any evidence that the support contravened any rules or laws.

The market support operations on the part of Guinness were in five parts which were essentially distinct, though they interlocked in places. First, there was the group masterminded by Morgan Grenfell and Cazenove. This represented the normal market support that one would always expect in a situation like this. Some of it was dubious, such as the deals for which Morgan Grenfell had been paid the £1,650 that figured on the Price Waterhouse list, but most was straightforward. We have noted that Rudani Corporation, for instance, which was also on the Price Waterhouse list, bought for Mrs Seulberger-Simon through Cazenove. This would have been passed through as a normal buying order and there is no reason to suppose that Cazenove knew of any dubious fee. Ansbachers' client Dr Marwan, whose sale of his shares after the bid originated the embarrassing 'interest-free loan' from Guinness to Ansbachers, comes into this category. The total support under this heading is impossible to work out.

Second, there was the group arranged by Sir Jack Lyons and Parnes. This comprises Lyons and Parnes themselves, Ronson, Margulies and Zentralsparkasse. This group accounts altogether for £18,205,000 of the invoices on the Price Waterhouse list. Just how large an investment in Guinness this represents is uncertain; Ronson's fee was 20 per cent of his investment, while that of Margulies seems to have been at least 22 per cent, based on the imprecise figures given by Roux in his evidence at Saunders' trial. On the other hand, Zentralsparkasse got only about 14 per cent. The total is unlikely to have been less than £100 million.

Third was Meshulam Riklis of Rapid-American Corporation. Riklis's interest was fairly straightforward; he wanted to maintain distribution of Distillers' whisky brands for Rapid-American's subsidiary Schenley, and if possible get more brands to distribute. He approached Argyll, but they did not talk to him: nor did Distillers when he approached them. Guinness were receptive, however, and made certain commitments in respect of which Riklis gave powerful support in the bid battle. He bought just over 5 per cent of Guinness for about £60 million.[2] He did break two rules, though probably through ignorance. Under the Takeover Code he should have declared his holding when it exceeded 5 per cent, and he should in any case have declared his holding since he had a commercial interest in the result of the bid.

Fourth was the arbitrageur, Ivan Boesky. He is said to have been first contacted by Gerald Ronson, who knew him and was in the habit of exchanging market tips.[3] This happened towards the end of the bid period, in April 1986. Ronson appears to have told Boesky that Guinness would make good any losses he might suffer. The relationship was then firmed up by Thomas Ward, who apparently organized Boesky's purchases during the last days of the bid, and the agreement finally arrived at was that Guinness should invest in his 'limited partnership'. Estimates of Boesky's purchases vary wildly. Kochan and Pym put the figure at about £70 million,[4] but another estimate I have received is of no more than £22 million. The latter figure is based on a story that Boesky at first supported Argyll, and that a great part of his service to Guinness was in ceasing to do so. He is said to have sold a large holding of Argyll shares, and unwound a short position in Guinness (that is, bought back Guinness shares he had sold without owning them in the first place). Warner's figure in the *Independent* is £41 million and his losses about $30 million or £20 million.[5] The latter figure, as Warner says, sounds exaggerated; certainly no other supporter lost anything like half his investment. Perhaps it includes the expenses of unwinding pro-Argyll positions.

Last and largest was Bank Leu, the Swiss bank whose chairman was Arthur Fuerer. Through two subsidiaries, and against deposits and guarantees by Guinness, it invested a total of about £200 million in Guinness shares and in Distillers shares when they effectively represented Guinness. The most crucial single purchase was the 10 million Distillers shares bought on 17 April 1986, the day before the end of the bid battle. This, it will be recalled, was done at 705p per share at a time when under takeover rules Guinness was only entitled to bid 630p, this being its cash offer. At the time, it was accepted that Bank Leu was not associated with Guinness. The fact that it was indeed so associated made this the most important single transaction in breach of the rules.

What was the total of the improper market support? This will never be known. It would be neat if we could simply take the Bank Leu total of £200 million, because much of this represented absorption after the bid of shares bought during the course of it; but it is certain that Bank Leu did not absorb all the other purchases. The difference of £50 million between the highest and the lowest estimates of Boesky's dealings is an obstacle. There is also the question of whether one counts Riklis's purchase as being positively improper, or whether he should more charitably be seen as being in a grey area. It will also never be known precisely how much of the first category, the Morgan Grenfell and Cazenove support, was improper and to what extent.

Shaun Dowling soon collected back most of the improper fees on the Price Waterhouse list. Some accuse him of ruthlessness, but he was capable of patience and, in the case of Anthony Parnes in particular, could strike up a good personal relationship which had more efficient results than confrontation would have done.

The inspectors interviewed me on April Fool's Day, 1987. They asked me about the family shareholding and the other family directors, also about my impressions of Ernest Saunders and his management of the Company, the role of Bain, and the acquisition policy. They also asked about Saunders' appointments, notably Fuerer and Ward. They asked me for my views on the Boesky investment, and examined me in particular about the view expressed by Saunders and Ward that an association with Boesky was a way of profitably getting into the American market. This part of the interview made me feel rather uncomfortable because the rationale for the Boesky investment does not really bear close examination; frankly, we were flannelled into it. They then asked me about Boesky's participation in the market support operation, and the operation in general. I told them that it was obvious there had been one because something of the sort happened in every major contested bid. They asked me why I was not angrier when the Boesky investment was mentioned at the Board Meeting on 8 July 1986. They asked whether I knew how much Ward was paid, and whether I knew that Sir Jack Lyons was close to the Company; on the latter subject, I told them what I knew of the Zentralsparkasse fee. I also told them that I had never liked the idea of taking over Distillers, or the Board arrangements proposed in the offer document; that I had been on Saunders' side during the Risk Affair and blamed the advisers for getting the Company to agree to the offer document arrangements. I added that Saunders had been unwise to drop Benjamin as Chairman. Altogether I found the inspectors friendly, and my meeting with them was not at all unpleasant.

The Annual General Meeting was held on 27 May and it was, as might be expected, even more interesting than the Extraordinary Meeting of the previous September. That meeting had been very one-sided, a walkover for Saunders. This was different: there was a debate of sorts, for Saunders retained support among many shareholders who were grateful for his performance as Chief Executive. Macfarlane had intended to put a resolution to the meeting removing Saunders as a director; knowing that this was coming up, Saunders resigned the day before, accompanying his resignation by a long letter to shareholders putting his point of view. He asked Macfarlane to read it to the meeting, and also distributed the letter to the Press; it got wide coverage, some newspapers printing it in full. Macfarlane said that since Saunders had resigned he would no longer propose the resolution dismissing him, and declined to read the letter. There were some protests at this, but Macfarlane made two points. One was more than doubtful, namely, that following Saunders' resignation his letter had become irrelevant. The other, though, was quite reasonable, namely, that anyone interested could read the letter in the newspapers. Distributing his letter to the Press may have been one of Saunders' rare mistakes in personal public relations; Macfarlane would no doubt have refused to read out what he had to say even if it had not been published, and in that event his refusal would have looked spiteful and unfair. Then again, in the unlikely event of Macfarlane yielding and reading out the letter, the meeting would have been held up and Saunders' vociferous supporters encouraged. Saunders seems here to have let his enemy off the hook, because he could always have got his letter into the papers next day.

From the floor, the speeches in favour of Saunders were at least as numerous as those against him. The wits had their day too; our old friend Declan O'Hegarty suggested that Mikhail Gorbachev should join the Board and introduce some *glasnost* into the Company. Robin Cook, MP, was there representing the Guinness shares held by the Labour Party pension scheme; he asked about the sale to Lonrho of the whisky brands, the operation that had enabled the new bid for Distillers to go ahead after the referral to the Monopolies and Mergers Commission. He also asked what part Sir Jack Lyons had played in events; since Lyons was known to be a friend of Mrs Thatcher, there was a political point to be made here. He also asked whether Guinness intended to keep Cazenove as its stockbroker, and was referred to the statement by Cazenove's solicitors on 29 January that they were not at fault. Robin Cook's intervention might have been one factor in persuading the authorities to pursue the firm's partner David Mayhew.

The most effective intervention came from Alan Wood, former Advertising Director and then Chairman of Guinness Overseas in the old days. Wood spoke briefly and to the point, saying that Saunders had brought disgrace to the Company. Referring to the efforts to get back the £25 million of improper payments listed by Price Waterhouse, he said it was humiliating for the Company to have to go round like a child asking for his ball back.

In the meantime Shaun Dowling was having a tussle with the Takeover Panel because of Guinness's last-minute purchase of Distillers shares, through others, at prices higher than its last cash offer of 630p. The most important of these was of course the 3 per cent holding bought at 705p by a subsidiary of Bank Leu, but it appears from the Panel's ruling that some shares were bought by Guinness allies or 'concert parties' at above even this level, the highest price paid being 731p. Under the takeover code, any cash purchase by a bidder at a higher price than his last cash offer has to be accompanied by a new cash offer of the equivalent. Therefore, the Panel was concerned that Distillers' shareholders should be given compensation by Guinness that would put them in the same position as if the cash offer had in fact been made at the price of 731p.

Fortunately for Guinness, this did not entail an instruction to pay more than £1 for every Distillers share. Having established their figure of 731p, they applied detailed reasoning to the question of who should get what. Since more than a year had elapsed since the bid, they treated shareholders differently according to whether they had received cash or Guinness shares, whether they still held Guinness shares, or whether they had sold them and at what price. The equivalent of a Distillers price of 731p was a Guinness price of 335.4p. Those who still held their shares, the Panel ruled, should receive nothing because there had been times when they could have sold at that price. Those who had sold at or above that price should also receive nothing. Nor should those who had sold after the price of 335.4p had been reached, even though they had not received that price: more fool them – as the Panel did *not* put it – for missing their opportunity. Essentially, then, the compensation went to those who had sold their Guinness shares between 15 April and 21 August 1986, in the form of an amount for each former holder to make up his proceeds to 335.4p a share. The full amount was awarded to holders who had accepted the cash offer of 630p per share, but they amounted to only 0.38 per cent of the Company. Nothing was awarded to holders of call options on Distillers, though they will certainly have lost out. Altogether, the Panel seem to have resolved the matter fairly, though there are distinct signs that, where they could, they leaned in the direction of lenience to the Company. The hearings before the Panel were in August and September 1987, but following an appeal the final decision was not promulgated until 13 June 1989. In view of the delay, interest was added to the compensation payments at a rate of 10 per cent per annum.

EIGHTEEN

Saunders in the Stocks

Public opinion has always had its own methods of punishing those it does not like. Persecution by journalists is a modern one, and it is affecting more and more sections of society. Gone are the days when only the rich, the prominent and the notorious were in danger. It can also be directed at people who are comparatively modest and obscure. It has something in common with the stocks and the pillory, except that these punishments, though intensified by the gleeful participation of the public, were imposed by authority. A closer parallel is the medieval charivari, in which an individual who had annoyed the community was compelled to ride in a ridiculous procession, perhaps facing backwards on a donkey with his hands and feet tied together. He was beaten, pelted with filth, and jeered at. Adulterers caught in the act used to be treated like this; the treatment by today's newspapers of those who have committed the same offence is an obvious descendant. The running pack of men in trilbies, the popping lights, the yelled, intrusive questions formed an early Hollywood cliché which is often presented as funny in films; in real life it is much less so, for the victim. Some people suffer under it more than others; perhaps no one exactly enjoys it. Power and money can provide very considerable protection, as demonstrated when Ernest Saunders was able to escape from the horde outside the Portman Square offices by holing up in the Inn on the Park. After his dismissal, though, Saunders had no power and very soon no money either. At the same time he was also deeply unpopular, as he has remained. The media tried him, condemned him, and carried out their informal punishment long before there was anything in the shape of a judicial verdict against him. This observation has nothing to do with any opinion as to Saunders' guilt or innocence. Many of the victims of lynch law had certainly done what they were accused of, but others had not, and the same, of course, is true of those who undergo the due process of law.

It will be recalled that Saunders went into Champneys health farm on Sunday, 11 January 1987, between the Friday when he stepped down and the Wednesday when he was dismissed. Stress had finally caught up with him. Champneys was not enough; on the Tuesday Carole had him admitted to the Lister Hospital in Chelsea where he was sedated and given treatment for high blood pressure. It was at the Lister that he received Macfarlane's letter sacking him without compensation.[1] At the end of that week, when he returned home to Knoll House, he was still ill; most of the time he was asleep.

It was therefore his family, more than he himself, who suffered from the media persecution which began in earnest at this time. As one who has been both at the receiving end and, as a young man, once or twice part of the pack, I can say that it is difficult to describe the experience to anyone who has not gone through it. Let James Saunders take up the story in *Nightmare*:

Every time a car went in or out [of their gates], or someone went for a walk, the press leapt into action. For long periods the leafy country lane outside would be quiet, its grass verges lined with an unusual number of parked cars, all with bored people sitting in them. But if one of the white gates opened, like collapsing dominoes a string of car doors would be flung back and reporters, photographers and TV camera crews would fumble with their various bits of equipment in a frantic effort to get a statement or a few pictures. . . . The house was to remain constantly under siege for the next two months, and then intermittently until we sold it in June 1987.[2]

The besiegers got rather little for their pains, it appears; as we have seen, Saunders was in bed much of the time. When he or Carole did leave the house they slipped out the back way, through the adjacent churchyard, where they could not be spotted. The Press mostly caught James and Joanna. As one does, brother and sister became quite friendly with some of them: 'One particular photographer turned up so many times that after a while he would bring his latest pictures to give to Jo, and then take a few more to please his boss.'[3] But often the persecution was terrible. James describes one Sunday lunch spoilt by constant banging on the front door, after which he and his sister tried to go for a walk and were actually driven back into the house.

The description rang a bell for me and I turned to the autobiography of my mother, Diana Mosley, where she describes how it was when she and her husband, Sir Oswald Mosley, were released from political imprisonment in the autumn of 1943.

It was not long before the journalists discovered our whereabouts. They laid siege to Rignell [her sister's house]; every laurel, shrub and hedge or ditch concealed some unfortunate half-frozen reporter. They got little change from the nearby villages because nobody had seen us arrive. They made up thrilling stories about a mansion, and baying hounds. The baying hounds were the Jacksons' dachshunds . . . M. stayed in bed, partly in order to cheat the journalists of their prey and partly because he was very weak.[4]

Apart from their modern habit of waving gigantic grey felt cylinders at their targets, the habits of reporters have not changed much in half a century.

But the Press charivari was not the worst of it. Saunders was now, suddenly, desperately short of money. He had few savings, and his share options in Guinness were forfeit under the terms of his sacking. It became clear that he would have to sell his house in Penn, which he did that summer. In the meantime, despite his weakened state of health, he had to face the DTI inspectors. This meant finding a new solicitor; David Napley could not act for him, as his firm had been retained by the Company for a period, and in *Nightmare* James explains that it was surprisingly difficult to find solicitors who had no connection with Guinness, Distillers, Argyll or the City regulators. In the end they went to Payne, Hicks-Beach, who retained counsel and naturally asked for money on account of costs. This was the first instalment of a process that would soon suck Saunders completely dry. According to *Nightmare*, the solicitors arranged for him to be accompanied by counsel and others in greater numbers than he could afford or than he saw the need for.[5] This is an area in which lawyers are apt to be insensitive.

With these helpers, Saunders had to face sessions with the inspectors. They questioned him 'in the manner of an inquisition'. Quite so. Their duty was to elicit the facts, and from what was already known it was certain that they would regard him as a prime suspect. 'When I made points that the inspectors did not want to know about, they listened briefly, then reverted to their original line of questioning.'[6]

Carole Saunders, who had been so strong, now crumbled. She became tearful and fell into a clinical depression. Early in March, she and her husband went to have a short rest in their flat at Les Diablerets, near Geneva. Unfortunately their train journey happened to be on the night of Fasching (Shrove Tuesday), and when they changed trains at Basle Carole was upset by revellers in comic masks jumping out at her. Saunders and Carole saw their Swiss doctor who booked them both into a clinic at Nyon. They could not afford to stay there more than a few days, so they

303

transferred to Les Diablerets. The Press tracked them down there and started the harassment again. They had to move.

Later that month Saunders faced the first legal action against him personally. This was a civil action by Guinness in connection with the payment of £5.2 million to Thomas Ward's Jersey company. The Company was getting back the rest of the Price Waterhouse list, in whole or in part; so it would have a go at recovering this payment too. Ward was in the United States, but Saunders was held personally responsible for the payment because it had never been authorized by the Board. Guinness secured what is known as a 'mareva' injunction against both Ward and Saunders, freezing all the latter's assets up to the full £5.2 million. The fact that £3 million of the payment had been temporarily lodged in Saunders' Swiss bank account was brought out in court and certainly told against him, even though the allegation that he had intended to keep it was dropped by Guinness and not made into a formal accusation. This did not prevent the allegation from being highlighted in the Press, and it was frequently mentioned, again without being actually made into an indictment, in Saunders' subsequent trial in 1990. The DTI inspectors, according to the account in the *Mail on Sunday* of their interim report, were to conclude that the £3 million was indeed destined for Saunders. Apparently, though, the evidence on which they based this opinion was not thought strong enough to be used in a formal accusation. In these circumstances the use made of it by the prosecution both before and during the trial seems a little dubious.

Saunders and Ward both submitted affidavits saying that the £5.2 million had been Ward's fee for helping with the bid and that its size was due to the fact that he was giving up all his lucrative activities as a Washington lawyer to devote his time to Guinness. Ward, from Washington, disclosed that he had all the money, less tax. He strongly denied the claim that £3 million had been destined for Saunders, and held to the contention that the whole amount was fair payment for his services during the Distillers takeover.

Now that everyone has had time to get used to it, the general attitude to the Guinness Affair in general and to Ward in particular has been transformed. It is hard to recapture the atmosphere in spring 1987. At that time no newspaper questioned the assumption that the £5.2 million payment was concrete evidence of criminality, and the courts took the same view. When Saunders and Ward tried to get the mareva injunction lifted by the Vice-Chancellor, Sir Nicholas Browne-Wilkinson, Guinness exerted such efforts into getting this refused as to induce even Kochan and Pym, no fans of Saunders, to comment: 'It was easy to forget that the proceedings were simply an attempt by two defendants to have an asset freezing order discontinued.'[7] The Company's lawyers, briefed by Shaun Dowling, gave what amounted to a preview of the subsequent criminal trials. In his judgement, Sir Nicholas not only refused to lift the mareva injunction on the grounds that Saunders might decamp to Switzerland, but said that the payment of £5.2 million 'could not have been lawfully made'. Saunders then began preparing with his solicitors a claim against Guinness for wrongful dismissal, a claim which still stands and of which we may hear more one day. But in the atmosphere of the·time there was no practical prospect of such a move succeeding.

The DTI inspectors wanted to continue their interviews with Saunders, and became impatient for him to return to Britain. Eventually, in early May, they used their power of threatening him with prosecution if he did not return, so he did so, against his doctor's advice.[8] Then on 6 May, when he was at the office of his solicitors, Saunders was arrested and taken to Holborn police station. He spent a night in the cells and was charged the following day with trying to pervert the course of justice and destroying documents. The police opposed bail, but Saunders' counsel successfully argued against this. The magistrate set a figure of £500,000 and imposed conditions; Saunders' passport had to be surrendered to the police, and he must not contact anyone who worked, or had worked in the past, for Guinness.

The bail money was guaranteed in equal parts by an old friend of Saunders and by Tiny Rowland, of Lonrho, who a few weeks before had contacted Saunders, met him in Switzerland, and made friends with him. Lonrho had done well out of the whisky brands whose hurried sale had enabled Guinness to bypass the Monopolies and Mergers Commission. Rowland saw Saunders as having outwitted Godfray Le Quesne of the MMC and Sir Gordon Borrie, Director of the Office of Fair Trading, both of whom Rowland disliked because he saw them as having prevented his acquisition of Harrods.[9] Rowland also helped Saunders and his family by lending them a flat for five months[10] and according to Tom Bower, his biographer, said he would offer Saunders a job in Lonrho when his problems were at an end.[11]

Carole Saunders was still ill in Switzerland, so it was mainly James who looked after his father at this time. After graduating from Cambridge in June he was in London reading for his bar examinations. Joanna, studying in Exeter, was supportive too. Saunders himself no longer had any financial resources at all, and the mareva injunction meant that the family even had to obtain permission from the court to get money released from the children's trust in order to live. A time of pressing worry, almost of indigence, began, which ended only in March 1988 when the court allowed enough money out of the children's trust to buy a small house for the family. Saunders ran out of money to pay lawyers in December 1987; he applied for legal aid in March 1988 and it was refused, with no reason given. This happened again in May. Legal aid was only finally granted in October for the civil case brought by Guinness; criminal legal aid was denied until December 1988. This meant that on a number of occasions Saunders had to appear before the court absolutely unrepresented. In fact, this may have done him little practical harm, for every one of these court appearance ended in adjournment. All Saunders could do was protest against the continuing delay, probably as competently as the counsel for the other defendants. But since the courts are quite accustomed to awarding legal aid to the formerly rich – Robert Maxwell's sons are a recent example – one casts about for reasons for this delay and cannot help wondering whether it had something to do with media-led prejudice against Saunders.

Guinness sued Ward for the return of the £5.2 million and was granted judgement on 17 July 1987. Ward, of course, was in the United States and out of reach, but Saunders was held to be liable to pay if Ward did not. However, he countered this by joining Olivier Roux as a third party to the action, thus giving notice that if he had to pay any of the money he would try to get it from Roux. Saunders also continued to be examined by the DTI inspectors.

So far, Saunders had been the only man to be arrested in connection with the Guinness Affair, but in the autumn of 1987 this changed. The Serious Fraud Office had been beavering away, in close touch with Dowling. One day Dowling received a telephone call: 'Parnes has done a runner.'

'I don't think he has,' said Dowling. 'I'm finding him helpful. He's gone to Los Angeles, but he'll be back.'

'Yes, he will,' said the policeman, 'because we are getting the Yanks to pick him up.'

'Must you? It will hold things up.'

It did indeed hold things up. Parnes was arrested off his aircraft as he arrived in Los Angeles on 1 October. He was refused bail and imprisoned in Terminal Island prison where he stayed for six months, in horrible conditions. He would have been wiser to return home immediately, but quite naturally he fought extradition for six months before throwing in the towel. As a result Dowling, and the Serious Fraud Office, were deprived of his help for all that time.[12]

Sir Jack Lyons was arrested on 8 October, and Gerald Ronson on 12 October. On the 12th, Saunders was summoned to Holborn police station where he was charged with thirty-seven further offences. Merely reading out these charges took half an hour and the charge officer had to pause for sips of water. Saunders appeared at Bow Street with Ronson the following day. What particularly upset Saunders was that for technical reasons he was charged under the Theft Act, which inevitably made it look as if he had stolen money from Guinness. Helped by his son James and his daughter Joanna, he gave an informal Press conference to complain about his treatment. Roger Seelig was arrested on 15 October and Lord Spens five months later, on 10 March 1988. Thereafter the law pursued its leisurely way until the start of the first trial in February 1990.

Ephraim Margulies, who as far as the outside observer can see had done much the same as Ronson, was never arrested or charged. The difference is that whereas Ronson asked for his indemnity, Margulies was paid his without having asked for it.

After the arrests the investigation took its leisurely course. Every few months the accused were hauled up before the magistrates; on each occasion the cases were adjourned at the request of the prosecution. The defendants, through their lawyers, if they had them, would protest; eventually the newspapers, too, became impatient as 1987 drew to an end, and 1988 passed without any cases being brought. On 30 April 1989 the *Mail on Sunday* published a letter from Ernest Saunders as the main article on its leader page, headlined 'Why am I denied justice?' This was a preview of James Saunders' book *Nightmare*, which was to appear in June, and Saunders made some telling points. The main one was the delay; already two years had passed since he was first arrested. There was the fact that he was denied legal aid for twelve months after his savings had gone, whereas the prosecution could call on all the resources of the State. There was the fact that under his bail conditions he was not allowed to talk to anyone in Guinness, whereas the prosecutors, of course, could.

The appearance of James Saunders' book was heralded by an article in the *Financial Times* saying that it might be banned, since it concerned matters that were *sub judice*.[13] This galvanized me into action; clearly I had to have a copy. I happened to be at Oxford that morning staying at Trinity, my old college, after a 'gaudy' or college dinner. I went next door to Blackwells bookshop and persuaded them to sell me a copy from the package they had received, before they had even put it on display. The book was never banned, as it happened. James had been careful to exclude anything to which exception might be taken. The possibility did of course also provide an excuse for evasiveness. As James puts it: 'I have been forced to omit any evidence which may be produced in court or discuss any matters with which a jury might be concerned.'[14] Quite so.

The DTI inspectors, who had held their last interview in October 1988, completed their report in September 1989. This was never published, although the *Mail on Sunday* was to get hold of a copy and publish extracts on 17 May 1992. It is understandable that the inspectors should have preferred to keep it to themselves, because it was extremely condemnatory not only of those who did get prison sentences but of a number of others who were acquitted, or not even charged. There was at one time an indication that the inspectors were thinking of composing a final report. Perhaps they still are. They wrote to me on 10 August 1994, to tell me so, and to invite my comment on an extract of it in which I am criticized, mildly and entirely deservedly, for not pursuing the matter of the Boesky investment with more determination. Whether in this secrecy-obsessed country the authorities will see fit to print it, or whether it will be for the minister's eyes only, is a matter of conjecture. Certainly the leaked report was only an interim effort.

What, then, have the inspectors achieved? Rather less than

309

nothing. They made their proceedings available to the police, and Saunders, at any rate, was arrested partly on the basis of information obtained from them. Chief Inspector Botwright of the Fraud Squad said as much under cross-examination at Saunders' trial. What proved in the end worse, from the prosecution's viewpoint, was that long transcripts of evidence given before the inspectors were read out in court, providing the prosecution with much of its case. Since those appearing before the inspectors were legally compelled to answer and therefore did not have the right to silence, the European Court of Justice has now ruled that the trial was unfair. There were gaps in the prosecution's case, but they would certainly have done better not to plug them with the evidence before the inspectors.

NINETEEN

Before the Court

It took the best part of three years for the case against Saunders and the others to come to court. Saunders and Lyons were both arrested in May 1987; Ronson, Seelig and Parnes were arrested in October 1987, Spens in March 1988 and Mayhew in May 1988. Even the preparatory hearings did not start until 27 April 1989. A good part of the delay was caused by Saunders' financial difficulties and the extreme reluctance of the authorities to grant him legal aid; he was turned down no less than four times before finally being allowed it in December 1988. By that time his capital had long disappeared into the pockets of the lawyers, and he was naturally behindhand with his defence, so it is not surprising that he applied for a further three months delay so that his senior counsel, Mr Richard Ferguson, QC, and the rest of his team, could prepare themselves.

Legal arguments started on Monday, 18 September 1989. The judge, who was to try all the defendants, was Mr Justice Henry. His background, until then, had mainly been in planning; he did, however, have the reputation of understanding computers, which was evidently thought useful in a case where he would need to master an immense quantity of evidence.

He was confronted with seven defendants: Saunders, Ronson, Parnes, Lyons, Seelig, Spens and Mayhew, and an immense number of indictments, especially against Saunders. A single trial for all seven could scarcely be contemplated; it would have been too long, and possibly too complicated, for any jury. The judge accordingly decided that there should be three trials: the first of Ernest Saunders, Sir Jack Lyons, Anthony Parnes and Gerald Ronson; the second of Roger Seelig, Lord Spens and Saunders again; and the third of Seelig again and David Mayhew. I shall follow custom and refer to them as Guinness 1, Guinness 2 and Guinness 3. After Saunders was convicted in Guinness 1, he was dropped from Guinness 2, so the eventual defendants in that trial were Seelig and Spens. Guinness 3 did not take place.

A determined attempt was being made to have Thomas Ward extradited from the United States so that he could be accused of stealing the £5.2 million that had gone to him through Marketing and Acquisition Consultants. He resisted this successfully, but came back later by the time feeling had subsided sufficiently for his case to be judged more coolly.

There was a further delay of five months until Guinness 1 opened on Monday, 12 February 1990. The four defendants appeared in Southwark Crown Court, an anonymous modern brick edifice with a great windowless wall embellished only by the royal coat of arms in a dung-coloured plastic which can only have been specified by a dedicated enemy of royalty. The courtroom was a large, wide rectangle with the rather low ceiling affected by cost-conscious modern architects; it needed to be large to accommodate the batteries of lawyers for the four defendants and for the prosecution. There was no dock; the four defendants sat in a row towards the back of the room. Two of them I had never seen before. Parnes was dark and lean – he could have been a chief of the Bedouin; Ronson was thickset and wore an air of authority as well as a gold ring or two. Lyons, whom I had once met in passing, was small, bespectacled and rather hunched. When they stood, Saunders towered over them all. Behind them sat the Press and the public, in front of them were the batteries of lawyers. The judge faced the gathering from behind a desk with the jury on his right and a witness stand on his left. The general consensus in the Press was that the case was likely to run for six months, an estimate which proved accurate.

I attended the court on some days, and I was also a witness. The trial reminded me of an immensely long game of cricket, in that it proceeded with the same calm deliberation that foreigners find so bewildering in the national game. It was punctuated, as cricket is, by moments of excitement that were somehow enhanced by the slowness of the rest of the proceedings. Yet the flavour is missed unless it is borne in mind that the following little scene, repeated endlessly with variations, occupied much of every day.

A bewigged barrister from the prosecution or the defence invites the judge to look at one of the papers in the cabinet beside him.

'Is it here, in the blue bundle?'

'No, my lord. I fancy you will find it in the yellow bundle underneath it.'

A pause.

'It doesn't seem to be in the yellow bundle.'

Another barrister: 'I think it is in the red bundle, about halfway down.'

'I don't seem to have a red bundle here.'

There is a short, whispered colloquy between the barristers, following which yet another barrister saunters up with yet another bundle. Unhurriedly he hands it over, unhurriedly the judge accepts it with a nod and a smile, unhurriedly he leafs through it. This time he finds the required document and the case continues. No objection is raised to the fact that the document was unavailable and had to be searched for; on the contrary, everybody exudes a quiet and complacent good humour. And so the long day wears on.

The slowness, very general in court cases, must have something to do with the fact that all the professionals in court are paid by the hour; they have no motive to speed up. In the

Guinness case at any rate it had its positive side; the fact that everyone took their time did, seemingly, make them immensely thorough. One did not get the impression that anything was ever left out; a clear and detailed picture emerged. Like the mills of God, those of the court ground slowly, but they ground exceeding small.

The chief prosecuting counsel, John Chadwick, QC, opened the proceedings by contending that the four defendants 'were so greedy for money and power that they were willing to cross the line which defines what can legitimately be done' in a bid battle 'from conduct which is dishonest'. Saunders, according to him, organized the share support scheme with the help of Parnes and Lyons, each of whom received millions unlawfully. Ronson was recruited as a supporter. They submitted false invoices to Guinness because true invoices would have revealed that the transactions were unlawful. Chadwick sketched the career of each of the defendants, emphasizing that they were all intelligent and successful men who must have known the implications of what they were doing. He also went into the question of Ward's £5.2 million, underlining the fact that this was not disclosed to the Board and that Price Waterhouse were kept in ignorance of the fact that any of it was going to Ward personally. The fact that £3 million of it had been temporarily in a Swiss bank account belonging to Saunders was brought out.

Chadwick also said that Saunders had given instructions for the shredding of letters and diaries connected with the bid, also his jotting pad, and that his own diary was never found; furthermore, he had borrowed address books from the office and returned them looking noticeably thinner. This point was to figure prominently in the evidence of his personal assistant, Mrs Margaret McGrath; Saunders' comprehensive denial that anything of the sort happened would be one of the less convincing parts of his evidence.

Olivier Roux was the first witness; he spent forty hours at the stand and gave a fairly clear picture of what happened. It will be recalled that he had immunity from prosecution; nevertheless, he must have been aware that Richard Ferguson, QC, Saunders' counsel, would do his best to incriminate him and to maintain that all the improper invoices which he had signed – in other words, most of them – were agreed without Saunders being in any way aware of what was done. Roux had little difficulty in refuting this. 'You must know that I could not go ahead and sign those documents off my own bat when I had no executive power in the company.' Strictly speaking, what Roux did not have was executive position, rather than executive power, in the strange set-up which existed in Guinness under Saunders. Even so, it would be highly unusual if, as (in form) a non-executive director, he had signed documents like this without checking.

Roux gave fairly complete accounts of the payments referred to on the Price Waterhouse list, the most interesting of which concerned Margulies.[1] His support, to the tune of £14–15 million, had been arranged at a meeting between Saunders and Margulies fixed by Parnes in March 1986 as the bid battle was nearing its climax. 'The essence of the meeting was that Mr Margulies would confirm that he was going to help Guinness and said he would expect nothing from Guinness except the same kind of help and comfort if he needed help in some trouble in the future,' said Roux. Roux had then discussed the matter with Saunders and they had agreed that it would be better to pay Margulies a fee, as they had paid Ronson, since otherwise he might expect more from Guinness than he had done for the Company. So Margulies was asked for invoices – £1,940,000 for CIFCO and £1,495,000 for Erlanger & Co. – and Guinness paid these. It seemed, said Roux, a reasonable amount for the support the Margulies group had given.

Then, in 1986, the DTI inspectors went in.[2] Soon afterwards, Roux went to dinner with Parnes who told him that Margulies was trying to make it look as if the whole of the CIFCO payment had been made to Parnes personally. Parnes said he had received £340,000 of it as a commission from CIFCO.

The evidence Parnes had given to the inspectors on this subject was more dramatic, if not quite clear.[3] At first he was reluctant to reply when they asked about Margulies because of what he called 'a threatening situation . . . which makes it difficult for me'.

INSPECTORS:	Threatening? . . .
PARNES:	Retaliation.
INSPECTORS:	Of what nature?
PARNES:	It could be anything.

David Donaldson, QC, giving evidence at the first Guinness trial, said Parnes had seemed to be genuinely afraid when questioned about Margulies. At one moment he was 'sobbing tearlessly'.[4] Finally, under some pressure, Parnes identified Ari Margulies, Ephraim's son. Parnes went on to say that he had tried to give his £340,000 commission back when he found out that it was not from Berisfords, Margulies' British quoted company, but this was refused. Why did he feel like this?

PARNES:	My instinct told me it was wrong.
INSPECTORS:	What more did you have to do other than sit on your money?
PARNES:	Lie.
INSPECTORS:	To whom?
PARNES:	To you.

The fact that the inspectors successfully pressurized Parnes into coming clean about Margulies caused some embarrassment for Roux, who had covered up for Parnes in front of the inspectors and now, in court, had to change his story. This was gleefully exploited by the defence, and some journalists thought it made all his evidence seem untrustworthy. However, it was only a comparatively peripheral matter. Did it in any way affect Roux's credibility with the jury? Probably not, or not much.

When Benjamin Iveagh gave evidence he sprang a surprise, to me at any rate. He said that when Saunders paid his flying visit to him in Ireland in January 1987, during the weekend after he stepped down and before he was dismissed, he had suggested that the Company should become Irish-registered. Benjamin had rejected this as 'ludicrous', as indeed it was; such a move at such a time would have been greeted by jeers, and the worst possible construction would have been put on it. How had the idea occurred to Saunders? It could perhaps be explained by something Benjamin had mentioned earlier in his evidence. In August 1985 Saunders had asked him to stand down as Chairman, but he had resisted, 'more especially because I was Chairman of Guinness Ireland, which was a subsidiary of the parent Company but had its own local Board and input. I was fearful that if I gave up the Chairmanship that company would simply be run from Mr Saunders' office in London.' Saunders, that final weekend before his dismissal, was grasping at straws; he remembered Benjamin's concern with Ireland and saw in it some dim hope of salvation.[5]

Much of my own evidence concerned the Zentralsparkasse, the fact that I was friendly with Horst Tiefenthaler and had been told that on Sir Jack Lyons' advice he had bought a holding of Guinness shares after the bid. I also remember reacting rather sharply to Richard Ferguson's suggestion that I might regard the Risk Affair as a 'storm in a teacup'. However, I expressed respect for Saunders' performance as Chief Executive and said I had supported him up to the end. I told the court that I had been against the Distillers takeover when first announced, on the grounds that the company was too big.[6]

The trial wore on. Margaret McGrath confirmed what she had already told the DTI inspectors about her destruction of certain documents on Saunders' orders. She seemed embarrassed; the judge was to describe her in his summing up as 'a grudging witness' and speculate that she was troubled by her old loyalty. Nevertheless, what she said was very clear. Saunders had told her to rub out certain entries in a desk diary, particularly those relating to a lunch with Ronson in April 1986, *tête-à-tête*, at which according to Ronson he had confirmed the arrangement to pay Ronson for buying Guinness shares.

Howard Hughes, senior partner of Price Waterhouse, detailed his growing suspicions and the way in which Saunders had put off talking about the Boesky investment, the deposits with Bank Leu and Ansbachers, and the mysterious payments. One rather odd episode was recalled. On 22 December 1986, that is, three weeks after the inspectors had gone in, Hughes had dined with Saunders and Benjamin and had not mentioned his worries. Nor had he done so at a directors' meeting as late as 7 January 1987. Neither was an appropriate occasion, Hughes told Richard Ferguson, QC. This does indicate that Hughes was trying, until the very last minute, not to rock the boat with Saunders in a way that might lose his firm this important client. The following day, 8 January, Hughes had advised Edward Guinness to keep an open mind and not give 'headlong' support either to Saunders or to the new non-executive directors.[7]

Then came the transcripts of the evidence given to the DTI, read out by the prosecution barristers. The inspectors had asked Saunders why, with two stockbroking firms already employed, he had used Parnes as well. Saunders told them that Cazenove was analytical, and had good contacts at golf-club level; Parnes was more 'streetwise'. Saunders could not recall encouraging Parnes to find buyers for Guinness shares; Parnes was 'very much on Olivier Roux's team'. He added: 'I got involved with the bid team when things were wrong and left them alone when things were right.'[8]

Saunders recalled a discussion with Roux and Ward when they persuaded him that Parnes and Lyons should have £3 million each. 'Roux particularly thought Parnes and Sir Jack had provided extremely valuable services to him. Ward seemed to agree.' Donaldson noted that Cazenove's fee had been £600,000 and asked, 'Do you take the view that Mr Parnes was worth five times Cazenove?' Saunders replied that Parnes had devoted all his time to providing exceptional market intelligence to Roux, perhaps to the detriment of his other business. As to Lyons, his contribution had been 'opening doors' and 'just providing damned good advice'.

DONALDSON:	You would have us believe, Mr Saunders, that you reached the decision to pay £3 million to each of these two gentlemen because, and solely because, your colleagues urged you in that direction?
SAUNDERS:	Yes.

As to Ward's £5.2 million, 'There was a stage . . . at which each time Mr Ward wanted to go home I almost took his passport away and said I absolutely needed him here, at which point he said to me, "In which case you are going to have to pay for it," and that was the fee we agreed.' He could not recall why the payments were not brought before the Executive Committee by the Finance Department.'[9]

The transcript of Ronson's interview with the inspectors provided one of the livelier moments in the trial. He told them he did not think Parnes or Saunders was doing anything wrong. He admitted that he had been naïve and stupid. He had been amazed to learn of Parnes's £3 million fee. 'If Mr Parnes had mentioned his fee at the beginning, I would have smelt that this whole thing was not right.'

He continued: 'I find it very, very irritating because that is not how I built Heron up . . . I built up a very positive business . . .

and . . . not . . . by doing funny deals. We do deals on a straight line.'

He described a scene with Parnes in which both talked like ethnic comedians:

' "I relied on you, Tony. Do I need this aggravation?" . . . "Gerald" – and he was in tears and . . . shaking like a jelly – "I swear on my children's life I did not know."' The inspectors asked why Parnes had done it. 'Maybe greed, maybe ego . . . Who knows the reasons people do things? The fact of life is he had tears in his eyes because I had nailed him on this situation.' He then agreed with the inspectors that he had bought a million Argyll shares in the last ten days of the bid and denied firmly Donaldson's suggestion that this might have been a breach of faith towards Guinness.[10]

Earlier in the transcripts, what Ronson told the inspectors was certainly very damaging to Saunders. He had met him face to face and said he would like to recapitulate 'what our deal is, because I don't want there to be any argument afterwards or any embarrassment'.

'He told me, "Yes, you are covered on any losses you have on the shares," and that if they were successful we would get a success fee of 20 per cent of our exposure. Ernie Saunders, when he speaks, speaks quite clearly and you do not misunderstand.'[11]

Another colourful passage from the inspectors' transcripts concerned Sir Jack Lyons, who told them: 'I am very concerned about our country . . . our political situation in what could be an election year and I do not want to give fuel that could be unfairly used and damaging to our Prime Minister, because that is the level at which I am dealing.' He feared a leak. Donaldson could give no total assurance but said, 'Nobody wants it to leak'. Lyons explained that he had written to Mrs Thatcher saying why the Guinness bid should not be referred to the Monopolies and Mergers Commission. Ten days later the bid had been cleared and Saunders 'wanted to almost throw his arms around me, I think'.

The inspectors asked him if he was on Christian name terms with the Prime Minister. He replied: 'I could be if she were not the Prime Minister. I always show my respect to the Prime Minister and call her "Prime Minister". She varies. She calls me either "Sir Jack" [or] ... often ... "Jack", and refers to my wife as "Roslyn". On other occasions ... she might refer to Roslyn as "your lady wife".'

He had persuaded the Prudential to assent its holding of Distillers to Guinness. The Chairman and Deputy Chairman, Lord Hunt and Lord Carr, were 'very good friends of mine ... particularly Lord Carr, and I used that friendship'.

His fee had been offered by Saunders and Ward, and included £750,000 for his flat in Watergate, Washington. He described this flat in the manner of a house agent's brochure, almost as if he was trying to sell it to the inspectors. It was a prime duplex with a patio and swimming pool in the most exclusive block in Washington. Its walls had been decorated with silks from Paris and its carpet was 'probably the most expensive you can get anywhere in the world'.

In due course Saunders was called. Alone of the defendants, he did not exercise his right of silence, but gave evidence for ninety hours over seventeen days. Richard Ferguson, his counsel, began by recapitulating the *Nightmare* thesis. Saunders had been made a scapegoat and cast aside by a company he had served loyally for five years. He had been stripped of the means of earning his livelihood, his personal life was in ruins, his health had been undermined. Ferguson was fairly sharp about the Guinness family, which he said was 'clinging to past glory while no doubt basking in the present value of the Guinness shares, a price attributable in very large measure to the man they dumped, Ernest Saunders'. Nor did he spare the new non-executive directors; they had been 'more concerned with their City image than with doing justice to the Chairman and Chief Executive'. They did not like Saunders' style; perhaps his face no longer fitted.

Ferguson, it has been suggested, advised Saunders against going into the box. If so, he made the best of his client's refusal to take this advice, saying that Saunders had felt that if he failed to do so it might be taken as an indication that he had something to hide. I suspect this was not really the only, or even the main, factor. Saunders may well have thought that since the transcripts of the evidence before the inspectors had been made public, there was in fact little point in trying to keep anything quiet. At least if he gave evidence he had a chance of putting his case. Also, he was a compulsive and skilled communicator who had been chafing under his enforced silence for all these years. One should not discount this emotional reason why Saunders had to have a say.

At first it went relatively well for him while he was being examined sympathetically by his own counsel. He went through his background and early life, recounted his time at Guinness, and made the point that his own financial expertise was 'rather primitive', leaving him dependent on Roux for this side of things.[12] Later, it became rougher. He not only had to face cross-examination by Chadwick and his team for the Crown, but also by the counsel for the other defendants. As *Observer* journalist Michael Gillard wrote, it was Ernest Saunders versus the rest. 'One by one,' Gillard remarked, 'the former Guinness Chairman refuted the Ronson/Parnes/Lyons version of the meetings or conversations they testified to having had with him.'[13] He did indeed. He denied Roux's evidence that he, Saunders, had approached Ronson for share support; he claimed they had only talked of property matters. He denied approving Heron's invoices. He denied Roux's statement that he had agreed to pay Margulies a success fee and indemnity. On this subject Saunders remembered that Margulies 'had wanted to meet him to consider investing in Guinness. At the end of their meeting Mr Margulies, a very religious man, had given [him] a sort of blessing.' He described the Roux letter as 'a buck-passing operation of the most cynical kind'. Gillard predicted that the rest of Saunders' time in the box 'is likely to prove somewhat like a batsman who has been regularly scoring sixes against underarm bowling suddenly facing the bumper barrage of the West Indian pace attack'.[15]

And so it was. When on 19 June the time came for Michael Sherrard for Ronson and Colin Nicholls for Parnes to have a go at Saunders, both accused him of lying. Saunders reacted heatedly, and Robert Harman, for Lyons, had to try, in his words, to 'lower the temperature'. This put Saunders under strain; the court adjourned until the following Monday, 25 June, because of his medical condition.

On that day he faced Chadwick, who began by asking what Saunders thought of paying Ward £5.2 million for eight weeks' work when his own salary was £225,000 a year. This invited a reply which would back up Saunders' portrait of himself as someone rather unconcerned about money for himself: 'I am not one of those people who worry about what I get paid in relation to what other people get paid.' There were certain aspects in winning the bid for which Ward had been uniquely valuable, and Ward said the fee had been necessary to keep him in England for eight weeks. He compared the sum with the fees budget of £100 million and the global bid cost of nearly £3 billion.[16]

Then Chadwick went into the question of the £3 million, part of the £5.2 million, which had temporarily resided in a Swiss bank account belonging to Saunders. Why had the amount transferred by Ward been in fact £3,029,421.23, which represented £3 million plus the precise interest on the amount prior to the transfer; and why had the money been treated in all respects as if it belonged to Saunders? Chadwick suggested it had been intended for Saunders before he had second thoughts. Saunders denied this vehemently.

On subsequent days, Saunders accused Lyons of 'a blatant lie', Benjamin and Simon Boyd of 'amnesia or lies'. He described a

323

weekend aboard Ronson's yacht in June 1986. The hospitality had been magnificent, but Saunders had felt under pressure, with Heron 'seeing what they could squeeze out of us'. He had returned to Guinness with a checklist of things in which Heron might help Guinness. There was no mention, he told Chadwick, of the £2.5 million that Guinness had paid ten days earlier. It had been Roux who had recommended the payments of more than £3 million to Lyons and Parnes.

Chadwick asked Saunders what he thought had justified Lyons' fee. Among other things, said Saunders, the letter to Mrs Thatcher. Also, Lyons had been in touch with Lord Armstrong, head of the Civil Service, and induced Lord Hunt to assent the Prudential's holding of Distillers to Guinness. He had given Roux strategic financial advice. Had it gone before the Board, 'I would wager with you that the Board would have accepted.' (A bet on an undisprovable past contingency is of course pretty safe.) What about the payment to Parnes? Roux, said Saunders, had pushed for this. Had it gone to the Board, it would have been for Roux to justify.

Three times Saunders described Lyons's verson of events as 'bullshit'. At last the judge intervened: ' "Utter nonsense" will do, Mr Saunders, for a man with your gift of language.'[17]

Saunders' verson of events, as it developed, involved at least two conspiracies against him. One concerned Freshfields, Price Waterhouse and Bains. He denied that any of them had spoken to him of the doubtful payments before Roux produced his letter. Chadwick said that both Hughes and Ian Taylor of Freshfields had said they had spoken to Saunders about matters of concern. Saunders: 'They would, wouldn't they?' He added: 'What we have here [is] a conspiracy amongst a group of professionals to keep quiet and, ultimately' remove 'the person who if he had known would have made Mrs Thatcher's night of the long knives seem a rather short night'. Was this, Chadwick asked, the same conspiracy as Sir Norman Macfarlane's? No, said Saunders, it was a distinct one. 'A number of groups of interested parties who have a highly convenient way of getting themselves out of trouble, and that is landing me in it.' Saunders also accused Margaret McGrath of lying about the destruction of documents and notebooks, but could produce no possible reason why she should have done this.

Some observers noted that Saunders seemed at times to be trying to 'psych' the jury, to establish a dominance over it. This did not succeed; some of the jurors would react by looking at each other with a nod, a smile and closed eyes, as if to say, 'Here we go again.' The judge at one moment warned: 'You risk boring the jury, Mr Saunders.' One unnamed 'expert' told Michael Gillard that after his long effort at defending himself his case was 'dead in the water'.[18] If this was so, one reason for it was undoubtedly the use that Chadwick made of the temporary sojourn of £3 million of Ward's fee in Saunders' account at the Union Bank of Switzerland. Why had Saunders not asked Arthur Fuerer to open an account for Ward at Bank Leu? Why had the precise amount transferred been £3 million plus £29,421.23, if the £3 million was always simply a part of Ward's fee of £5.2 million? Why had Saunders given instructions that he was not to be identified as the source of the money when it was transferred back to Ward? Without formulating a charge against Saunders on this matter, the prosecution succeeded in undermining him by using it to the full.

It was downhill all the way after that, for Saunders and for the other defendants. The judge took two days to sum up, and did so with great lucidity; the jury, none of whom looked as if they were business people, were presented carefully with the alternative facts on which they had to pronounce, as they had emerged in the trial.

All the defendants were found guilty, though not quite of everything. After some charges were dropped during the trial, there remained twenty. Of these, Saunders was accused of fifteen,

Ronson of five, Parnes of six and Lyons of six. The details were as follows:

Charge	Accused, Verdict
Conspiracy re Heron share support:	Saunders, Ronson both guilty
Breach of Companies Act re Heron:	Saunders, Ronson no verdict
False Accounting, Heron invoice for £2.875 million:	Saunders, Ronson both guilty
Theft of £2.875 million from Guinness:	Saunders, Ronson both guilty
Theft of $4.8 million from Guinness:	Ronson, Parnes both guilty
False accounting re $4.8 million, PIMA:	Saunders guilty
False Accounting re £3.35 million, Consultations et Investissements:	Saunders, Parnes both guilty
Theft of £3.35 million from Guinness:	Parnes guilty
False Accounting re £1.94 million, CIFCO:	Saunders, Parnes both guilty
Theft of £1.94 million from Guinness:	Parnes guilty
False Accounting re £1.495 million, Erlanger:	Saunders, Parnes both guilty
Conspiracy re Z-Bank:	Saunders, Lyons both guilty
False Accounting, £0.254 million, Z-Bank:	Saunders, Lyons both guilty
Breach of Companies Act re Z-Bank:	Saunders, Lyons no verdict
False Accounting, £3 million, Konsultat:	Saunders, Lyons both guilty
Theft of £3 million from Guinness:	Lyons guilty
False Accounting £5.2 million Marketing and Acquisition Consultants:	Saunders guilty
Theft of £5.2 million from Guinness:	Saunders guilty
Destroying Company documents:	Saunders not guilty.

The Press applauded loudly. The *Daily Telegraph* exulted in its main leading article: 'Yesterday's verdicts in the Guinness Case will be welcomed by the City of London, as well as by the community at large. . . . The defendants had been engaged in systematic deceit on a huge scale. Their acquittal would have appeared to endorse the tactics employed by Mr Ernest Saunders and his confederates during the Distillers takeover.'[19] As usual when someone disapproved of is found guilty, freeing journalists from the risk of being had up for contempt of court, the press really went to town on the defendants, especially Saunders. The crash of the high-flyer is always good for a bit of a gloat. To Michael Gillard of the *Observer*,[20] Saunders was 'an arrogant, autocratic Icarus' and a 'ruthless exploiter and manipulator of all around him'.

Saunders was sentenced to five years in jail, Ronson to two, Parnes to two, and Lyons was fined £2 million but not sent to jail because he was seventy-four years old and ill with cancer. Later, his knighthood was taken away from him. The general opinion was that these sentences were fair and necessary, and would stop all the nonsense.

TWENTY

The Tide Turns

It is looking a little different now; in fact September 1990, when the verdicts and sentences were handed down in Guinness 1, now appears to be the high point of this particular effort by the authorities to bring takeover practice under control through the legal system. It took a year from the end of the first Guinness trial for the second one to come to the same court before the same judge; this time the defendants were Roger Seelig of Morgan Grenfell and Lord Spens of Ansbachers. Seelig was accused of fraudulently attempting to induce the disposal and acquisition of shares, and of false accounting. Spens was charged with conspiracy to defraud, in connection with the deal that resulted in the interest-free loan to Guinness. There is a rather odd feature about the decision to prosecute Spens, which is that he was apparently not singled out by the DTI inspectors for any criticism; the *Mail on Sunday,* in its summary of the interim report of the inspectors that had been leaked to it, says he 'is the only Guinness trial defendant who is not specifically criticised for his conduct'.[1]

One illuminating point to come out of the opening speech of prosecuting counsel Elizabeth Gloster, QC concerned a New York bank called L. F. Rothschild, which Seelig induced to buy 6 million Guinness shares to support the bid. However, they only in fact bought about 2 million, buying the rest after the price had fallen after the bid and making a cool £1.7 million for themselves.

Since Seelig did not know this, they were of course indemnified as if they had bought the whole amount before the bid. 'Ironic', Ms Gloster called this. One can think of other descriptions.

At the beginning of March 1992 the trial collapsed; the judge brought it to an end when it seemed to him that Seelig, who was conducting his own defence, was heading for mental breakdown. Guinness 2 had lasted five months and cost an estimated £1.3 million, a modest amount compared with Guinness 1 which is said to have cost over £20 million. Seelig's mental breakdown was doubted by some sections of the press, in a preview of the later fuss about Ernest Saunders and Alzheimer's. The *Evening Standard* said that what it rather pompously called an 'Evening Standard investigation' had 'revealed' that he was driving a red Porsche around Gloucestershire in search of antiques;[2] and nearly a year later, the *Daily Telegraph* reported with a discernible sneer that Seelig was 'back in rude health'.[3] No one who reads the transcripts can doubt that Seelig's breakdown was perfectly genuine. It can be attributed to the expense of getting justice. His glittering career in merchant banking had naturally made him a rich man, but his millions were, one suspects, in units rather than in tens. A full-scale defence, with solicitors, juniors and a QC, for a trial lasting months, would certainly have cost some of those millions; conceivably, he might have had to spend them all. So he decided to conduct his own defence.

The mental strain to which this exposed him would be particularly severe on someone with a mind of his type. He was, we remember, the star deal-maker of Morgan Grenfell. For this he had to be quick-witted and constantly aware. He had to have the ability to see all the factors in a situation at once, as a picture, a *Gestalt*; and the corollary of this is liable to be an inability to avoid seeing it in this way. The procedure of the court, in which clever but slow-spoken people would be carefully building up over weeks an image that to him was obvious throughout, must have maddened him. In addition, there was the leisureliness described above, the slow shuffling of bundles of documents, the sauntering of highly paid people around the court in a lumbering slow-motion ballet. The only way any accused can cope with all this is an ability to switch off. Someone of Seelig's type is not good at this. With lawyers on whom he relied he could probably have managed it, but as his own advocate, feeling that his white-hot brain needed to be kept at full awareness for every second, it was clearly too much for him.

However, Seelig's breakdown may perhaps not be the only explanation for the premature ending of Guinness 2. Some evidence, highly embarrassing for the prosecution, emerged at about the same time. Not long after the defence had shown signs that it intended to make full use of this new evidence, the prosecution announced its decision not to proceed against Mayhew and Seelig in the case that had been scheduled against them: Guinness 3. This was on 7 February 1990. Guinness 2 came to an end a month later.

Strictly speaking the evidence was not new, though it had been withheld from the defence in Guinness 1, a decision which was later to attract judicial criticism. The most important item had been lying around since October 1986; that is, since a time after the success of the bid for Distillers and before the DTI inspectors were sent in. It concerned a decision of the Takeover Panel concerning an offer by Turner and Newall for an automotive parts company called AE, formerly Associated Engineering. This, we remember, was the bid that caused the ruin of Geoffrey Collier.

The directors of AE wanted to remain independent, so they resisted the bid and called in the merchant bank Hill Samuel to help them. Hill Samuel induced Midland Bank and another buyer to purchase shares in AE so as to keep their value above the bid price, thus making the bid unattractive to AE shareholders. It was fairly certain that if the manoeuvre succeeded and the bid lapsed, the price of AE would fall and the buyers would suffer a loss; so Hill Samuel promised to indemnify the buyers for that loss.

The Panel's appeal committee took the view that this arrangement, in itself, was not precluded by the City Code which the Panel administered, but that it ought to have been publicly disclosed. The practical effect of such disclosure would of course have deprived the arrangement of most of its effectiveness, because it would have indicated to AE shareholders that the price only stood above the bid offer for artificial reasons. They would have been likely to accept the bid, which as it was only failed by 1 per cent.

This slim margin indicates strongly that it was the purchase with secret indemnity which turned the trick. Turner and Newall complained, and the matter came before the Panel's Appeal Committee. Midland Bank, Hill Samuel and Cazenove all maintained that disclosure was not required, but the Appeal Committee decided to the contrary. However, it was thought necessary to make this point clear in the rules. The following provision was inserted in the notes on Rule 8 (page E15): '2.(c) When dealings are disclosed, details of any arrangement in relation to the securities in question, which exists for the offeror or any person acting in concert with it, or for the offeree company, to bear any associated liability or risk (for example, indemnity or option arrangements), must be disclosed at the same time.' The result of the manoeuvre was allowed to stand, and the possibility of a criminal prosecution was not even suggested.

The significance of this to the Guinness Affair is that Hill Samuel's scheme of secretly indemnifying purchasers of shares in a bid was clearly analogous to the support operations around Guinness-Distillers. The fact that the Panel, though disapproving, felt it necessary to change the code at a date after the Distillers takeover gave the Guinness defence a potential argument that anything of the same nature which happened before that change was acceptable.

But long before the glacier-like procedures of British justice had brought Saunders and the others to trial, there was another decision in the same sense. This was given in December 1988 by a Licensed Dealers Tribunal set up by the Department of Trade and Industry. It was dealing with an appeal by a company called TWH Management Ltd whose dealing licence the DTI had proposed to withdraw.

The background was as follows. A rich Arab family called Algosaibi had established TWH Management Ltd in London as an investment and dealing company; it was a subsidiary of another company they owned in the Dutch West Indies. Chairman of the British company was a merchant banker called Philip Watson, who had experience at Hill Samuel and Robert Fleming; his co-directors, one of them of Iraqi origin, also had a respectable financial background. TWH Management's main task was to provide investment services for the Algosaibis, but they also had some other clients. The company had a Principal's Dealing Licence which the Secretary of State for Trade and Industry intended to revoke because of certain dealings done through Ansbachers and arranged by Lord Spens. The company appealed, and the Department of Trade and Industry, as was the practice, appointed a Licensed Dealers' Tribunal to decide on the matter.

It emerged that the Algosaibi family had been thinking of buying Ansbachers, the attraction to them being its banking licence. After a long delay they decided not to go ahead, but they evidently felt guilty about this, and they instructed TWH Management to develop business with Ansbachers. This was in 1984, the same year as Lord Spens took over as Managing Director at Ansbachers.

In Autumn 1985 Spens suggested that TWH Management could deal in shares involved in takeovers on the basis of an indemnity; that is, any losses would be made good, and any profits – in practice this would be rarer – would go to Ansbachers. TWH Management would end simply with the interest on its money.

The first such deal took place in late 1985. TWH bought 600,000 shares in United Newspapers for £1,830,606.90 in October of that year, then in December sold them at a loss which Ansbachers made up, with interest, by a payment of £208,000. At the time United Newspapers was bidding for Fleet Holdings which was resisting. An increased offer succeeded on 18 October, a few days after TWH's purchase, which probably made the price of United Newspapers higher than it would otherwise have been and may well have been the reason for its success.

During 1986 Spens suggested and Watson carried out six further similar transactions, all purchases of shares involved in bids which were done on a basis of no profit no loss. One of these was Guinness at the height of the Distillers battle. In March 1986 TWH bought 250,000 Guinness shares. These were then sold in May and formed part of the holding related to Guinness's interest-free deposit with Ansbachers.

All the payments made by Ansbachers to TWH Management were made on the basis of invoices whose wording – to put it kindly – was not objectively correct. They were said to be 'in respect of investment advisory services' or for 'currency and investment advice' or for 'introductory fees re potential new clients' and so on. Spens had suggested the wording, according to Philip Watson.

Timothy Barker, the Director-General of the Takeover Panel who had been seconded from Kleinwort Benson, argued that the transactions were improper because people in the securities industry 'must not engage in any activities which could result in a false market being created'. During takeovers in particular, 'there should be no covert activity which could influence the share price of either the offeror or the offeree company. The use of unconnected parties, supported by indemnities, to purchase shares in companies' involved in a bid 'clearly contravenes this general principle'. Philip Watson would have known that the arrangements were made to avoid disclosure, especially because of the steps taken to disguise the payments. In the cases where Ansbachers was advising the company whose shares were bought, the deals contravened not only the City Code administered by the Panel, but also Section 151 of the Companies Act 1985 (which prohibits a company from purchasing its own shares).

Under cross-examination Barker had to admit that not all his strictures applied equally to all the deals, but on the general principle he stood firm; until, that is, counsel for TWH brought up the decision in the matter of AE. Confronted with this, Barker conceded that a bank involved in a takeover was not stopped from using its own money to further the deal. All the same, he maintained that Watson ought to have found the deals very strange, and insisted on an explanation.

Watson, in his reply, pushed responsibility off on to Ansbachers. For each of the deals he had asked Lord Spens if the share purchase contravened the code or the Companies Act; each time he had been reassured, and had informed the Algosaibis of this. As to the false invoices, Watson had used words suggested by Spens, though he regretted that the entries in the books of the company were not written in more precise terms. He maintained that it was reasonable to have trusted the word of Lord Spens, whose reputation at the time was unblemished; a fact which a character witness corroborated.

The Tribunal decided that the evidence had not shown that the transactions had been designed to create a false market. A false market, the Tribunal ruled, was created when the price of a security was not purely governed by supply and demand, but was affected either by misleading rumours or by abnormal dealing methods. All the transactions by TWH Management had been normal dealings at the current market price. This definition of a false market is unusually narrow. Following it, however, the Tribunal said that there was nothing intrinsically improper in buying or selling shares in the market under an indemnity arrangement between the dealer and a third party. Nor was it improper when this occurred in shares of companies about to feature in bids. This view was supported by the Panel's ruling in the matter of AE. If in some of the deals there was a liability to disclose, this fell not on TWH but on Ansbachers. The AE decision made it clear that many practitioners at the time did not appreciate that indemnity share transactions needed to be disclosed under the City Code. The only criticism of Watson was in the matter of the false invoices, where his conduct was deserving of censure but not so much so as to justify revocation of his licence to be a dealer, or that of TWH.

If this decision seems unexpectedly permissive, an explanation is that all the deals under scrutiny took place before the Panel tightened up the City Code in October 1986 to compel disclosure of indemnity arrangements. This did not prevent Barker, the Panel's Director-General, from opposing the exoneration of TWH, though his arguments were sabotaged by his own organization's decision in the matter of AE.

The Tribunal's decision knocked a hole in the prosecution's case against all the Guinness defendants. In Guinness 1 the prosecution suppressed it. The Serious Fraud Office took this decision in 1989. According to the SFO this was on independent legal advice, though the *Sunday Times* said the 'independent' adviser was none other than Barbara Mills, QC, a key member of the prosecution team in Guinness 1 and later herself head of the SFO and, later still, Director of Public Prosecutions.[4] This allegation was never challenged, and the Home Office was sufficiently uneasy about the propriety of excluding the evidence to agree to refer back the Guinness 1 case to the Court of Appeal. This was to be sure not announced till December 1994, in accordance with the leisurely habits of the system. We shall never know whether, if the defence had been able to use the material in Guinness 1, there would have been different verdicts.

In Guinness 2 it was used, because Lord Spens saw to it that it was. He had of course been a prime mover in the TWH operations, so knew all about it. There was resistance to introducing it from Miss Elizabeth Gloster, QC, the prosecuting counsel, and some support for her in this by the judge on the grounds that panel decisions ought to remain confidential. All the same, once the defence had raised it there could be no question of excluding it. Had the judge done this, justice could not have been seen to be done. It is possible to suppose, as Lord Spens does, that it was the introduction of this evidence that caused Guinness 2 and 3 to abort. On this view, the premature ending of both trials was a damage limitation exercise; if the defendants had been found not guilty, fair and square, on this evidence, it would have provided convincing grounds for those convicted in Guinness 1 to seek a referral back to the Court of Appeal. They did so anyway, as we have seen; but in 1990 it was possible for the SFO to believe that this might be avoided. A very large section of official opinion had been pleased and relieved at the verdicts in Guinness 1, led by the SFO for which it had been the only major triumph since its foundation in 1988. Anything likely to endanger those verdicts could well have been seen as inconvenient.

As a matter of fact Spens now says that had Guinness 2 continued he would have brought up other matters, even more inconvenient to the prosecution than the AE and TWH material. He told me that a main focus of the defence would have been to 'bring into the open the activities of the Argyll supporters, and to analyse, in public, the other cases of market support operations. The whole concept of the false market and the so-called "grey area" would have been the subject of intense cross-examination under oath and in the full glare of the press.' He added that both inspectors would have been called to explain their actions.[5]

But who knows? Perhaps the real reason for ending the two trials was the ostensible one, namely that Seelig broke down. The breakdown was real enough; transcripts of the trial and accounts from those present make this very clear. On 7 February 1992, the prosecution announced that it would not proceed with Guinness 3, and the judge accordingly gave not guilty verdicts to Mayhew and to Seelig on the counts to be dealt with in Guinness 3. These had to do with the purchases of shares by Bank Leu near the end of the bid. Then on 21 February he discharged on health grounds the case against Seelig in Guinness 2, without a verdict. Later, on 13 March, he did the same for Spens. The grounds given were that Spens had suffered a heart attack the year before, he had faced the strain of the trial, the events had occurred six years before, he was not a central figure, and the end of the trial would save public money. But he refused to rule Spens not guilty; the indictments against him and Seelig should remain on the file. Spens asked for costs, upon which the judge went through the prosecution against him and refused costs on the grounds that he had brought the prosecution on himself. The Divisional Court later reversed these decisions, giving Seelig and Spens their not guilty verdicts and awarding Spens his costs.

There does seem to be an inconsistency between the judge's leniency in ending the trials as he did and the severity of his strictures on Spens at the end. He need not have ended Guinness 2 when Seelig broke down; he could have allowed him to rest for a couple of weeks. Alternatively, he could have continued the prosecution against Spens alone. Instead, he let him off in a way that was clearly grudging. 'You do not leave this court without a stain on your character,' a judge once told a defendant when acquitting him on a technicality. Mr Justice Henry did not say this in so many words, but in implying something of the sort was he trying to minimize the effect of AE and TWH on the verdicts in Guinness 1?

In the meantime, Ernest Saunders had applied to the Court

of Appeal to have his sentence cut. It was in fact halved, to two and a half years, and he served ten months in Ford Open Prison, being released on 28 June 1991. The Appeal Judge, Lord Justice Neill, said that the original sentence had been 'substantially too high'. The Court also took into account Saunders' medical condition, but this was only a subsidiary factor, as is shown by the fact that his release was not immediate. The medical report concerning his mental and physical condition noted that he seemed confused and listless; it mentioned as a possibility that Saunders might have been suffering from premature Alzheimer's Disease. This was in no sense a diagnosis, just a reference to a possibility. Nor was it based on nothing; I have referred to the occasion when Saunders fell asleep at the end of dinner. That was in January 1987, showing that already at that time he was under intense strain, and he had been through a great deal in the subsequent years. Dr Eric Rochat, his Swiss doctor, giving evidence in Guinness 1, had diagnosed deep psychological depression, mentioned the possibility of suicide, and said that it was against his advice that Saunders had returned in May 1987 to face the inspectors. What he really needed was three or four months in hospital. He had been talking to himself, it was impossible to hold a normal conversation with him.[6] Clearly he was able to pull himself together; his performance in front of the court proves that. Dr Rochat would have seen him at his worst. But the strain still showed when he was in Ford. It is hardly his fault if the doctors who saw him there should have mentioned the possibility of a premature onset of Alzheimer's. Being scientists, rather than publicists, they saw no harm in bringing it up.

It was most unfortunate for Saunders that they did so. Alzheimer's Disease, unfortunately for him, was newsworthy. The Press, still limitlessly spiteful towards him, hinted that he had been shamming, and either gulled the doctors, or even conspired with them. The public, at least as spiteful as the Press, caught on and made the affair into a catchword. To this day, when the name

Saunders is mentioned in the public bar, he is as likely as not to be described as the only man who has recovered from Alzheimer's.

After the collapse of Guinness 2 in March 1992, there was a lull. Benjamin Iveagh died of cancer in June. Then at the turn of the year Thomas Ward went on trial. For six weeks the Guinness Affair was replayed in front of a jury at the Old Bailey. There was only one charge: the theft of £5.2 million from Guinness. We remember that in April 1987 a judge had ruled that the payment, to Ward's company Marketing and Acquisition Consultants, 'could not have been lawfully made', and that a mareva order had been issued to freeze the assets of both Ward and Saunders. In July of the same year the High Court again ordered Ward to repay the money to Guinness, this time with interest of about £700,000. In March 1988 a warrant was issued for Ward's arrest; a month later he applied to the Appeal Court to overturn the order for repayment. This was refused. Then in October 1988 he was given leave to appeal to the House of Lords, who in February 1990 ruled against him. The case was taken to the United States, and in August 1990 the Baltimore District Court of Maryland also ruled that the money was not a proper fee. The inspectors, in their secret interim report, take the same view and also state that just over £3 million of the money was intended for Saunders. Mr Justice Henry, in his summing up at the end of Guinness 1, said the payment was too large to be lawful; a statement that may seem to accord with common sense but is nevertheless full of difficulties. One can say an amount is excessive, but this is purely in the eye of the beholder; there is no law laying down sums. As to the question whether the amount was authorized, it seems to have been accepted throughout that Saunders had *carte blanche* with the Company's money during the time of the bid. In any case Ward finally agreed in June 1991 to come back to England to stand trial, though the trial did not start, as we have seen, till early January 1993. Supported by some excellent character witnesses, he maintained that the £5.2 million was a success fee properly agreed with Saunders. This was accepted by the jury and he was triumphantly acquitted.

A factor in this decision may have been that the amount was less than 0.2 per cent of the general bid total of £2.6 billion. 'Thank God and thank you all,' said Ward to the jury. Outside the court he rubbed in what by any reckoning was a humiliation for the Serious Fraud Office, saying: 'I regret that a lot of very good people have been hurt by what I think are totally misplaced prosecutions.[7]

This acquittal created a radically new situation. Given that, as was now established, the £5.2 million had been properly paid to Ward, two guilty verdicts against Saunders were proved wrong, namely theft and false accounting with reference to the payment. But that was by no means all. It is not too much to say that most of the structure of accusation mounted against the Guinness defendants in the courts was undermined. The authorities would beat a fighting retreat and score at least one further victory when Saunders and the other defendants in Guinness 1 lost their appeals in November 1995. But as the comprehensive re-establishment of discipline that had been intended when the prosecutions were instituted, the operation had failed and failed expensively. Despite all, the area remained grey.

Jeremy Warner's comments on Ward's acquittal in the *Independent on Sunday* are of interest because he was perhaps the best-informed and most judicious of all the pack of financial journalists following the affair. 'It is hard these days to get overly worked up or incensed about what happened during the Distillers takeover,' he wrote. As time passes, memories fade, and the Guinness Affair had in the meantime been superseded by that of Robert Maxwell. Yet Warner still recalled the outrage that was felt by many people when the details of the Guinness affair emerged. 'The use of numbered bank accounts, secretive offshore tax havens, shadowy schemes to manipulate share prices, the payment of multi-million-pound commissions and "success fees" for a few months' work; somehow I doubt if these were ever the stuff of ordinary business and commerce . . . The Guinness affair lifted the lid on a corrupt and greedy world.' Yet Warner admitted that to acquit Ward was 'perhaps the only realistic thing a jury could have done'.[8]

TWENTY-ONE

Still a Grey Area

Whatever view one takes of the Guinness Affair, something certainly went very wrong. The final outcome is a series of contradictions. It is beyond the scope of this book to analyse these, in fact anyone attempting such analysis would probably be advised to wait many, many years until time has neutralized the mines in his path. What is certain is that few of the authorities covered themselves with glory over the Guinness Affair. This applies to the Takeover Panel, the Serious Fraud Office, the courts, the Department of Trade and Industry and its inspectors; it most certainly applies to the politicians, both Government and Opposition. There was one imaginative decision which had good results, namely the imposition – it would seem at the initiative of the DTI – of the new non-executive directors in July 1986. This ensured that the Company itself and the decent people who worked for it at every level came through the affair without serious damage. The trouble with all the other entities is that each was pursuing its own agenda, incurring the suspicion that it was sometimes acting in its own interest rather than in that of justice or of truth.

But it is only fair to note that the problem they faced was not new, and had always proved intractable. What is known as white-collar crime has always been difficult to police. In cases like the Guinness Affair the difficulty is compounded because it did not involve straightforward theft, or fraud in the normal sense. It concerned deception of the market, breach of its rules and the breaking of promises: a far less straightforward set of offences. Much of the relevant law and practice is new and comparatively untried, the result of quite recent changes designed to provide a level playing field for the new entrants into markets attracted by 'shareholder democracy'.

Those accused of white-collar offences of this rather technical nature tend to be more intelligent than those who pursue them. They are often rich and sometimes well connected. Evaluating the offences requires specialist knowledge which is more likely to be found among financial practitioners than anywhere else; and there is a tendency in these circles, certainly shown by the Take-over Panel in the early stages of the Guinness Affair, for dog not to eat dog.

Ever since the capitalist system got going, some practitioners have broken and bent the rules, and they have often got away with it. George Robb, in his study *White-collar Crime in Modern England,* makes out that most practitioners have done this: 'The stereotypical image of the virtuous and respectable Victorian businessman is almost wholly the creation of twentieth-century sentimentalists and conservative ideologues.'[1] This is an exaggeration so gross as to make one suspect that Robb is rather an ideologue himself, though he may simply have been led astray by his researches into the scams of the time. In any case his remark is absurd. To take an example: if fraudulent bank failures had been, as he implies, the rule rather than the exception, then all money would have been kept in mattresses and the Victorian economic expansion would never have been financed. No, there were plenty of respectable Victorian businessmen, many of whom were even virtuous; the early Guinnesses and Pursers fitted the 'stereotypical image' rather well. Even the behaviour of Barings at the time of the Guinness issue, though 'hot', was in no way criminal.

That said, there was white-collar crime which did, quite often, go unpunished; and the creation of a legal framework to control it was slow and inefficient. Parliament can be said to have been over-indulgent in this area. This would have been a more valid point to make than the wholesale rubbishing of Victorian businessmen. They were as a rule honest, not because legislation forced them to behave properly but because religion and ethics had formed their conscience. The social climate, too, tended to enforce good behaviour. Those who believe in the effectiveness of the law in this area might say that Victorian businessmen were more honest than the authorities deserved, for Robb tells us that nineteenth-century England had 'the most permissive commercial legislation in all of Europe, if not the world'.[2] But is the law effective here? Zola's novel *L'Argent*, which is quite closely based on actual Parisian scandals, shows that French fraudsters managed quite nicely. The book shows them effectively frustrating the tighter rules which prevailed in France.

In this country the 1844 Companies Act was no more than rudimentary, and it was weakened, not strengthened, in 1856. Between 1862 and 1900 there were several Companies Acts but they were mostly 'ad hoc attempts to patch up holes' which 'did little to change the permissive tone' of company law.[3] No truly effective Companies Act was passed until 1928, and only in 1948 was there a Companies Act as tough as those in Europe and America. It was also in 1948 that the Fraud Squad was initiated. This police outfit is not to be confused with the Serious Fraud Office, a prosecuting institution that was not set up until 1988.

This lax legal framework did not stop the company sector from flourishing. Robb tells us that by 1900 the British had invested about two-fifths of their national wealth in company shares, more than twice the corresponding figures in France and Germany combined. 'Corporate organisation facilitated British domination of the world economy and enriched many members of the investing public.'[4] Quite so, which indicates that fraud must have been the exception rather than the rule. But it could happen in the highest circles. Robb says of a famous swindler of the 1890s: 'Many persons felt that Ernest Hooley escaped prosecution at the time of his 1898 bankruptcy because he knew too much about the activities of highly placed officials, including a number of peers . . .'[5]

That is why white-collar crime has always been so peculiarly disquieting. When pursuing the rich, powerful and intelligent people who are often concerned, the law approaches its limits; the limits, that is, beyond which its writ does not in practice run. In effect, such people are often untouchable. They flit abroad, they engage tricky lawyers, they trip up their pursuers in legal and accounting tangles. Even if they are caught, the authorities may find they need to bargain with them, as happened with Ivan Boesky. Justice seems mocked; it is mocked. When white-collar offenders are convicted, their sentences seem light compared with the sums they have got away with – and compared with those meted out to people who may have stolen much less. Robb cites a Victorian clerk who embezzled £3 and was transported for seven years.

The contrast with the millionaire swindlers, pictured as celebrating with champagne, irritates public opinion. Such irritation comes in waves. 'Criminal prosecutions in cases of commercial fraud in this country are apt to go by fits and starts; sensation trials take place at the call of an angry public . . . Some unfortunate dupe or over-sanguine capitalist becomes the scapegoat of the sins of others.'[6] Things have not changed much; this was exactly the emotion which powered the reaction to the events at Guinness. It was trenchantly expressed by a member of the Guinness 2 jury, Mrs Edna Wijeratna, who wrote to the *Financial Times* that she and her colleagues were disappointed and angry when the trial ended 'with justice neither done nor seen to be done'. She said that many of the jurors had wondered whether the consideration extended to Roger Seelig would have been forthcoming for someone in humbler circumstances.[7]

Much, then, has stayed the same as it was in Victorian times; yet much has also changed. Society's standards have become sporadic; day to day and in normal life people do not impose them on each other as reliably as they did. Another way of putting this is that personal tolerance has increased. I have found myself knowingly in the company of an interesting swindler who had done a stretch in prison and been intrigued by his knowledge and quiet charm. My grandfather would certainly not have given this man the time of day. Yet just as God is proverbially not mocked, so the innate feeling for right and wrong in our collective psyche may sleep but is not dead and can rear up ferociously. Periods of cynical acceptance are followed by episodes of frantic indignation.

Such indignation was a feature of the public mood of the mid-1980s. Business transgressions were increasingly blatant, and public opinion, all the way up to Lady Thatcher as Prime Minister, was increasingly resentful. Such resentment may have been a reason for the elephantine size of the Companies Act 1985, running to 630 pages. A particular feature of that Act is the granting of unusual powers to DTI inspectors of the type sent in to look at Guinness. In Section 434, subsection 5, it is laid down that an answer given by a witness to a question by inspectors 'may be used in evidence against him'. However, it is further enacted in Section 436 that if a person refuses to appear, or to answer any questions, he will in effect be held guilty of contempt of court. It appears to have escaped Parliament's attention that if such a person is then prosecuted, and if the judge allows in evidence the answers he has given under this duress, it is hard to maintain that he has benefited from the right to silence which every accused person is supposed to enjoy under the English system.

It does look as if this provision was an unnecessary piece of overkill. It was under an earlier act that inspectors without these special powers concluded that Robert Maxwell was not a fit person to run a public company. Thanks partly to the suppressive power of the law of defamation, but mostly because of the naïvety of certain bankers, this opinion had precisely no effect in preventing Maxwell from running numbers of public companies with results that have become notorious. But the remedy here is for more notice to be taken of what inspectors say, not for Parliament to give them inquisitorial powers which, it now appears, make their evidence inadmissible in the courts.

In a confused sort of way Parliament in passing the 1985 Act seems to have cast the inspectors in the role of a French *juge d'instruction* or examining magistrate. In the French system, known as inquisitorial whereas ours is adversarial, the examining magistrate investigates the case and interrogates the prisoner with a view to deciding whether he should be brought to court. In court there are still prosecuting and defending counsel, as in Britain. Many people consider that the French system has merit, and it looks as if the general perception that accused businessmen are slippery customers, cunning and well-heeled, made legislators think that something of the sort was required in this special area.

The trouble is of course that DTI inspectors are not examining magistrates. In the Guinness case it seems clear that the granting of these special inquisitorial powers, together with political and public pressure, made the inspectors forget their true functions. As a result their efforts have been entirely wasted. The purpose of an investigation of this nature is not to provide evidence for use in criminal trials. Anything of this sort which may emerge is essentially a by-product, even if it turns out to be a useful one. The primary function of the inspectors is to produce a report which should be published. Delay in publication is a violation of the rights of taxpayers who have after all paid for the report. The report should suggest necessary action against companies and individuals; sackings and disqualifications perhaps more often than prosecutions. Above all it should be demonstrably objective. When it criticizes, such criticism should be as near as possible incontrovertible.

There is a particular reason for the inspectors to exercise extreme caution in suggesting prosecutions, which is that they may state that an offence has been committed and the accused may then be found not guilty. This tends to discredit the report and may even make it impossible to publish it.

This is what has happened here. The inspectors' *oeuvre*, a massive and closely argued thesis in three substantial volumes, has remained like the wings of an earwig. This creature, under its carapace, apparently possesses gorgeous iridescent wings like those of a dragonfly, fully formed, which it never uses. The ways of nature are strange, but hardly stranger than those of a Government which can commission a report costing millions and keep it more secret than a design of a thermonuclear warhead. To be sure the report is styled 'interim', and perhaps a final report will one day be issued; as said earlier there have been signs that this may be the case. If so it will hardly be of more than historical interest.

We do have a general idea of what the interim report says because it was leaked to the *Mail on Sunday*, which published a good summary on 17 May 1992. Most of what follows can be found in that article.

Saunders is directly accused of intending to keep the £3 million plus interest that went into his Swiss bank account from the £5.2 million paid to Ward. 'It was not credible that anyone would deposit over £3 million in the bank account of another with no control over the operation of the account.' They also cite the fact that the £29,000-odd that was paid over and above £3 million coincided with the interest that would have been due on the money between the time when Ward received it and when it was paid to Saunders. The inspectors go to town on Saunders' evidence, saying it 'bore the deep stamp of unreliability, a systematic evasiveness, extensive gaps of recollection in sensitive areas contrasted with his powers of recall on subjects where he could judge himself to be under no threat'. They add: 'By the time he was dismissed in 1987 he was without scruple or honesty. We do not consider that he can again be entrusted with the charge of a public company.' Ward, too, is bitterly criticized over the payment as one who should never be trusted again. This is clearly a passage that will have to be revised following Ward's acquittal.

Ronson is criticized not only for the share support for which he was convicted, but also because he apparently bought some Argyll shares during the bid, breaking his implied agreement with Saunders to be a Guinness supporter. This was a 'shabby and opportunistic breach of faith unpalliated by the illegality and impropriety of that agreement'. He is also taken to task for introducing Guinness to Boesky when he must have known that the purpose of this was to support the share price with an indemnity.

Lyons, Parnes and Margulies are all criticized much as one might expect, though Parnes is praised for his honesty in giving evidence. As to Lyons, the inspectors think that the size of his remuneration implies that he may have played 'a more active role in relation to the less savoury aspects of the bid than we have been able to establish'. Seelig is severely criticized, but so are other directors of Morgan Grenfell who, it is implied, sought to unload their responsibility unfairly on to Seelig. These were the Chief Executive, Christopher Reeves, the Head of Corporate Finance, Graham Walsh, and the Finance Director, David Ewart. 'We found quite implausible the idea that Mr Seelig was a lone and secretive wolf whose style and methods of operation were known only to himself.'

It is when we come to David Mayhew that fundamental doubts begin to arise about the whole approach of the inspectors. We recall that his firm, Cazenove, throughout maintained that he had done nothing improper, and that they were backed in this by their solicitors; also that the charges with reference to the purchase for Bank Leu, that he had been going to face in Guinness 3, had been dropped. The inspectors express the suspicion here that he did not tell them the whole truth, which may or may not be so. Where serious doubts arise is in their strictures on a quite different deal.

It appears that Lord Rothschild's company, J. Rothschild Holdings, gave Mayhew an order to buy £25 million worth of Guinness shares, and that he used this order to support the price at important times during the bid. The inspectors say: 'He placed himself in a serious conflict of interest poised between the obligation to buy at times and prices most favourable to JRH and the desire to make purchases at times and prices most helpful to the success of the bid.' Yet they also say that Rothschild wished to be helpful to Cazenove in the hope of doing future business and that he genuinely wanted a holding in Guinness. What they are describing here is technically known as 'sloppy dealing'; that is, dealing not neatly in the interests of securing the best price for the client but clumsily in order to use the deal to influence the price to the greatest possible extent. To imply that this is inherently improper, as the inspectors do, shows no understanding of the way markets work. Any regulation to ban the practice would be quite unenforceable, and it is clear anyway that this particular example of sloppy buying was done with the full knowledge of the client who expected some benefit in return. This is how the City works, and has always worked. The fact that the inspectors make such a song and dance about it reduces their credibility.

The inspectors' report might have had more practical use if they had taken some expert evidence from a member of the Panel, to get some idea of what actually goes on in markets and temper their abstract ideas. But the Panel itself, it has to be said, was as surprisingly permissive as the inspectors were surprisingly restrictive; beginning with the rejection of Spens' complaint on behalf of Bells, and continuing with their acceptance of the arrangement which killed Turner and Newall's bid for AE, which in turn frustrated their attempt to oppose TWH's appeal before the DTI tribunal. From the severe standpoint of the inspectors, the Panel might seem to have sold the pass. Certainly the contrast between Panel and inspectors contributed to the confusion in which the Affair ended – if indeed it has ended.

The greatest mistake of the inspectors was not to cast their net widely enough. They in fact missed the opportunity to produce an account of the whole bid battle for Distillers, which would have had a permanent value far beyond any immediate prosecutions. Misled perhaps by a rush of blood to the head at the genuinely shocking revelations about Guinness and its supporters, they made no attempt to discover what happened on the other side. It was well known that Argyll, as well as Guinness, was extensively supported during the bid, though there is no evidence that the Argyll side did anything improper. We cannot know this, though, because the matter has not been investigated. It should have been, in order to get a comprehensive view of the whole story. Even if there was no impropriety, it would be illuminating to know what was done. As it is, the story resembles the Zen saying about the sound of one hand clapping. Argyll instituted civil proceedings against Guinness which were settled out of court by a payment of £100 million in December 1992. A tidy sum, but rather little in relation to what Argyll would have made if its bid had succeeded, therefore much less than they might have been awarded after a successful action if the evidence was all against Guinness. Very likely the failure to pursue this case was simply due to a desire by Argyll's board to put everything behind them, but there are other possibilities. On Guinness's side everything might have remained hidden if Boesky had not 'sung', and if the Risk affair had not frustrated Roux's attempt to market surplus Guinness shares at a price that did not trigger the indemnities.

Lord Spens is scathing about the inspectors,[8] although he has no personal reason to feel ill-will against them because he is the only one of the Guinness defendants whom they did not criticize. He did, it is true, encourage TWH to be economical with the truth in their invoices, as well as accepting the 'interest-free loan' from Guinness against their own shares which got him into trouble; but these are his only known lapses and he was after all cleared. His opinion, as an old City hand, is worth recording, and many of his points hit home. He says the inspectors omitted to look at all 5719 transactions in Guinness between 20 January and 18 April 1986, only examining some of them and those mostly on the bought side and connected with identifiable individuals. This, Spens thinks, seriously discredits the report. He draws attention to short sales of Guinness just before the second underwriting was organized for the increased bid in mid-February 1986. He charges the inspectors with being diverted from their original terms of reference and confining their attention to individuals identified by the press. On market practice, the inspectors ought to have interviewed market makers to contribute some professional expertise. He asks: 'Was the support operation the cause of the increase in the Guinness share price from mid-March to the end of the bid?' He points out that the 1986 budget on 18 March had reduced income tax and not increased drink tax, and that other brewery shares had gone up in about the same proportion as Guinness's. The inspectors' assumption as to the effect of the market operations on the Guinness share price was 'guesswork'.

The cases of the four Guinness 1 defendants were eventually referred back to the Court of Appeal so that the AE and TWH evidence could be heard on their behalf. 'Eventually' is right, because the reference back did not occur until December 1994, more than two and a half years after the end of Guinness 2 and twenty-two months after the Home Secretary, Michael Howard, had been asked for it. The delay indicates that there was strenuous resistance behind the scenes, This is not to be wondered at; the move was a severe slap in the face for the SFO which had withheld the evidence. A spokeswoman for the SFO showed definite irritation, telling *The Times*: 'We are not talking here about new material. This is unused material which at the time was not regarded as relevant and therefore not disclosed.' She said the SFO would be strongly contesting any argument that the convictions were unsafe or unsatisfactory.[9] No wonder: the SFO had had a bad run since its success with Guinness 1. *Private Eye* estimated: 'The score in major trials after Blue Arrow, Guinness and Barlow Clowes reads SFO 6, Defendants 13 (including those like Mayhew, Seelig, Spens and two Barlow Clowes defendants not proceeded against).'[10] To lose the four Guinness convictions would have altered this score to Defendants 17, SFO 2.

In a quite separate procedure Saunders had taken his case to Europe, arguing that the acceptance by the court of the transcripts from the DTI inspectors vitiated his right of silence and was therefore unfair. The first hearing, before the fifteen European Commissioners on Human Rights, decided in his favour in December 1994, the same month as his case was referred back to the Court of Appeal. The vote was fourteen to one, and the British commissioner, Nicholas Bratzer, QC, voted with the majority.

The verdict read as follows:

> The Commission finds that the applicant was in effect compelled to incriminate himself . . . The Commission considers this must have exerted additional pressure on the applicant to take the witness stand rather than exercise the right of silence. The Commission finds that the use at the trial (of the DTI evidence) was oppressive and substantially impaired his ability to defend himself against the criminal charges facing him. He was therefore deprived of a fair hearing.

As is usual in these cases, the opposing parties, namely Saunders and the British Government, were invited to get together to resolve their differences during a period of three months before being referred to the nineteen judges of the European Court of Human Rights. The British Government met this invitation with stony silence, presumably hoping against hope that the problem would go away.

The Court of Appeal, consisting of three judges led by the Lord Chief Justice, Lord Taylor, eventually sat in November 1995. They gave against the defendants, but the SFO's relief at this must have been somewhat tempered by the ruling that the material on AE and TWH ought to have been disclosed to Guinness 1. However, Lord Taylor and his colleagues were satisfied that the 'procedural irregularity which occurred as a result of non-disclosure' did not penalize the defendants, whom the jury would have convicted anyway.[11] There seems to be a flaw here. One can follow the argument that what went on at Guinness was so obviously outrageous that it scarcely mattered whether or not something like it had happened elsewhere and been accepted. All the same, to rule that certain evidence ought to have been disclosed and simultaneously to say that disclosure would have made no difference seems on the face of it to be logically contradictory.

Most of the judgement, though, turned on the same matter that had been brought up by Saunders before the European Commissioners, namely the question whether the judge ought to have allowed the transcripts of evidence given under duress to the DTI inspectors. Here, Lord Taylor and the others ruled that Parliament could override the general principle that no person should be required to incriminate himself, and that in enacting the relevant provisions of the 1985 Companies Act it had done this, knowing what it was doing. The trial judge was therefore right to admit as evidence the interviews before the DTI inspectors. The issues in the case were simple: 'A combination of indemnities paid by Guinness to purchasers of its own shares, huge success fees even to the Guinness board, provided ample evidence of a dishonest scheme in which all the appellants played their part.' Lord Taylor also mentioned the fact, however, that Saunders had taken his case to Europe and the European Commission on Human Rights had referred it to the European Court in Strasbourg. 'Should he succeed there, treaty obligations would require consideration to be given to the effect of the decision on the United Kingdom.'[12] Leave to appeal to the House of Lords was refused.

After the appeals were rejected, Saunders spoke out, describing the ruling as a 'politically convenient judgement' in conflict with the ruling in his favour by the European Commission of Human Rights. He said that 'legal gymnastics' had been used to excuse 'improper behaviour by the Government and the prosecution'.[13] He would, of course, say something of the sort. The significant thing, though, is not that he said it, but that it was respectfully reported in *The Times* and elsewhere. This showed that the verdict was no longer accepted as gospel truth; there was an enormous difference from the attitude at the original conviction of Saunders and the others, the general view that the sentences expressed absolute and final justice.

A little more than a year after the Court of Appeal's verdict, in December 1996, the European Court of Human Rights in Strasbourg ruled that Saunders' trial had been unfair because of the use of evidence given before the inspectors without the right of silence. The headlines in the press next day were very varied. The *Independent* said the UK was 'red faced' at the verdict. This was fair enough, but it is doubtful if the Serious Fraud Office was 'stunned' by it, as the *Guardian* maintained. The result had been amply signalled by the opinion of the Commission on Human Rights given two years before. It is extremely rare for the Court to go against the Commission.

There was some comfort for the British authorities in the fact that the Court threw out Saunders' American-style claim against the Government for a total of nearly £4.7 million, and reduced his application for costs from £336,400 to £75,000. The *Sun*, anti-Saunders like most of the popular press, made the most of this by coming up with the headline 'Saunders beaten on £4.5 million bid,' which was rather misleading considering that Saunders had in fact won a stunning victory. The *Evening Standard* achieved some sort of balance, coming up with 'Victory for Guinness crook Saunders.'

Saunders' press conference, which should have been triumphant, was marred by the journalists' obtuse insistence on asking questions about Alzheimer's Disease, and Saunders' exasperated refusal to answer them. The legend that Saunders secured his release from jail by shamming Alzheimers with the connivance of his doctors has no basis in fact, as we have seen, and its persistence must be extremely annoying to Saunders. It even annoys me, especially when people come out with it as if it was some original insight. It is by no means only the dim who do this; Stuart Bell, MP, produced this decaying rabbit out of his hat when talking to the *Sun* after the European verdict, and he is only one of many who should know better.

But when a myth is as persistent as this one is, it is not enough to deny it; we need to examine its psychological roots. In this case there is little difficulty. It stems from the general resentment that white collar offenders, as a class, receive more lenient treatment than the public thinks they deserve; and that Saunders, in particular, was let off far too lightly when he served 'only' ten months in Ford Prison.

Those who think like this can be reassured. Saunders suffered from more and worse than his spell in prison, and the authorities made very sure that this was the case. Their spiteful delay in according him legal aid helped to precipitate him down from prosperity to penury, their refusal to release the Turner and Newall-AE material hobbled his defence.

Should we be indignant on his behalf about all this? Perhaps not unconditionally so. It is impossible not to be shocked by what happened during the Distillers takeover. Lies were told, promises were broken and the City rules on acquisitions were insolently ignored. With hindsight, the Company never ought to have gone for Distillers; the batttle with Argyll as an equally powerful opponent ensured that victory would have been impossible without cheating. My instinct and that of Simon Boyd were not far wrong.

Have the gross mistakes of the authorities shown that in the end anyone can get away with anything? It may seem so, yet one need not be too pessimistic. The rules on share support schemes, too lax in 1986, were tightened up in 1987. Some lessons will have been learnt; specifically, it may be hoped that the City Panel will in future rein in its tendency to rulings that are eccentrically permissive. If this means that more future cases are dealt with outside the courts, so much the better.

In the meantime, the Guinness Affair is still not quite settled; at the time of writing there is a stand-off between the British courts and the European court. Eurosceptics in politics and the press have been sounding off, and will no doubt go on doing so. If 'Europe' can be saddled with Ernest Saunders this will discredit it further in the eyes of the public. Whether this is right or fair is not the point; it is a fact.

As to Saunders himself, he is clearly on the way up again. He is working successfully as a management consultant and seems both prosperous and fulfilled. To his young colleagues, the Guinness affair is history. He still accepts no responsibility for anything that happened, blaming Roux and the advisers for irregularities during the bid, and Macfarlane for getting together with other Scots, including Argyll, to remove him. He also now claims that it was Benjamin Iveagh who instructed him to drop Risk. This is corroborated nowhere – it is not in *Nightmare*, for instance – and I can only conclude that his memory is playing tricks. But he deserves his new success. Nothing can take away from him the brilliance he showed in the first years at Guinness. He simply overreached himself. Let us leave it at that.

357

Afterword: The End for the Family

Norman Macfarlane talked to me privately twice in the autumn of 1987. First, he took me aside after a Board Meeting and said, 'I notice you are only on £4,000 a year, whereas the other non-executives get £10,000.'

'Well,' I said, 'I suppose it was thought that the others were appointed for a special function.'

'No, it's quite wrong; all non-executives should have the same fees. This is clearly most improper, and typical of Saunders. I'll get it put right.'

Sure enough, in a few days I not only received a notification that I was now on £10,000 a year, but also a cheque for the extra I would have received if I had been put up to that figure when the new non-executives were appointed.

Not long after that, Macfarlane invited me to tea at Grosvenor House. This time he gave me the sack.

'You come up for re-election at the next Annual Meeting,' he said, 'and I note that you have been a director for twenty-seven years. Perhaps you ought to stand down; I think the right term for a non-executive director is three years.'

I said, 'I don't sit as an ordinary non-executive, but as a representative of the family holding. All the same, that is now at most 3 per cent of the Company, and two representatives are probably too many. Obviously, between the two of us Benjamin is the senior. Certainly I will stand down.'

Macfarlane may have expected to have more trouble with me; at any rate he seemed relieved when the interview was over. It still seems strange to me that he produced the specious and arbitrary idea of a three-year term rather than coming straight out with the reduction in the family's proportionate holding, something of which I was well aware and which was already making me half expect an invitation to retire. I stood down as requested at the 1988 Annual General Meeting the following May. At a lunch shortly afterwards Macfarlane presented me with a miniature wooden barrel full of whisky, saying he expected me to buy a refill. Not being a whisky drinker, I never did this; my guests had the odd dram, but it seemed to empty rather quickly, I suspect through evaporation. Bottles, at the end of the day, are probably more economical. The barrel is still around somewhere. I regard it mostly as a memento of my father's losing battle to retain the Guinness cooperage.

Now there is nobody from the family on the Board, because Benjamin contracted cancer and died in June 1992. He was only 55. I saw him a few months before his death, when I was already planning this book. He did not seem ill at that time. We spent a pleasant evening together but he told me precisely nothing of interest. To me, and to others, he remained an enigma to the end.

Anthony Tennant took the Company in hand and made it perform extremely well. He told one or two people that all he was doing was carrying out the plans already laid down by Saunders, but in this he was not fair on himself. Notably, the association with the French drinks and luggage group LVMH was imaginative and profitable. I have remarked earlier that Saunders' personality, though strong, was perhaps not quite strong enough. The same can certainly not be said of Tennant, who as a negotiator is agreed to be formidable.

Vic Steel left at the same time as I did, also scoring a whisky barrel. As head of the distilling arm of the Group he was succeeded by none other than Tony Greener, who it will be recalled was one of the new non-executives. When Tennant himself retired as Chief Executive in 1990, Greener took over. But the current performance of the Company, now that the family is no longer in it, is not part of my subject.

Appendix A: The Name Guinness

The name Guinness, in my opinion and most others', comes from the Irish Mac Aonghusa, and is one of several versions current in the seventeenth and eighteenth centuries in which the 'Mac' is dropped leaving a 'g' as its only vestige. This derivation seems much the most probable, but nobody can be quite sure.

Some of us have tried to discover that our ancestry was distinguished. Most genealogy since Homer has had a similar purpose. However, in the case of the Guinness family there was in some quarters another bias cutting across the more usual hankering after noble descent: namely, the wish not to have been descended from native Catholic Irishmen. A link with the French Counts of Guines would have suited both these preferences; but the only trace that anyone may ever have envisaged this satisfying possibility is the presence, in the strongroom at Elveden Hall, of a magnificent folio volume, dated 1631, about the de Guines family. Whoever acquired this book evidently drew a blank. My own opinion is that our ancestry is both obscure and entirely Irish, because this entails making the fewest assumptions. But let us look at the facts and theories.

Back as far as Richard Guinness of Celbridge, Arthur's father, everything is clear. Richard was land agent to Archbishop Price of Cashel. He was probably born in 1680 or perhaps a little later. He married Elizabeth Read; tradition in the Read family had it that he had worked for Elizabeth's father as a groom and eloped with her. He had a brother, William, who was apparently a little older and became a gunsmith in Dublin. But who was Richard and William's father?

The romantic view of the family origins is that the brothers were in some way connected with Bryan Viscount Magennis of Iveagh in County Down. Lord Magennis was a Catholic clan chief who supported James II at the Battle of the Boyne in 1690. After that battle was lost the Viscount was attainted, that is, deprived of his title and his land. He left Ireland with most of the Catholic aristocracy in what became known as the 'Flight of the Wild Geese'. On this theory, Richard and William must have kept quiet about their origins either because of the attainder, or because they were illegitimate. In itself the theory is suspect, simply because it is so much of the type that upwardly-mobile families desiring noble credentials used to invent. All the same, it is interesting that Arthur Guinness the first, that no-nonsense character, himself used a version of the Magennis coat of arms. When in 1761 he married Olivia Whitmore, and her silversmith cousin John Locker made a silver cup for the couple as a wedding present, Arthur had it engraved with these arms impaling those of Whitmore. This cup is still in existence. Then in 1814 Arthur's eldest son, the Reverend Hosea Guinness, took it into his head to get the use of the coat of arms properly authenticated: he asked Ulster Herald to agree the family's right to use it. The Herald did so, but as a new grant, not a confirmation of an existing right, implying that he doubted any connection with the Magennis family. So why had Arthur used the escutcheon? Whether or not social pretension entered into it, his choice certainly implies that he regarded his surname as a version of Magennis or Mac Aonghusa.

Fortified by Ulster Herald's grant to Hosea, members of the family went on using the coat of arms when they felt like it, without bothering too much about their antecedents, until in the 1860s Arthur's grandson Benjamin was awarded a baronetcy.

This meant that the question of ancestry had to be looked at seriously, and Benjamin engaged Sir Bernard Burke to do this. Sir Bernard was an obvious choice, being one of the most respected genealogists of the time; unfortunately he was also an incorrigible romantic. The modern, scientific principle in genealogy was once given me by a Herald: 'if we find two alternatives, it's generally right to choose the less interesting.' Sir Bernard Burke had no truck with this. He spent his life preparing ancestries for numerous families including a good proportion of the peerage, always when in doubt going for the more interesting possibility. It made him very popular. In the case of Guinness he naturally seized on the Magennises of Iveagh, and the lineage he endorsed is only one among a number which were later discredited. (Sir Bernard gave my mother's family, the Mitfords, a pedigree going back to the Saxons. Alas, it was quite imaginary.)

However, in the course of his researches Sir Bernard also encountered a completely different theory about the name Guinness, and from a highly respectable source within the family. Richard Guinness MP, father of Adelaide who was to marry Benjamin's son Edward Cecil, wrote to him as follows:

> My father (Richard Guinness, Barrister-at-Law) was the eldest grandchild of Richard of Celbridge, who died when my father was 6 years old, viz., in 1763, at the age of 83, so he [the first Richard] must have been born near 1680. I always heard that the father of Richard had come into Ireland from Cornwall with Cromwell.

Sir Bernard Burke ignored this letter, probably because it contained nothing more solid than an assertion of what 'I always heard'. Even so, as a serious researcher he ought at least to have looked into it. The Cornish theory was more strongly held than Sir Bernard was aware, and a monograph on the family origins printed privately in 1924 by Henry Seymour Guinness was to come down in its favour. Henry's work is painstaking and it is at first sight rash to differ from him. But while his rejection of various possible theories is impressively argued, his positive conclusion seems to be backed by no hard evidence. Let us look at it.

It concerns a family called Gennys in Cornwall. Henry concedes that 'no direct reference has been found to connect any member of the Gennys family with Ireland'. However, the Gennyses were related by marriage to a family called Vigors; and a Dean Bartholomew Vigors was the executor of Archbishop Price's will under which Richard Guinness and his son Arthur were beneficiaries. Also, Henry found references to a certain Owen Guinneas, of Murphystown, Co. Dublin, of whom four children were baptized between 1687 and 1690. These were Sarah, John, William and George – a William, to be sure; but no Richard. Later, in 1726, a lease on some land at Donnybrook is granted to George Guines, dairyman, and his brothers William and Richard Guines. 'It is more than probable that these three men were all the sons of Owen Guinneas,' says Henry. Is it? Owen Guinneas himself occupied some land together with a Welsh family called Davis, and his Christian name was 'at that period essentially a Welsh one'. Welsh, we note, not Cornish, which makes it all something of a non sequitur, and in any case the name Owen was most certainly used in Ireland – Owen Roe O'Neill springs to mind. It was an anglicization of Eoin.

The only other reference to Richard Guinness's father gives him the improbable Christian name of Ever. Rupert Guinness, in 1925, exchanged letters with a statistician called R. A. Fisher, later to be knighted as Sir Ronald, whose wife was born Ruth Eileen Guinness. Fisher traced his wife's descent, correctly, through the first Arthur Guinness and back to Richard Guinness; but he took it one generation further back, giving Richard's father's name as Ever Guinness. Rupert replied: 'In spite of protracted research nothing authentic can be ascertained regarding [Richard's] parentage and Ever Guinness seems to be a purely mythical personage.' Ever could be Owen, or more probably Euen, hurriedly written. But nobody seems to know R. A. Fisher's source.

The Cornish theory first surfaced with barrister Richard (1755–1829), whose son, Richard Guinness, MP, proposed it to Sir Bernard Burke. Henry's monograph tells us that in the diary of Henrietta Guinness, the youngest daughter of Richard the barrister, 'there is a note that Mr Henn-Gennys [Henn-Guinness in the diary] dined with her family at Stillorgan, co. Dublin, in the month of March 1824. This gentleman was presumably Edmund Henn-Gennys of Whiteleigh House near Plymouth, and the representative of the ancient Cornish family of Gennys.' The Henn-Gennyses kept up with that branch of the Guinness family, but the second Arthur never agreed that they were relations: a nephew of his told Henry that he 'distinctly remembered Richard Samuel Guinness MP . . . introducing to Arthur Guinness about the year 1854 a Captain Gennys from Cornwall who claimed connection with the Guinness family of Dublin' but that 'Arthur Guinness did not consider that Captain Gennys adduced any satisfactory evidence of the connection.' The theory seems to have been a castle in the air constructed by Richard Guinness's family and Edmund Henn-Gennys over the dinner-table and fortified, on the part of Richard Guinness, by a preference for Protestant ancestry.

Henry's monograph refutes various other theories for Guinness origins. He disposes of Ginnis of Derbyshire and Co. Kerry, Gunnis of Carnarvonshire, Lincolnshire, Co. Fermanagh and Co. Tyrone, and Gynes of Essex and Ireland. He shows that the Magennis of Iveagh theory has no real basis, despite being apparently confirmed by a detailed narrative from a Church of Ireland clergyman called Fahy, based on what he had been told by a great-aunt. Henry found glaring discrepancies with other records, and when he asked Mr Fahy to produce his aunt's notes, it turned out that they had been destroyed by damp; this at least, in Ireland, does ring rather true. But it is in this Magennis section that Henry Guinness gives a clue to what I think are the facts.

> It has been suggested ... that following the enactment of the Penal Laws [against Catholics] ... in 1690, the father or ancestor of Richard Guinness of Celbridge ... changed his name from Magennis to Guinness and conformed to the Protestant religion. This suggestion may be set aside as most improbable, as long before ... William of Orange the name of Gennis, Ginnis, Gennys, Guinneas and Guinness were [sic] known in Dublin and elsewhere in Ireland, and in several instances the occurrence of the name indicates that the individual was a Protestant.

It is strange that Henry thinks that this fits the Cornish theory. If versions of a name like Guinness were common in Ireland 'long before William of Orange' in 1688, the families who bore it can hardly have all been descended from a soldier coming over with Cromwell in the 1650s. The clan Magennis or Mac Aonghusa becomes much the most likely origin. Certainly the dropping of the first syllable – Gaelic for 'son of' – need have had nothing to do with becoming a Protestant after 1690, although this was a practice among some Irish Protestant converts who wanted to deny their native origin. Sir Bernard Burke found recognizable versions of the name as early as Tudor times, some already without the Ma(c)-. The name, he said in a letter to Edward Cecil Guinness, 'occurs in the State Papers of Ireland of 1542 and its various forms of spelling are therein shown, viz: Fitzguinneys, McGuinez, Guinez, Guineys'. He even found reference to a Sir Arthur Guinez, Knight.

Then again, when Arthur wanted a coat of arms he chose the Magennis one. All this suggests that the father of Richard Guinness and his brother William was an ordinary, humble Son of Angus, possibly called Owen or Euen, not closely related to the

Lord Magennis of Iveagh but belonging to his clan, personally or by ancestry. (Most Campbells, after all, have nothing to do with the Duke of Argyle.) However Richard spelt his surname, he can hardly have foreseen that his descendants would make it known all over the world as the name of a dark, smooth, hop-tangy beer with a 'baby in every bottle'.

Appendix B: Some Other Brewery Families

Apart from the Guinnesses, the most important family in the Brewery was undoubtedly the Pursers, together with the Geoghegans who were the sons of a daughter of John Purser Junior, one of whom also married his Purser first cousin. In the family tree below, all the men except Dr T. G. Geoghegan worked in the Brewery. Not all were equally successful; Benjamin Purser left to found a brewery of his own in Sligo which apparently failed, and his son Edward also resigned early; one story has it that he had to go because he married a Catholic. Of the three Geoghegan brothers, the most important was William Purser Geoghegan who was Head Brewer from 1880 to 1897.

Other Brewery families of which we are aware, at Brewer level, are as follows.

The Wallers: G. A. Waller, Head Brewer 1867–80, had two brothers in the firm, William and Edmund.

The Usshers: Simeon Ussher, a Brewer from 1844 to about 1860, was son of the Head Clerk.

The Phillips: E. L. Phillips, Head Brewer 1911–23 and his son W. E. Phillips, Assistant Managing Director 1948–66.

The Jacksons: Arthur Jackson, Assistant Managing Director 1935–41 and his son Guy Jackson.

The McMullens: Alan McMullen, Head Brewer 1931–7 and his son Launce McMullen, Head Brewer, Dublin, 1960–69.

APPENDIX B: SOME OTHER BREWERY FAMILIES

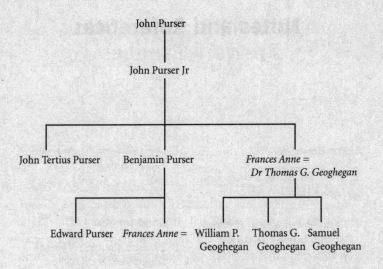

John Purser

John Purser Jr

John Tertius Purser — Benjamin Purser — *Frances Anne =*
Dr Thomas G. Geoghegan

Edward Purser — *Frances Anne =* William P. Geoghegan — Thomas G. Geoghegan — Samuel Geoghegan

Notes and References

1 The Brewery

1. Michele Guinness, *The Guinness Legend*, Hodder & Stoughton, p. 38.
2. Gourvish and Wilson, *The British Brewing Industry, 1830–1930*, p. 100.
3. ibid.
4. ibid., p. 101.
5. ibid.

2 From Partnership to Company

1. Gourvish and Wilson, op. cit., p. 103.
2. Figures from Philip Ziegler, *The Sixth Great Power, Barings 1762–1929*, p. 200.
3. ibid.
4. ibid., p. 201.
5. *Bankers' Magazine*, quoted by David Kynaston, *The City of London*, vol. 1, p. 407.
6. Ziegler, op. cit., p. 201.

7. Owen Williams, *Nonsense Book*, unpublished.
8. ibid.

3 Good for You

1. Elizabeth, Countess of Fingall, *Seventy Years Young*, Lilliput, 1991, p. 302.
2. Bryan Guinness, 'Dairy Not Kept', unpublished version.
3. Countess of Fingall, op. cit., p. 337.
4. *Guinness Time*, December 1949.
5. Julian Amery, *Approach March*, p. 315.
6. Brian Sibley, *The Book of Guinness Advertising*, Guinness Superlatives, 1985, p. 38.
7. ibid.
8. ibid., p. 74.

4 Symbiosis and Growth

1. *Guinness Time*, December 1960.
2. ibid., Spring 1967.

5 The Fading of the Family

1. James Saunders, *Nightmare*, Hutchinson, 1989. p. 57.

6 The Brewers' Last Spurt

1. Gourvish and Wilson, op. cit., p. 481.
2. *Guinness Time*, Spring 1971.

7 Heading for the Weir

1. Nick Kochan and Hugh Pym, *The Guinness Affair: Anatomy of a Scandal*, Christopher Helm, 1987, p. 190.
2. *Sunday Telegraph*, 27 February 1994.
3. Saunders, op. cit., p. 60.

8 Ernest Saunders

1. Saunders, op. cit., p. 58.
2. ibid., p. 60.
3. ibid., p. 50.
4. ibid., p. 52.
5. ibid., p. 59.
6. ibid., pp. 64–5.
7. ibid., p. 62.
8. Kochan and Pym, op. cit., p. 8.
9. Peter Pugh, *Is Guinness Good for You?: Bid for Distillers – the Inside Story*, Financial Training Publications, 1987, p. 24.
10. Saunders, op. cit., p. 64.
11. *Daily Telegraph*, 16 December 1981.

9 Resurgence

1. Saunders, op. cit., p. 60.
2. Kochan and Pym, op. cit., p. 18.
3. Saunders, op. cit., p. 65.
4. Kochan and Pym, op. cit., p. 8.
5. Saunders, op. cit., p. 79.
6. ibid., p. 155.

10 Towards the Big League

1. *Investors' Chronicle*, 20 January 1984.
2. Saunders, op. cit., p. 109.
3. ibid.
4. ibid.
5. ibid., p. 111.
6. Dominic Hobson, *The Pride of Lucifer: Unauthorized Biography of a Merchant Bank*, Mandarin Books, 1991. p. 323.
7. Pugh, op. cit., pp. 44–5.
8. Saunders, op. cit., p. 128.
9. Hobson, op. cit., p. 330–31.

11 Going for Distillers

1. Kochan and Pym, op. cit., p. 71.
2. ibid., p. 77.
3. Saunders, op. cit., p. 138.
4. Kochan and Pym, op. cit., p. 84–5.
5. Saunders, op. cit., p. 139–40.
6. ibid., p. 138.
7. ibid., p. 139.
8. ibid., p. 140.

9. Olivier Roux, evidence to Serious Fraud Office.
10. Saunders, op. cit., pp. 148–9.
11. ibid., p. 149.
12. Roger Seelig, interview with author.
13. Saunders, op. cit., p. 150.
14. Kochan and Pym, op. cit., p. 101.
15. ibid.
16. ibid., p. 104.

12 The Battle in the Market

1. Saunders, op. cit., p. 153.
2. Kochan and Pym, op. cit., p. 111.
3. Anthony Salz, evidence given in Guinness 2.
4. Olivier Roux, evidence to Serious Fraud Office.
5. Hobson, op. cit., p. 374.
6. Saunders, op. cit., p. 158.
7. ibid.
8. Kochan and Pym, op. cit., p. 96.
9. Financial Times, 22 January 1986.
10. Kochan and Pym, op. cit., p. 118.
11. Roger Seelig, interview with author.
12. Saunders, op. cit., p. 162.
13. Financial Times, 8 June 1990.
14. Saunders, op. cit., p. 162.
15. Olivier Roux, evidence to Serious Fraud Office.
16. Simon Boyd, letter to author, 13 September 1994.

17. Saunders, op. cit., p. 165.
18. Financial Times, 21 February 1986.
19. Kochan and Pym, op. cit., p. 120.

13 Making Enemies

1. Quoted in Pugh, op. cit., p. 101.
2. Quoted in Kochan and Pym, op. cit., p. 162.
3. Quoted ibid.
4. ibid., p. 144.
5. Saunders, op. cit., p. 174.
6. Kochan and Pym, op. cit., p. 143.
7. Saunders, op. cit., p. 173.
8. ibid.
9. Kochan and Pym, op. cit., p. 150.
10. Saunders, op. cit., p. 175.
11. ibid.
12. Kochan and Pym, op. cit., p. 150–51.
13. Saunders, op. cit., p. 176.
14. ibid., p. 178.
15. Pugh, op. cit., p. 104.
16. Kochan and Pym, op. cit., p. 151.
17. Saunders, op. cit., p. 177.
18. Kochan and Pym, op. cit., p. 151.
19. ibid., p. 152.
20. Saunders, op. cit., p. 181.
21. ibid., p. 176.

14 Saunders Takes the Halter

1. Saunders, op. cit., p. 183.
2. Roger Seelig, interview with author.
3. Simon Boyd, interview with author.
4. Saunders, op. cit., p. 183.
5. Ivan Fallon, *Sunday Times*, 13 July 1986.
6. Kochan and Pym, op. cit., p. 157.
7. Saunders, op. cit., pp. 183–4.
8. ibid., p. 180.
9. Kochan and Pym, op. cit., p. 160.
10. Saunders, op. cit., p. 184.
11. Ivan Fallon, *Sunday Times*, 20 July 1986.
12. Saunders, op. cit., p. 186.
13. ibid., p. 173.
14. Kochan and Pym, op. cit., p. 164.
15. Saunders, op. cit., p. 182.
16. Alan Scrine, interview with author.
17. *Financial Times*, 14 November 1986, quoted Hobson, op. cit., p. 305.
18. 16 November 1986, quoted ibid.
19. 11 October 1987, quoted ibid., p. 311.
20. Fenton Bailey, *The Junk Bond Revolution; Michael Milken, Wall Street and the Roaring Eighties*, Fourth Estate, 1991.
21. Kochan and Pym, op. cit., p. 170.

15 The Fabric Unravels

1. Quoted Hobson, op. cit., p. 369.
2. John Humphries in interview with author.
3. Hobson, op. cit., p. 373.
4. *Financial Times*, 30 December 1986.
5. *Sunday Times*, 4 January 1987, quoted Hobson, op. cit., p. 374.
6. Roger Seelig, interview with author.
7. *Financial Times* and others.
8. Brian Baldock, interview with author.
9. *Sunday Times*, summary of court proceedings of Saunders' trial, week 10.
10. Saunders, op. cit., p. 213.

16 The Sacking of Saunders

1. Saunders, op. cit., p. 220.
2. ibid.
3. *Mail on Sunday*, 17 May 1992.
4. Saunders, op. cit., p. 222.
5. ibid.
6. Ian Gilmour, *Inside Right*, Hutchinson, 1977, p. 257.
7. *Business*, 7 June, quoted in Hobson, op. cit., p. 376.
8. *The Times*, 21 March 1988.

17 Clearing Up

1. Shaun Dowling, interview with author.

2. Kochan and Pym, op. cit., p. 137.
3. Jeremy Warner, *Independent*, 28 August 1990.
4. Kochan and Pym, op. cit., p. 138.
5. Jeremy Warner, *Independent*, 28 August 1990.

18 Saunders in the Stocks

1. Saunders, op. cit., p. 221.
2. ibid., p. 224.
3. ibid., pp. 224–5.
4. Diana Mosley, *A Life of Contrasts*, Hamish Hamilton, p. 199.
5. Saunders, op. cit., p. 228.
6. ibid.
7. Kochan and Pym, op. cit., p. 183.
8. Saunders, op. cit., p. 236.
9. Tom Bower, *Tiny Rowland, A Rebel Tycoon*, Heinemann, 1993, p. 516.
10. Saunders, op. cit., pp. 245–60.
11. Bower, op. cit., p. 516.
12. Shaun Dowling, interview with author.
13. *Financial Times*, 27 June 1989.
14. Saunders, op. cit., Prologue.
15. *Financial Times*, 19 May 1990.

19 Before the Court

1. *The Times*, 21 February 1990.
2. ibid.
3. Transcripts seen unofficially.

4. *Financial Times*, 18 May 1990.
5. *Daily Telegraph*, 15 March 1990.
6. *Sunday Correspondent*, 18 March 1990; *Daily Telegraph*, 15 March 1990.
7. *Financial Times*, 30 April 1990; 1 May 1990; 3 May 1990.
8. *Financial Times*, 5 May 1990.
9. ibid., 9 May 1990.
10. ibid., 11 May 1990.
11. ibid., 10 May 1990.
12. *Daily Telegraph*, 6 June 1990.
13. *Observer*, 17 June 1990.
14. *Financial Times*, 12 June 1990.
15. *Observer*, 17 June 1990.
16. *Financial Times*, 26 June 1991.
17. ibid., 3 July 1990.
18. *Observer*, 2 September 1990.
19. *Daily Telegraph*, 1 September 1990.
20. *Observer*, 2 September 1990.

20 The Tide Turns

1. *Mail on Sunday*, 17 May 1992.
2. *Evening Standard*, 2 March 1992.
3. *Daily Telegraph*, 16 February 1993.
4. *Sunday Times*, 1 January 1995.
5. Lord Spens, interview with author.
6. *Financial Times*, 12 July 1990.
7. *The Times* and *Daily Telegraph*, 16 February 1993.
8. *Independent on Sunday*, 21 February 1993.

21 Still a Grey Area

1. George Robb, *White-collar Crime in Modern England*, Cambridge University Press, 1992, p. 3.
2. ibid.
3. ibid., p. 149.
4. ibid.
5. ibid., p. 163.
6. Henry R. Grenfell, *Nineteenth Century*, March 1879, quoted ibid., pp. 162–3.
7. *Evening Standard*, 2 March 1992.
8. Lord Spens, interview with author.
9. *The Times*, 23 December 1994.
10. *Private Eye*, 13 March 1992.
11. The *Times*, 28 November 1995.
12. *Times* Law Report, 28 November 1995.
13. *The Times*, 28 November 1995.

Index